SOCIOLOGICAL REVIEW MONOGRAPH 36

Social Anthropology and the Politics of Language

The Sociological Review

SOCIOLOGICAL REVIEW MONOGRAPH 36

Social Anthropology and the Politics of Language

Edited by Ralph Grillo

Routledge
London and New York

First published in 1989 by
Routledge
11 New Fetter Lane, London EC4P 4EE

Set in Times
by Hope Services, Abingdon
and printed in Great Britain
by Billings & Sons, Worcester

British Library Cataloguing in Publication Data
Social anthropology and the politics of language
(Sociological review monograph; 36)
1. Language. Political aspects
I. Grillo, R.D. (Ralph D)   II. Series
401'.9
ISBN 0–415–03765–4

Cover: Honoré Daumier '*You have the floor: explain yourself; you're free*': 14 May 1835

Contents

Contributors

Dr Deborah Cameron, Department of English, Digby Stuart College, Roehampton Institute, London, SW19.

Dr Elizabeth Frazer, New College, Oxford.

Professor Michael Gilsenan, Magdalen College, Oxford.

Professor Ralph Grillo, School of African and Asian Studies, University of Sussex, Falmer, Brighton, BN1 9QN.

Dr Roger Hewitt, Thomas Coram Research Unit, Institute of Education, University of London, 41 Brunswick Square, WC1N 1AZ.

Dr Caroline Humphrey, King's College, Cambridge.

Dr Marilyn Martin-Jones, Department of Linguistics and Modern English Language, University of Lancaster, Bailrigg, Lancaster, LA1 4YT.

Dr Maryon McDonald, Department of Human Sciences, Brunel University, Uxbridge, Middlesex, UB8 3PH.

Professor David Parkin, Department of Anthropology, School of Oriental and African Studies, University of London, London, WC1E 7HP.

Dr Johan Pottier, Department of Anthropology, School of Oriental and African Studies, University of London, London, WC1E 7HP.

Dr Jeff Pratt, School of African and Asian Studies, University of Sussex, Falmer, Brighton, BN1 9QN.

Gill Seidel, The Modern Languages Centre, University of Bradford, Bradford, W. Yorks, BD7 1DP.

Anthropology, language, politics

Ralph Grillo

Introduction

In Autumn 1986 the Editorial Board of the Sociological Review invited me to edit a Monograph on some aspect of anthropology and language. Recent developments in British social anthropology and in other subjects suggested that a focus on the politics of language would make an appropriate special issue.

In the last fifteen years a number of studies have appeared bearing titles which suggest a concern with this subject (e.g. Balibar and Laporte 1974; Bloch (ed.) 1975; Calvet 1974; Fowler *et al*. 1979; Kremerae *et al*. (eds) 1984; Lafont *et al*. 1982; O'Barr and O'Barr (eds) 1976; Paine (ed.) 1981; Parkin 1984; Pateman 1980; Smith 1984; Wolfson and Manes 1985; and many others). One striking feature of this work is its multidisciplinary (and international) character. British social anthropology is far from being the only or even the principal discipline interested in the relationship between language and the political, though it is one which has made a significant contribution to understanding that phenomenon.

The articles in this volume, not all by professional anthropologists, illustrate that contribution, which stems partly from a methodological orientation towards an ethnographic perspective (see later in this paper). They also illustrate the wide range of empirical material in which a politics of language may be located. There is, however, no claim that the cases presented here in any way constitute a representative sample, or offer, as yet, a potential for systematic comparison. The intention is precisely to demonstrate the varied empirical and intellectual nature of the field, and one objective is simply to explore the several theoretical and analytical traditions which have emerged in anthropology and in other disciplines. To that extent the volume is deliberately eclectic. Nevertheless, all the papers share a common focus on the relationship between the politics of use and the politics of meaning in what can be termed 'discursive practice'.

The social in the linguistic

The widespread interest in the politics of language is associated with a more general dissatisfaction with what has happened in mainstream linguistics. Following Chomsky's 'transformational' revolution, that mainstream adopted an increasingly 'asocial' stance. This comment by Chomsky himself is illuminating. It is from a conversation with Mitou Ronat where he has been discussing 'sociolinguistics': 'Sociolinguistics is presumably concerned not with grammars in the sense of our discussion, but rather with concepts of a different sort, among them, perhaps, "language", if such a notion can become an object of serious study' (Chomsky 1979: 190). He goes on to say, and one can but agree, that 'questions of language are basically questions of power' (p. 191), but these are not the sort of questions linguists address. Indeed, some would deny that their discipline is a 'social' science at all, and it is wrong to expect it to be one. Yet there the emphasis on (universal) 'competence' and the central place accorded to 'grammar' did not simply marginalize the social and cultural in linguistic analysis, but robbed language of what is a defining characteristic: its role in social communication. (Similarly, the cognitivist thrust in psychology is in danger of undermining that discipline's attempts to grapple with culture.)

This is not a new point. Mallinowski's reservations about Saussure's distinction between *langue* and *parole* were published in 1937. The powerful critique of Saussure contained in the writings of the Soviet linguist Voloshinov came even earlier, though his work has only recently become widely known in the West (trs. 1973). Specifically regarding Chomsky, in the United States, Dell Hymes and others associated with the 'ethnography of communication' have since the early 1960s argued the case against him (see Gumperz and Hymes (eds) 1964, 1972), drawing on a long-standing concern with the links between language, culture and society, shared by pre-Chomskyan linguisticians. The importance for American anthropology of Boas's insistence that his pupils not only speak the language of their informants but engage in serious analysis of it is well-known. In part it is the Boasian tradition (as applied to Native Americans) which Hymes wishes to reclaim for linguistics. The multi-lingual, multi-ethnic, character of urban American society also provided a significant incentive for the development of a social linguistic orientation.

In their different ways, linguistic anthropologists, 'sociolinguists' (such as Labov in the United States and Trudgill in Britain), and 'sociologists of language' (outstandingly Fishman and Haugen) have each helped rescue language from the transformationalists. Not all deal equally satisfactorily with the social or cultural dimensions of language, nor are they all equally concerned with the political dimension (however that may be defined), but together they represent a serious challenge to the currently dominant linguistic paradigm, and one reflected in other work by more orthodox linguists (cf. Le Page and Tabouret-Keller 1985). Interestingly, this challenge is now as strongly represented in Britain as anywhere.

Interesting because until relatively recently the study of language in society was poorly developed in this country. There was by contrast with, say, France, nothing comparable to the social linguistic perspective which produced Brunot's magnificent multi-volume study of French (1930) – perhaps the finest socio-historical account of a language ever written – and which continues to inform writing on language, as in Furet and Ozouf's review of literacy in the nineteenth century (1982), or in different ways the work of a Balibar, Foucault or Pêcheux.

In Britain, over the last twenty-five years or so the relative neglect of language in society has been transformed into something closely resembling the obsession it has long been in social reality. Among historians, Asa Brigg's interest in the language of class in England (1960) has generated a range of studies (e.g. Phillips 1984) well-complemented by the research on contemporary urban English by sociolinguists such as Cheshire, the Milroys, Trudgill and many others. The discussion of the social significance of language and class in education is too well-known to require further comment. More recently there has been an explosion of research on language and urban ethnic minorities (e.g. LMP 1985). Social and socio-historical studies of the regional minority languages in Wales and Scotland now abound (e.g. Durkacz 1983; Mackinnon 1977; Williams 1979). There has been important, indeed fundamental, research on language and gender relations (see Cameron 1985 and Coates 1986 for recent summaries). And this is to say nothing of work in literary theory where structuralism and after has brought greater awareness of the social in the linguistic in Britain as elsewhere.

The multidisciplinary nature of this endeavour may again be emphasized, though in all these fields and others besides a number of significant contributions have come from those trained in anthropology. The collections by Ardener (ed.) 1975 and 1978, Bloch (ed.) 1975, Parkin (ed.) 1982, and books and articles by Chapman 1978, Delamont 1976, Hewitt 1986, Saifullah Khan 1980, and Street 1984, provide varied and representative examples.

Though this is not the place to document past neglect of language by British social scientists as a whole, in order to appreciate anthropology's relatively recent interest in the study of language in society, and the form it has taken, it is necessary to reflect on the history of that discipline.

Language in British anthropology

The general position can be summarized as follows. Post-World War One British anthropologists were, usually, expert speakers of 'native' languages, but, as Parkin (1984: 346) points out, for them 'Language was a tool of discovery but not the discovery itself'. The position is well set out by Nadel (1951: 39–48). Apart from providing a means of communication, and the establishment of 'rapport', with informants, language was important because of the way it gave access to 'the natives' point of view'. As a 'vehicle of conception' (Geertz 1964: 59), it was a carrier of social categories, hence an intimate knowledge of the language (though not necessarily of 'language') was essential for the study of kinship (e.g. Fortes), of law (e.g. Gluckman, or Bohannan), and of conceptual systems generally (e.g. Evans-Pritchard).

There were exceptions to the general rule that British anthropologists had little to say about the linguistic. Of these much the most important was Malinowski, whose 'supplement' to Ogden and Richards' 'Meaning of meaning' (1923), with its discussion of what he called 'phatic communion', remains a landmark for all interested in social linguistics (cf. Parkin 1984: 345). In fact Malinowski's work on language attracted greater interest outside the discipline than within – it was a significant influence on the linguist J.R. Firth (Henson 1974: 67 ff.), and thence on Firthians such as Halliday (1978). Possibly it was more widely appreciated in the United States than in Britain, one reason being the much closer institutional relations between anthropology and linguistics in North American universities (Grillo, Pratt and Street 1987). In

Britain, on the other hand, the two subjects underwent what Henson (1974) has called 'separate development'.

Although there were major inadequacies in Malinowski's functionalist approach to language, it is perhaps unreasonable to blame the sterility of this perspective for the general neglect of language in British anthropology (Grillo, Pratt and Street 1987). None the less, it was not until the 1960s, when British anthropology entered a post-functionalist era, that the linguistic became a serious object of inquiry under the influence of French structuralism. The structuralist intervention, however, led anthropologists toward what was perhaps in the long run an unhelpful view of language as the embodiment of, primarily, intellectual signification (cf. Crick 1976). Moerman's objection (1988: 87 ff.) to Geertz's 'semiologic' approach to cultural symbols is well-founded: it ignores the linguistic practices – for Moerman epitomized by 'conversation' – through which signs are given meaning.

This orientation was coupled with a concentration on features of society 'either . . . extremely remote from economic and political processes, or . . . presented in such a way that no connection could be established' (Grillo, Pratt and Street 1987: 287). Thus the initial re-discovery of language within British anthropology occurred within a framework which diverted attention from – indeed could not conceptualize – a relationship between language, as concept-bearer, and the practices and processes in social life which might be identified with the political. An interesting contrast is Leach's handling of language in 1954 and 1976, and conversely Parkin's analysis of 'naming' (in this volume) compared with earlier structuralist accounts.

American linguistic anthropology might have been of assistance, but it was not well known in Britain. Certainly orthodox political anthropology offered no way out of the cul-de-sac. If there was in the past of British anthropology a general lack of interest in language as such, in traditional political anthropology that interest was minimal. Nowadays, political anthropology scarcely exists as a specialization outside undergraduate courses – very few list it as their professional theoretical area. This partly reflects the assumption that the 'political' is everywhere (or alternatively nowhere). However, in so far as a traditional (functionalist) political anthropology could be defined by its specific concerns – e.g. comparison of the way in which power and authority were distributed and organized or violence controlled in centralized and non-centralized systems – its literature contained almost nothing about language.

Again there were exceptions, but the insights contained in, for example, Evans-Pritchards' paper on the 'Sanza' style of Azande speaking (1956) and the themes which it appeared to place on the agenda of political anthropology were largely ignored – especially by Evans-Pritchard himself. Leach's discussion of language in *Political Systems of Highland Burma* (1954) too made little impact, though his and others' analyses of the political categories and concepts within a culture were undoubtedly influential. An excellent example in this vein was Beattie's account of the idea of *mahano* in Nyoro society (1960).

This omission was perhaps understandable if it is accepted that language in traditional societies did not look political, in an obvious, common-sense way. Or rather, in traditional societies language seemed hardly ever to have been the politicized, contested object it had been and was in Europe, and later was to become in some Third World countries. Whether or not traditional societies were indeed different in this respect, even when anthropologists did investigate European societies where language use was or had been conspicuously politicized (as in the many communities around the Mediterranean) language was not generally seen as a significant phenomenon for political investigation (cf. Boissevain and Friedl (eds) 1975; Cole 1977; Davis 1977). Nor did the overt politicization of language in colonial or post-colonial societies (e.g. pre- or post-independence South Asia) attract much attention.

Given this history, the second re-discovery of language, through which a political dimension is finally located, seems all the more surprising. There are perhaps several reasons for this. One is, quite simply, that the general level of interest in language has itself risen significantly over the last twenty-five years throughout the social sciences, and anthropologists have been carried along with the tide. During the same period, however, there has been a rapidly changing appreciation of the way in which language can be understood as a social and cultural phenomenon, and of what are appropriate data for linguistic inquiry. By 1971, certainly, other voices were beginning to be heard, including for example that of Edwin Ardener[1] whose (premature?) anti-structuralism (1971) suggested another way forward (cf. McDonald, this volume). Subsequently, a range of quite disparate influences (e.g. Austin, Bernstein, Foucault, Hymes to name but a few), enabled language to seem more amenable to a different kind of anthropological investigation.

There were changes, too, indeed successive changes, in the understanding of what may constitute the political (cf. Brenneis and Myers (eds) 1984; Fardon (ed.) 1985). In anthropology, as elsewhere, there came a moment when there could be a politics of anything – hence why not language? Here the several strands of what Cohen (1969) called the 'actor-oriented approach', which dominated thinking in the sixties and early seventies, undoubtedly left their residue, as in the work of Bailey (e.g. 1969) and of some of the contributors to Kapferer (ed.) 1976, a volume whose focus changed significantly between its inception (in 1972/3), when the key concept was 'exchange', and its publication when the crucial term was 'meaning'. Equally important, post-structuralism, Marxism (structural and other), and not least feminism have each been a profound influence on how anthropologists and others have conceptualized politics, language and their relationship (cf. Fardon (ed.) 1985 *passim*; Grillo, Pratt and Street 1987: 288 ff.).

Yet in both anthropology and in the social sciences at large there remain important divergences in the way the political has been constituted in the study of language in society. Thus Parkin has attacked anthropologists who

> quite arbitrarily, carve out domains of social behaviour, dub them political, and proceed to analyze the ways in which people talk about them and within them. They draw on some of the ideas of the performativists and linguistic philosophers but are held together by a specific interest in the creation and distribution of power. This is, of course, deliberate epistemological naivety. (1984: 348)

In fact, as his title ('Political language') implies, Parkin's remark is addressed to an area of inquiry which represents only one of several ways in which anthropologists have engaged with the political in the linguistic, albeit an important one. Here I will look at three ('Language as political object', 'Language as political resource', 'Language as control'), concluding with some emergent themes in the study of the politics of discursive practice. These fields (or approaches) are neither discrete nor homogeneous – currently they interlink in complex ways. But their identification may permit a clearer view of the varieties of the politics of language, and of the ways in which the linguistic and political have been connected.

Language as political object

The first approach may be characterized as one in which language is seen as a significant object of action or contest in situations where it is thought of as an attribute differentiating one group of people from another (cf. O'Barr 1976: 8). This is now almost a traditional way of approaching the politics of language, well-developed in one field: the study of the relationship between language and social differentiation in the formation of national systems. The political is defined by reference to large-scale, inter- and intra-national relationships, predominantly those pivoting on the nation-state, and the politics of language are about ways in which the domains of language use are defined by the forces which determine those relationships.

A good, wide-ranging, example is Anderson's account of languages of state as part of his wider account of nationalism (1983). One orientation within this general perspective may be termed the 'Political Economy of Language'. Here the politicization of language within the context of the formation of the nation-state is treated as a function of the peripheral or marginal status of particular groups within the economic system. Regional minorities, for example, are seen as 'internal colonies' whose fate is determined by their 'dependent' or 'peripheral' situation in the social and economic order (see Hechter 1975). Language and culture are generally seen as epiphenomena, though not always. In the work of the French regionalist, Robert Lafont, for example, the way in which southern France ('Occitanie') was incorporated in a French-speaking state crucially involved not only an economic, but also a cultural and linguistic imperialism. This theme has been taken up by a number of writers in and from the Third World, e.g. Ngugi wa Thiongo (1986) and earlier Franz Fanon, concerned with the cultural effects of colonialism and neo-colonialism.

In general, most attention has been focused on European experience where, until recently the anthropological contribution has been limited to what has emerged from research on regional minorities in Britain and France (but see Gellner 1983). In the last decade, however, British anthropologists have turned their attention to linguistic differentiation in contemporary cities where a major theme has been language policy in multicultural education (e.g. Saifullah Khan 1980; LMP 1985; and Hewitt, on the 'political grammars' of West Indian Creole, in this volume). Within the important field of Third World language planning, however, anthropologists have generally been content to let the 'sociologists of language' make the running (but see O'Barr 1976).

Implicitly or explicitly anthropological work on language policy is also fundamentally concerned with language and ethnic identity, in particular the way in which language symbolizes (subjective) difference rather than marks differentiation. It thus deals with collective, and individual, identification, and currently of considerable interest (see the papers addressed to the 1987 conference of the Association of Social Anthropologists) is the way in which ethnicity is constructed in and through history. Here, language is sometimes seen, quite straightforwardly, as one (but only one) factor in self-identification and thus an issue in communal conflict (e.g. in Sri Lanka, Nissan and Stirrat 1987). In other instances, especially again in Europe, language is seen as central to a different process of identification, one external to some collectivity whose identity is in question. This is associated with the 'symbolic appropriation' of the 'other' (cf. Chapman 1978), at times reminiscent of writing on the political economy of the nation-state ('the minority is the creature of the majority context it inhabits', McDonald 1986: 339), albeit without the economic reductionism to which that approach is prone. McDonald's paper in this volume develops this general theme through an examination of the ideological salience of the Breton language – including some of its specific linguistic features – for those active in the Breton movement.

Interest in language and identity is not, however, confined to this first field. At the opposite end of the scale to the perspective which locates the political in terms of national structures is that which locates it at the level of personal interaction. The political is seen as embedded in what might otherwise be thought of as the personal. Within this 'micro-politics of language' there is often a common focus on what is conventionally called 'discourse' (i.e. conversation), and language is seen as a resource within verbal exchanges.

Language as political resource

Some work on language and identity has been strongly influenced by methodological individualism. The political is defined by the power that one person (*qua* individual) can exercise over another within a conversation. Social psychologists of language are often concerned with this (cf. Giles and St Clair (eds) 1979). So, mostly, is 'pragmatics'. Or rather in so far as pragmatics deals with the political it is with power of what is essentially an interpersonal kind. This poses a problem. For although the personal may be a *site* of the political, as feminists and others argue, this does not mean that the political can be understood as a function of interpersonal relationships (see discussion by Martin-Jones in this volume). Other writing within the 'Micropolitics of language' has a more 'sociological' character, e.g. Delamont (1976) or Moerman's *Talking culture* (1988). Though Moerman himself is not especially concerned with the power dimension, his insistence on the 'culturally contexted' analysis of conversation leaves open that avenue. For those who do share that concern, Parkin's term 'Local Level Politics of Language' might be appropriate (1984: 347, and in this volume), though Parkin himself is not referring to discourse analysis of this kind.

The work of John Gumperz, discussed here by Martin-Jones, provides one example. Like other ethnographers of speaking, Gumperz emphasizes the heterogeneous nature of 'speech communities'. The totality of languages or linguistic varieties constitutes the 'code matrix'. Individuals possess or have competence in a subset of this totality which is their 'linguistic repertoire', and this 'provides the weapons of everyday communication. Speakers choose among this arsenal in accordance with the meanings they wish to convey' (Gumperz 1964: 138). This is illustrated in his account of code-switching in northern Norway (Blom and Gumperz 1972), and other recent work on the communicative strategies employed by social actors in conversation (Gumperz 1982; and Gumperz (ed.) 1982).

Gumperz is also concerned with the way in which cultural conventions structure discourse. This is important in an intercultural context, especially in societies (such as Britain), where 'communicative resources . . . can be every bit as essential as real property resources were once considered to be' (in Gumperz (ed.) 1982: 5). Here the political is defined in terms of the control of the (bureaucratic) channels, communicative and other, which give access to jobs, housing, social services, etc. In such contexts, lack of competence in the appropriate codes may allow the emergence of go-betweens who undertake a variety of 'brokerage' tasks – in this case they might be termed 'language brokers'.

Laurence Goldman's study (1983) of language use in legal disputes among the Huli people of New Guinea is also focused on linguistic resources in speech exchanges. Certain of these are predetermined by rights. For example, an essential part of land disputes between clans or subclans is the recitation of a *malu* (clan genealogy). 'Political leadership', says Goldman, 'is defined . . . as the authoritative right to perform *malu*' (p. 147). It is an attribute of headmanship, which is an inherited office. It is difficult for some categories of people (notably women and young men) to get a word in: in effect they need permission. This is despite what Goldman calls 'the egalitarian nature of talking in Huli' (p. 231) illustrated by a belief in the value of speech reciprocity. However, within these (important) limitations Huli speakers are able to deploy a variety of linguistic resources and strategies in an effort to achieve 'rhetorical efficacy' (p. 272).

Goldman suggests that 'Huli appreciation of "good usage" represents as much an interest in form as in the content of words' (p. 275). His work, and that of Gumperz, is in fact centrally concerned with form, sometimes at the expense of content. What is important in the exchanges they analyse is not what is said, but how it is said, and what the form signals. To that extent their work (Goldman's in particular) may be linked with much recent writing on 'Political Language', which earlier I suggested was an important focus of anthropological interest in the relationship between the linguistic and the political. Once more, variety is the norm, though there is a general concern with the 'performative' effects of linguistic form.

Anthropological interest in what came to be called the 'performative' can be traced to Malinowski's writing on 'phatic communion', a way of speaking which 'does not serve any purpose of communicating ideas' (Malinowski 1923: 316) but a social function (Malinowski thought of establishing human solidarity). This conception of language as performative resource was developed by the linguistic philosopher J.L. Austin whose discussion in *How to do things with words* (1962) of the 'illocutionary force' of language was taken up by Tambiah (1968, 1979), and by Bloch (1975). Gumperz's account of the communicative consequences of the use of different linguistic forms, for example what is signalled by code-switching (especially what he calls 'metaphorical' code-switching), is clearly relatable to this theme, as is the work of O'Barr on legal language where he argues: 'Form is communication; varieties of form communicate different messages; and speakers manipulate form, but not always consciously, to achieve beneficial results' (1982: 11).

This interest in form (and in greater or lesser degrees content) has been pursued in a number of studies of political rhetoric which focus on metaphor, as indeed does much of Goldman's Huli ethnography.

Parkin draws attention to a 'view of rhetoric as negotiated political persuasion' (1984: 356), and it is an emphasis on 'persuasion', or in more general terms the 'different effects of illocutionary speech and of intentionality' (Parkin 1984: 347), which has characterized many of the anthropological accounts of political language (cf. Gilsenan's paper in this volume). Noting an earlier absence of interest in rhetoric in political anthropology (p. 345), Parkin points to the influence of F.G. Bailey's ideas about speech as a 'strategy of control' (e.g. Bailey 1969) which he sees of more significance for recent work in this field than the work on rhetoric by the (American) ethnographers of speaking (Parkin 1984: 357). A collection edited by Sapir and Crocker (1977) was also important in drawing the attention of political anthropologists to this area.

One illustration of the concern with rhetoric is Robert Paine's edited volume (1981), to which Bailey also contributed (1981). Paine says at the outset that the 'leitmotif' of the book is 'politics as rhetoric'. This he identifies with how 'politicians attempt to sway, and even mould the experience and knowledge of their public'. For Paine, who draws on Kenneth Burke (1966, 1969), the 'politics of speaking' is defined as 'the way a speaker . . . works for the attention of his audience' (p. 5). The analysis of this phenomenon involves consideration of how meaning is 'selected, constructed and communicated – or "lost"'. The 'kernel of rhetoric' is 'saying is doing' (p. 9). 'Rhetoric is action' (p. 19); it is 'saying while doing'. Adopting Austin's terms, he equates 'performatory speech' with the symbolic, while 'propositional speech' is identified with 'pragmatic action'. It is in the symbolic form of a political message that is to be found its legitimation. The art of persuasion involves mastery of rhetorical devices among which Paine singles out for special attention what classical rhetoricians called 'enthymeme' (truncating an argument, leaving things unsaid) and which Paine associates with slogans and 'banner-words' (p. 14). (For a different perspective on truncation see Seidel 1975.)

Underlying at least some of this is an extremely cynical view of politics (if not of the human condition). This is illustrated in the Paine collection in the chapter by Bailey (1981). Bailey identifies three axes along which rhetoric works or may be analysed: 'hortatory/deliberative referring to the orator's objective; grandiloquent/tempered, concerning his style; and cardiac/pseudo-cerebral, words that recognize the fact that persuasion can be addressed to the heart or (apparently) to the head' (1981: 25). Note 'pseudo' and 'apparently'. 'In the presence of a rhetorician', says Bailey, 'caveat auditor'. 'Rhetoric, it seems, would have no place at all if decisions were reached by reason, if all men could see reason, and if seeing reason moved them to action.' This theme is continued in his distinguishing between both hortatory and deliberative rhetoric on the one hand, and 'decision-making by reasoning' (p. 27). All rhetorical 'devices', 'cardiac' and 'pseudo-cerebral' alike, 'stray from the matter-of-fact, step-by-step presentation of propositions logically connected and/or offered for empirical testing' (p. 30).

Returning to rhetorical devices, Paine (1981: 188) contrasts metaphor with metonym, and argues that 'whereas metonym always endorses power . . . metaphor is used to speak against it as often as it is used to endorse it' (p. 198). The following figure (taken from Paine, p. 199) illustrates this contrast.

	Metaphor	Metonym
Control	–	+
Creativity	+	–
Identity	+	+

Figure 1

This argument operates at a level of generalization which makes me, at any rate, extremely uncomfortable. Is there not a danger of confusing stylistic practices common in Transatlantic societies (or rather, perhaps, those influenced by the Graeco-Roman tradition), with supposedly universal tendencies? Parkin, too, is concerned by possible ethnocentrism, pointing out that rhetoric is not always action: 'Persuasion may itself sometimes be an aesthetic device, having no other end than its own satisfaction' (1984: 355). And there is a further problem relating to the conception of the political in terms of actors and resources. Certainly, *pace* Parkin's remark about Bailey, this approach can have little to say about language and control, but as Parkin also says there is another view of rhetoric which sees it as 'reinforcing traditional authority' (1984: 356). This leads to a longstanding theme in the politics of language: the way in which language enters into processes of social and cultural domination.

Language as control

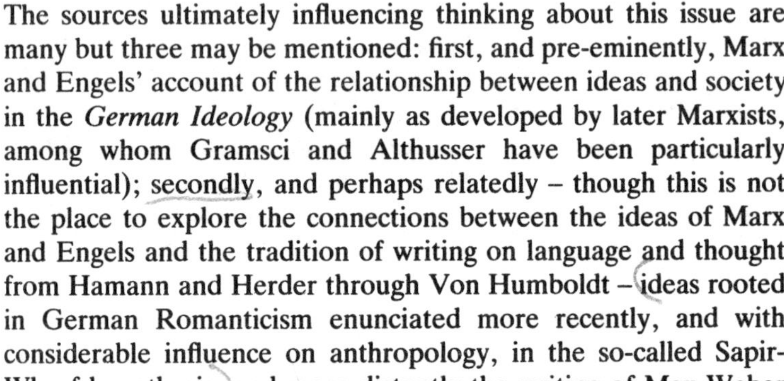

The sources ultimately influencing thinking about this issue are many but three may be mentioned: first, and pre-eminently, Marx and Engels' account of the relationship between ideas and society in the *German Ideology* (mainly as developed by later Marxists, among whom Gramsci and Althusser have been particularly influential); secondly, and perhaps relatedly – though this is not the place to explore the connections between the ideas of Marx and Engels and the tradition of writing on language and thought from Hamann and Herder through Von Humboldt – ideas rooted in German Romanticism enunciated more recently, and with considerable influence on anthropology, in the so-called Sapir-Whorf hypothesis; and more distantly the writing of Max Weber on the legitimation of authority.

Among the many questions that arise here is that of the extent to which language itself has power, i.e. is a dominating force in and of itself (working through the subject to create a sort of Orwellian world), and the extent to which language, in a less determinist way fashions, reflects, articulates, reinforces other structures of domination. This is one of the issues raised by the work of Maurice Bloch. Building in part on Austin's ideas, Bloch (1975) has developed an argument about the relationship between forms of speech and forms of control in traditional societies. Among the Merina of Malagasy he observed that speeches in village councils generally took a set form: an apology for speaking; thanks to all from God downwards for permission to speak; the main part of the speech; a final round of thanks and blessings (Bloch 1975: 7–8). The speech itself is highly formalized with restrictions on syntax, the use of set expressions, archaic terms and so on. This has an important political effect stemming from the way in which one formalized speech must be followed by another whose content is shaped by the first. Assuming that speakers accept the rules of discursive practice, 'communication becomes like a tunnel which once entered leaves no option of turning either to left or right' (p. 24). When an opponent has been placed in this situation, he (in this case definitely 'he') can only acquiesce or revolt. He is in a 'double bind'.

'Double bind', a psychoanalytical concept developed in work on schizophrenia, is used by Pateman (1980) in discussing what he calls 'repressive discourse', i.e. that within which the power inherent in a relationship is effectively disguised. So:

> Whilst a speaker may innocently make a meaningless statement and have this pointed out to him, a speaker in a position of superior power can attempt to strengthen his position by presenting meaningless utterances *as* meaningful, and this is more easily effective if the hearer does not even have the chance of replying. (p. 86)

Powerless listeners may convince themselves that they are inadequate because they fail to understand what is said. For the Merina speaker the double bind is that the only acceptable reply is one which acknowledges the previous speech and its premises. Like the psychiatric patient, he (again) may be 'reduced to silence' (Pateman 1980: 109), or revolt.

It has been suggested that something comparable characterizes the situation of women in many societies. In his contribution to Shirley Ardener's edited volume (1975), Edwin Ardener examines the phenomena of inarticulacy and 'mutedness'. The latter is not in any simple way 'silence', though that may be a manifestation of relationships within which mutedness appears. Mutedness refers rather to a structural situation in which a group may be muted 'simply because it does not form part of the dominant communication system of the society' (Ardener, E. 1975: 22). What is said has to be articulated, if it is to be articulated at all, through the dominant mode of communication – in this instance the dominant *male* mode, though the mutedness concept may also be applied to those in a subordinate class position.

Cameron (1985), and Cameron and Frazer (in this volume) indicate a number of problems with the Ardener model of female inarticulacy, but it is relevant to the discussion of the 'double bind'. It is in no way intended here to suggest that the position of the inferior Merina speaker, the schizophrenic patient, and women *tout court* are in any way directly comparable, nevertheless Bloch, Pateman and the Ardeners each point to important ways in which language and control operate in situations where 'the repressive forms and use of discourse [are] built into the existence and exercise of unequal power' (Pateman 1980: 113).

Bloch's work, and to a certain extent that of the Ardeners, raise in a precise way the question posed at the outset of this section: to what extent is 'control' a direct function of language? Does power in any sense reside in particular kinds of linguistic form or content? Here I have to agree with Parkin (1984) who questions 'Orwellian' assumptions: 'It is people who retain the power to name, entitle and objectify others, who determine the course of discourse' (p. 359). Pateman puts it bluntly: 'Most cases in which words are supposed to have power turn out to be situations in which people have power' (1980: 238).

This, I think, is what emerges from the concept of mutedness, which is a function of exclusion from a dominant system of articulation. This is not to deny the supreme importance of language in systems of social control, nor is it to subscribe to any simplistic duality of 'language' and 'society' (cf. Parkin's comment, 1984: 360, on the 'mutual irreducibility of the linguistic and the social'). It is, however, to question the philosophical priority accorded to language by some writers (e.g. Spender 1980). What is crucial is the way in which use is socially controlled, and a web of authoritative meaning constructed.

Bloch's argument raises another, related, aspect. This concerns, ultimately, creativity and the nature of the 'subject' or 'agent'. Paine takes issue with Bloch's conception of rhetoric as 'frozen', seeing rhetoric rather as 'moulden'. Bloch associates 'formalization with an absence of negotiation between speaker and audience. Bloch sees coercion where we see persuasion' (1981: 2). 'It is difficult to imagine', say Cameron and Frazer (in this volume), 'that some group could assume authority over the *totality* of communication and construction of meaning within a speech community, encompassing all forms of social interaction'. Elsewhere, in fact, Bloch himself acknowledges this when he posits, co-existing within the same social formation, 'systems by which we know the world', and 'systems by which we hide it' (1977: 290). That is, at the very least an alternative *conception* is always possible even if in practice it cannot be voiced other than as an interior monologue or in the privacy of the home (cf. Caroline Humphrey's account of political language among the Buryat of the Soviet Union, in this volume).

It is possible that the apparent closure of debate in Merina culture is a function of the type of society Bloch is discussing. Merina political oratory indeed shares many of the features of what Bakhtin calls 'the authoritative word . . . which binds us quite independently of any power it may have to persuade us internally' (1981: 342), but the authority here is in Weberian terms, of the 'traditional' kind (Grillo, in press). In fact, Parkin shows that rhetoric varies considerably in such cases only sometimes approximating to Bloch's formal oratory (p. 350 ff.). Brenneis and Myers (eds 1984), too, in their discussion of 'indirection' in discourse in the Pacific suggest at the very least that the language of politics works differently in 'egalitarian' and 'hierarchical' societies. Pratt's account of the political language of Italian Communists also explores the relationship between hierarchy and language use at different levels of Party organization. Pottier's analysis of debates in a Rwandan co-operative (also this volume) additionally shows that the formal political language of a society which Maquet described as built, traditionally, on the 'premise of inequality' can no longer be fully sustained under changing circumstances. As Parkin puts it, 'It is not formalism in language which represses people and their thoughts, but the degree to which speakers impose such discourse on others' (1984: 362), a point illustrated by his discussion, in this volume, of the differential control over naming among Giriama men and women.

Each of these examples land us squarely in the world of institutional power, and the authority exercised over, as well as through, discursive practice.

The politics of discursive practice: some emergent themes

For Bloch, the formalized language of traditional oratory is close to devoid of propositional content (1975: 22, and see Pratt in this volume). Control resides in the form. Other work, also concerned with control, has focused more closely on meaning. In different ways, Chilton (1985), Fairclough (1985), Fowler *et al.* (1979), to cite but a few anglophone writers, develop this theme, as does Seidel, in this volume (see also Chuter and Seidel 1987). Much of the data analysed through their work are derived from written texts (or are 'media' based), but some of the issues have been taken up by anthropologists working with much more scattered corpora of oral materials gathered in fieldwork (cf. Grillo 1985). As Seidel (1985) points out, the link at the linguistic level is in 'discourse', a term not limited in this case to verbal exchanges or conversation as it was in work considered earlier, but encompassing all aspects of linguistic organization at or above the phrase level (see Grillo 1985: 8, Parkin 1984: 360, Seidel, 1985: 44, among many others).

Discourse is a multi-faceted notion. In a recent discussion, Sherzer, who retains a definition which is 'purposely vague' (1987: 296), describes it as an 'elusive area, an imprecise and constantly emerging and emergent interface between language and culture' (ibid.), and argues for a conception of discourse as 'the nexus, the actual and concrete expression of the language-culture-society relationship. It is discourse which creates, recreates, modifies, and fine tunes both culture and language and their intersection' (p. 296). This view is one echoed in much recent work, including that of several contributors to this volume, with the addition, perhaps, of an assumption that analysis must always be concerned with the *practice* of discourse – *inter alia* the social activity through which discourse is produced and in which it is located (see further Grillo, in press).

At this point a number of traditions come together. A good example is Hill and Hill's *Speaking Mexicano*. Drawing on, but by no means confined to, the 'ethnography of speaking' pioneered by Gumperz and Hymes, and Labov-style sociolinguistics, the Hills have produced a fascinating account of what they call the 'syncretic project' of speaking Mexicano in the small towns around the Malinche volcano in Central Mexico. 'Mexicano' is the preferred term for an Indian language sometimes called Nahuatl, which coexists with Spanish in a dynamic form of diglossia. Its speakers are peasants with a high proportion owning their own land, though 80 per cent of their income comes from (male) labour migration to the factories of the larger towns of the region, or to Mexico City. In the colonial period Mexicano was the language of the 'inside', Spanish of the 'outside', bilinguals were rare and acted as brokers between the two societies. Nowadays most people 'speak two', as they say. Spanish is widespread and dominant in religion, law, work (except agriculture), commerce, education and the media, and may exert such a strong influence on the way Mexicano is spoken that it is sometimes unclear, from a technical linguistic viewpoint, whether someone is speaking Hispanicized Mexicano or switching between two languages. In complex ways Spanish actualizes an external, Hispanicized Mexicano an internal, 'power code'. Opposed to both is a 'purist code' which seeks to re-create an idealized form of the traditional language.

The Hills's 'translinguistic' approach to these data in which they compare code-switching with what Bakhtin calls the 'juxtaposition of voices', deserves the closest attention, not least for their methodology. The evidence for what these codes signify, how they are realized in daily speech, who uses them, comes mainly from tape recordings of formal interviews. Designed initially to collect examples of linguistic usage to be counted and correlated with social factors, these provide a much richer type of data when seen as speech events. Interviewers and interviewees engage in verbal duels embodying the 'symbolic strategies' through which individually and collectively the people of the Malinche attempt to manage their changing relationship with national Mexican society.

The broad shape of the Hills's approach is close to that of much recent work in Britain, indeed the influences – e.g. Bakhtin/Voloshinov – are often the same. However, unlike the Hills and others raised in American anthropology (e.g. Gumperz, Moerman, Sherzer), British anthropologists pay relatively little attention to the more 'technical' aspects of language (phonology and syntax). This comes from a lack of appropriate expertise and, perhaps, from the feeling that in the study of, say, language and class, there are more important things than the 'postvocalic r'. Our *forte* has been semantics, though our conception of it is rather different to that found in orthodox linguistics (Grillo, Pratt and Street 1987). None the less it is through this and similar work that the nature of the anthropological contribution – but not only the anthropological contribution – to the study of language and politics becomes apparent.

Crucial here, as indicated earlier, is a very broad conception of language as discourse and of politics as its practice (cf. Seidel 1985: 45). Discourse analysis encompasses all that is socially and culturally worked in and through language whether the focus is a single-word utterance (as in a famous passage in Voloshinov, 1973) or a complex corpus of writing and speaking (as in Seidel's account of European Parliament debates on sanctions against South Africa, or Hewitt's discussion of the 'political grammars' of West Indian Creole, both in this volume.

Such analysis is, or should be, fully 'contexted' (Moerman 1988) socially and culturally. There has been much recent discussion in linguistics of 'context' (cf. debates following publication of Sperber and Wilson, 1985), often thought of as a backdrop or framework to which language might be attached. It is important, rather to see it as a process of *contextualization* which occurs both in linguistic (or discursive) practice and in our analyses of it. This is relatable to Ardener's insistence, throughout his work, on anthropology as an 'act of translation'.

Both translation and contextualization also imply analysis worked in and through ethnography, usually but not always collected through fieldwork (cf. McDonald, this volume). A strategic advantage of this methodological orientation is that it helps avoid 'the vacuity of theoretical propositions divorced from indigenous statements, or distanced from the experiential complexity of case material' Goldman (1983: 290). It has, consequently, both an emic and etic dimension (which need not necessarily lead to the same result), forcing a balancing of structure and construction, actor and observer, and their interplay, an enterprise in which reflexivity also has a part to play (cf. the papers by Gilsenan, McDonald and Parkin in this volume). This is inevitably open-ended, but it enables many linkages to be made including those between what are generally thought of as macro and micro 'levels'. It is also in complex ways associated with a comparative perspective which though at times carrying with it the danger of a thorough-going relativism at least avoids the pitfalls of a premature and inappropriate universalism.

Ethnographic methodology also points towards the centrality of process. The emphasis is on language (or discourse) in action. 'Process' is another vague term, but here I take it to refer to the way in which practice (including, for example, verbal exchanges or conversation as do Moerman or Gumperz) is in important ways constitutive of culture and society. It is at this point that the anthropology of language can or should acquire a political focus, or at any rate one concerned with power. For, to paraphrase the *Eighteenth Brumaire*, men make their own meaning (Marx says 'history'), but do not do so under circumstances of their own choosing. One way of demonstrating this is to substitute 'women' for men in that misquotation. For nowhere has the political in the linguistic been more clearly demonstrated than in the field of language and gender relations (see in various ways the papers by Cameron and Frazer, Parkin and Pottier in this volume).

In no sense, however, should this process be seen as passive. As Seidel puts it: 'Discourse is a site of struggle. It is a terrain, a dynamic linguistic and, above all, semantic space in which social meanings are produced or challenged' (1985: 44). The papers in this volume contain many illustrations. Thus Cameron and Frazer are concerned precisely with 'competing world views contained in ordinary discourse', as indeed are Humphrey and Hewitt. Pottier's

account of debates within a Rwandan farming co-operative shows how 'through being clever with words, by forcing their president to shift language modes from formal to informal style [the] more vocal members undermined cultural stereotypes (the language of the dominant ideology)'.

Power, for the anthropologist, is not, can never be, predominantly a personal matter, but must be located within a nexus of social and cultural relationships. This is elementary, but fundamental. Equally fundamental, now, must be the assumption of the social in language. Hence the political in language, and the linguistic in politics. The chapters in this volume try to show how in various ways language is relatable to political processes, not as 'a mere epiphenomenon' (Cameron and Frazer) but as something quite central to them.

Note

1 Edwin Ardener, who died in 1987, was to have been a contributor to this volume. From the late sixties onwards (e.g. Ardener (ed.) 1971) he constantly stimulated thinking about language in British anthropology.

References

Anderson, B., (1983), *Imagined communities*, London: Verso.

Ardener, E., (1971), 'The new anthropology and its critics', *Man* NS 6(3): 449–67.

Ardener, E., (1975), 'Belief and the problem of women', in S. Ardener (ed.), (1975) q.v., pp. 1–27.

Ardener, E. (ed.), (1971), *Social Anthropology and language*, ASA Monographs in Social Anthropology No. 10, London: Tavistock Publications.

Ardener, S. (ed.), (1975), *Perceiving women*, London: Dent.

Ardener, S. (ed.), (1978), *Defining females*, London: Croom Helm.

Austin, J.L., (1962), *How to do things with words*, Oxford: Clarendon Press.

Bailey, F.G., (1969), 'Political statements', *Contributions to Indian Sociology*, 3: 1–16.

Bailey, F.G., (1981), 'Dimensions of rhetoric in conditions of uncertainty', in R. Paine (ed.), (1981) q.v., pp. 25–38.

Bakhtin, M., (1981), *The dialogic imagination*, Austin: University of Texas Press.

Balibar, R. and Laporte, D., (1974), *Le français national: politique et pratique de la langue nationale sous la Révolution*, Paris: Librairie Hachette.

Beattie, J., (1960), 'On the Nyoro Concept of *Mahano, African Studies*, 19: 145–50.

Bloch, M., (1975), 'Introduction', in Bloch (ed.) (1975), q.v., pp. 1–28.

Bloch, M., (1977), 'The past and the present in the present', *Man* NS 12(2): 278–92.

Bloch, M. (ed.), (1975), *Political language and oratory in traditional society*, London: Academic Press.

Blom, J.P. and Gumperz, J.J., (1972), 'Social meaning in linguistic structure: code-switching in Norway', in J.J. Gumperz and D. Hymes (eds) q.v., pp. 409–34.

Boissevain, J. and Friedl, J. (eds), (1975), *Beyond the community: social process in Europe*, The Hague: Department of Educational Science of the Netherlands.
Brenneis, D. and Myers, F. (eds), (1984), *Dangerous words: language and politics in the Pacific*, New York: New York University Press.
Briggs, Asa, (1960), 'The language of "class" in early nineteenth century England', in A. Briggs and J. Saville (eds), *Essays in labour history*, vol. 1. London: Macmillan, pp. 47–73.
Brunot, F., (1930), *Histoire de la langue française des origines à nos jours*, Paris: Armand Colin.
Burke, Kenneth, (1966), *Language as symbolic action*, Berkeley: University of California Press.
Burke, Kenneth, (1969), *A rhetoric of motives*, Berkeley: University of California Press.
Calvet, L.J., (1974), *Linguistique et colonialisme: petit traité de glottophagie*, Paris: Payot.
Cameron, D., (1985), *Feminism and linguistic theory*, London: Macmillan.
Chapman, M., (1978) *The Gaelic vision in Scottish culture*, London: Croom Helm.
Chilton, P. (ed.), (1985), *Language and the nuclear arms debate: nukespeak today*, London and Dover, N.H.: Frances Pinter.
Chomsky, N., (1979), *Language and responsibility*, Sussex: Harvester Press.
Chuter, C. and Seidel, G., (1987), 'The AIDS campaign in Britain: a heterosexist disease', *Text*: 7(4): 347–61.
Coates, J., (1986), *Women, men and language*, London: Longman.
Cohen, A., (1969), 'Political anthropology: the analysis of the symbolism of power relation', *Man* NS 6: 428–48.
Cole, J.W., (1977), 'Anthropology comes part-way home: community studies in Europe', *Review of Anthropology* 6: 349–78.
Crick, M., (1976), *Explorations in language and meaning: towards a semantic anthropology*, London: Malaby Press.
Davis, J., (1977), *People of the Mediterranean*, London: Routledge & Kegan Paul.
Delamont, S., (1976), *Interaction in the classroom*, London: Methuen.
Durkacz, V., (1983), *The decline of the Celtic languages*, Edinburgh: John Donald.
Evans-Pritchard, E.E., (1956), ' "Sanza": a characteristic feature of Zande language and thought', *Bulletin of the School of Oriental and African Studies*. (Reprinted in E.E. Evans-Pritchard, (1962), *Essays in social anthropology*, London: Faber & Faber.)
Fairclough, N., (1985), 'Critical discourse analysis', *Journal of Pragmatics* 9 (6): 739–63.
Fardon, R. (ed.), (1985), *Power and knowledge*, Edinburgh: Scottish Academic Press.
Fowler, R., Hodge, B., Kress, G. and Trew, T., (1979), *Language and control*, London: Routledge & Kegan Paul.
Furet, F. and Ozouf, J., (1982), *Reading and writing: literacy in France from Calvin to Jules Ferry*, Cambridge: Cambridge University Press.
Geertz, C., (1964), 'Ideology as a cultural system', in D. Apter (ed.), *Ideology and discontent*, New York: Free Press, pp. 47–78.
Gellner, E., (1983), *Nations and nationalism*, Oxford: Basil Blackwell.
Giles, H. and St. Clair, R.N. (eds), *Language and social psychology*, Oxford: Basil Blackwell.
Goldman, Laurence, (1983), *Talk never dies: the language of Huli disputes*, London: Tavistock Publications.
Grillo, R.D., (1985), *Ideologies and institutions in urban France: the representation of immigrants*, Cambridge: Cambridge University Press.
Grillo, R.D., (1989), (in press), *Dominant languages*, Cambridge: Cambridge University Press.
Grillo, R.D., Pratt, J. and Street, B., (1987), 'Anthropology, linguistics and language', in J. Lyons *et al.* (eds), q.v., pp. 268–95.

Gumperz, J.J., (1982), *Discourse strategies*, Cambridge: Cambridge University Press.

Gumperz, J.J. (ed.), (1982), *Language and social identity*, Cambridge: Cambridge University Press.

Gumperz, J.J. and Hymes, D. (eds), (1964), *The ethnography of communication*, American Anthropologist Special Publication, vol. 66, no. 6, pt. 2.

Gumperz, J.J. and Hymes, D. (eds), (1972), *Directions in sociolinguistics: the ethnography of communication*, New York: Holt, Rinehart & Winston.

Halliday, M., (1978), *Language as social semiotic*, Baltimore: University Park Press.

Hechter, M., (1975), *Internal colonialism: the celtic fringe in British national development, 1536–1966*, London: Routledge & Kegan Paul.

Henson, H., (1974), *British social anthropologists and language*, Oxford: Clarendon Press.

Hewitt, R., (1986), *White talk, black talk: interracial friendship and communication amongst, adolescents*, Cambridge: Cambridge University Press.

Hill, Jane H. and Kenneth C., (1986), *Speaking Mexicano: dynamics of syncretic language in Central Mexico*, Tucson: University of Arizona Press.

Kapferer, B. (ed.), (1976), *Transaction and meaning*, ASA Essays 1, Philadelphia: Institute for the Study of Human Issues.

Kramerae, C., Schultz, M. and O'Barr, W.M. (eds), (1984), *Language and power*, London: Sage.

Lafont, R. *et al.*, (1982), *Langue dominante, langues dominées*, Paris: Edilig.

Le Page, R. and Tabouret-Keller, A., (1985), *Acts of Identity: Creole-based approaches to language and identity*, Cambridge: Cambridge University Press.

Leach, E.R., (1954), *Political systems of Highland Burma*, London: Bell.

Leach, E.R., (1976), *Culture and communication*, Cambridge: Cambridge University Press.

Linguistic Minorities Project (LMP), (1985), *The other languages of England*, London: Routledge & Kegan Paul.

Lyons, J., Coates, R., Deuchar, M., and Gazdar, G. (eds), (1987), *New horizons in linguistics 2*, London: Penguin Books.

Mackinnon, K., (1977), *Language, education and social processes in a Gaelic community*, London: Routledge & Kegan Paul.

Malinowski, B., (1923), 'The problem of meaning in primitive languages', in C.K. Ogden and I.A. Richards (1923) q.v., pp. 296–336.

Malinowski, B., (1937), 'The dilemma of contemporary linguistics', *Nature* 140: 172–3.

Marx, K. and Engels, F., (1965), *The German Ideology*, London: Lawrence & Wishart.

McDonald, M., (1986), 'Celtic ethnic kinship and the problem of being English', *Current Anthropology* 27(4): 333–41.

Milroy, James and Lesley, (1985), *Authority in language: investigating language prescription and standardisation*, London: Routledge & Kegan Paul.

Moerman, M., (1988), *Talking culture: ethnography and conversation analysis*, Philadelphia: University of Pennsylvania Press.

Nadel, S.F., (1951), *The foundations of social anthropology*, London: Cohen & West.

Ngugi wa Thiongo, (1986), *Decolonising the mind: the politics of language in African literature*, London: James Currey.

Nissan, E. and Stirrat, R.S., (1987), 'State, nation and the representative of evil: the case of Sri Lanka', *Sussex Research Papers in Social Anthropology*, 1.

O'Barr, W.M., (1976), 'The study of language and politics', in W.M. O'Barr and J.F. O'Barr (eds), q.v., pp. 1–27.

O'Barr, W.M., (1982), *Linguistic evidence: language, power and strategy in the courtroom*, New York: Academic Press.

O'Barr, W.M. and O'Barr, J.F. (eds), (1976), *Language and politics*. Contributions to the sociology of language, 10, The Hague: Mouton.
Ogden, C.K. and Richards, I.A., (1923), *The meaning of meaning*, London: Kegan Paul.
Paine, R. (ed.), (1981), *Politically speaking*, Philadelphia: Institute for the Study of Human Issues.
Parkin, D.J., (1984), 'Political language', *Annual Review of Anthropology*, 13: 345–65.
Parkin, D.J. (ed.), (1982), *Semantic anthropology*, ASA Monographs in Social Anthropology, no. 22, London: Academic Press.
Pateman, Trevor, (1980), (2nd edn), *Language, truth and politics*, Lewes: Jean Stroud.
Phillips, K.C., (1984), *Language and class in Victorian England*, Oxford: Basil Blackwell/Andre Deutsch.
Saifullah Khan, V., (1980), 'The "mother tongue" of linguistic minorities in multicultural England', *Journal of Multilingual and Multicultural Development* 1(1): 71–88.
Sapir, J.D. and Crocker, J.C. (eds), (1977), *The social uses of metaphor: essays on the anthropology of rhetoric*, Philadelphia: University of Pennsylvania Press.
Seidel, G., (1975), 'Ambiguity in political discourse', in M. Bloch (ed.), (1975), q.v., pp. 205–26.
Seidel, G., (1985), 'Political discourse analysis', in T. Van Dijk (ed.), *Handbook of discourse analysis*, vol. 4, London: Academic Press, pp. 43–60.
Sherzer, J., (1987), 'Language, culture and discourse', *American Anthropologist* 89: 295–309.
Smith, Olivia, (1984), *The politics of language 1791–1819*, Oxford: Clarendon Press.
Spender, D., (1980), *Man made language*, London: Routledge & Kegan Paul.
Sperber, D. and Wilson, D., (1985), *Relevance: communication and cognition*, Oxford: Basil Blackwell.
Street, B.V., (1984), *Literacy in theory and practice*, Cambridge: Cambridge University Press.
Tambiah, S.J., (1968), 'The magical power of words', *Man* NS 3(2): 175–208.
Tambiah, S.J., (1979), 'A performative approach to ritual', *Proceedings of the British Academy* 65: 113–56.
Voloshinov, V.N., (1973), *Marxism and the philosophy of language*, New York/ London: Seminar Press.
Williams, Glanmour, (1979), *Religion, language and nationality in Wales*, Cardiff: University of Wales Press.
Wolfson, N. and Manes, J. (eds), (1985), *Language of Inequality*, Berlin/ New York/Amsterdam: Mouton.

Knowing what to say: the construction of gender in linguistic practice

Elizabeth Frazer and Deborah Cameron

> The thing is, in this kind of discussion group, well, you know, you can't think of anything to put, you can't think of how you really feel, but you say something anyway, you know what to put. (Janette, 15 year old youth club member)

Introduction

In this paper we address the problem of how what people say should be taken to relate to what they mean and/or the truth about their condition. What is the status, in other words, of people's *accounts*, to a researcher, to their peers, or to themselves? Many fieldworkers, in anthropology, sociology, psychology, or linguistics, have to face the particular problem of how to interpret and account for apparent contradiction in what their informants tell them or say. This has been an issue of particular significance in studies of gender and class consciousness, and this paper will draw on a study of this kind, in which the researcher recorded talk about gender, class and race produced by girls from a number of different social groups (Frazer 1988). Many researchers have analysed the ways in which girls both accept the appropriateness of labellir g certain sorts of behaviour or appearance as that of a 'slag' or a 'slut' and yet resent the way it is used against girls and even recognize its function of policing their sexual and other behaviour (Lees 1986; Wilson 1978). When a girl says

Simone (YP0402 26)	Donna, Donna round the flats, she's a real slag.

and also says

Simone (YP2101 5)[1]	I hate it when boys calls us slags, when they're sleepin around more, it's alright for them.

we want to explain how this apparent contradiction is held with comfort.

Between language and reality: explanations of contradiction

One answer is to elaborate a notion of 'false consciousness' or its psychologistic equivalent 'cognitive dissonance' (Elster 1983; Festinger 1957). For a social theorist, of course, an account of these psychic conditions must relate them to the social world, or even collapse the psychological/social distinction altogether. The concept of 'ideology' is usually brought into play in some form, touching as it does both individual 'attitudes' or 'beliefs' and their social determination. Ideology functions to legitimate power imbalances, and smooth out contradictions and disjunctions between appearances and reality. Language is usually seen as the medium in which ideology is manifest, and as the tool through which ideology works to obscure reality, to instil beliefs or worldviews in subjects, and to impose frameworks on our apprehension of the world (Barthes 1956; Thompson 1984).

In the specific case of femininity and gender differences the idea of language as a determinant of people's worldview has been particularly influential. In its most familiar version, represented for instance by Dale Spender (1980) this idea is supported theoretically from the writings of anthropologists such as B.L. Whorf (1965) – although it must be said that Spender reads Whorf rather eccentrically (for elaboration on this point see Cameron (1985: 109–10)) – and Edwin and Shirley Ardener (1975; 1978). The central argument is that men, as the more powerful gender, have been able to appropriate and control the means of representation and communication, forcing women to internalize a 'male' worldview contrary to their interests (the strong version of the thesis); or (the weaker version), denying women resources with which to encode their competing worldview systematically in language, and thus give it legitimacy in the culture. Both Spender and Shirley Ardener waver between the strong and the weaker versions of this argument, as is shown by Cameron (1985: 104, 112–13).

A contrasting account, which also stresses the founding importance of language acquisition as the means whereby women internalize the patriarchal order of things is proposed by writers working with the theory of subjectivity outlined by Lacan, and developed by writers such as Kristeva and Irigaray (for a useful summary see Moi 1985). This account is couched in a very different terminology, and has different theoretical underpinnings with regard to language – not anthropological, (that is, seeing language as a cultural practice deeply embedded in human *activity*), but 'structural' in the tradition of Saussure (that is, seeing language as an abstract system of signs). However, what it shares with the first account is the view that language has been constructed in such a way as to put women 'outside' it, so that using language – as all social beings must – becomes, for women, a process of alienation from their own reality.

Having constructed these accounts of women as a 'muted group' (to use the Ardeners' term) or 'marginal to the symbolic order' (in more Lacanian language) the next step is to consider the *mechanism* by which muting and marginalization are achieved. Here we run into serious problems, particularly if our goal is a materialist analysis, locating the mechanism in actual social practice (instead of, for instance, the allegedly trans-cultural, mythic symbol of 'the phallus' which many Lacanians would invoke at this point).

Concentrating, for the sake of argument, on the Whorf-Ardener-Spender version of the theory, it is clear that male control over language is a postulate without which the entire account falls. But how, exactly, is this control effected? The answer to this depends on defining what is meant by 'language'. It is obvious that some aspects of language can be appropriated and controlled on a short or long term basis by specific groups. For example, the use of one language rather than another (say English rather than Welsh) in certain settings, like the class room, or the law courts, can be legislated for. Decisions about the contents of dictionaries and grammars, or the prescribed style for official documents, religious liturgy, legal discourse, etcetera, can be made by individuals or small groups and handed down by *fiat*. The public speech of women or children (or other powerless or oppressed groups) can be tabooed more or less explicitly. But all these examples depend on the existence of an authority able to command and impose sanctions for disobedience. What is much more difficult to imagine is that some group could assume authority over the *totality* of communication and construction of meanings within a speech community, encompassing all forms of social interaction. Even if we believed that some legitimate authority existed, how would it be enforced in practice?

The adherent of the 'male control' theory might reply that such authority does not need to be enforced, because those who might challenge it have internalized the controllers' view of the world already in acquiring language. But this argument conflates 'language' with official or *legislated* language: a view which surely cannot be sustained empirically. In any society the vast majority of exchanges – particularly, one might argue, among powerless people – are of a 'vernacular' kind, unregulated by the sort of linguistic authority which plays a crucial role in institutions and 'high' culture.

This is not, of course, to argue that in the artless chatter of village women we will find a pure, unmediated expression of female sexuality; we will find no such thing! Rather, we are arguing that existing accounts fail to explain in any empirically satisfying way how women are prevented from encoding an 'oppositional' worldview in language, (as opposed to 'in some areas of a culture's linguistic practice'). More theoretically, we would claim that since meaning *tout court* is not strictly controllable, we cannot give 'language' the status some writers give it in fixing or determining social reality. Indeed, Simone's remarks which we quoted earlier bear witness to the existence of competing or 'contradictory' worldviews contained in the ordinary discourse of this group of young women.

On the other hand, we do not subscribe to the opposite argument, that language is a mere epiphenomenon, reflecting a social reality which is essentially independent of it (the view of social researchers whose orientation is positivistic). Since language-use is a fundamental social activity, we take it that the construction of meanings and social realities must be done to a significant extent in and through that activity. The question is, therefore, one of identifying the constraints and norms which affect speakers in social situations – causing them, for instance, to produce contradictions like those in Simone's talk.

One theoretical framework that does give due weight to the role of language in constructing social realities and meanings without supposing that those meanings are fixed absolutely in advance by language itself, is ethnomethodology. Ethnomethodology and other phenomenological sociologies emphasize the continuous construction of social 'reality' – the life world – by social actors (Schutz and Luckmann 1973; Berger and Luckmann 1966). For a phenomenologist, we cannot discuss or attempt to study 'social reality' *qua* an external object with an independent existence, because we have no access to it except in so far as we have experiences or apprehensions on a moment to moment basis (Husserl 1970; Garfinkel 1967). We, subjectively, unify our momentary experiences by a series of *ad hoc-ing* or *as if-ing* techniques – we act *as if* there is an objective world of social structures out there, *as if* we live in an orderly and law-governed social universe, *as if* the meanings of words and actions are fixed. We purport to follow rules which are like the laws governing the physical realm; but actually these rules are continually 'written' in the very process of our obeying them. Social life, and the taken-for-granted, then are *accomplishments*. The social world itself, or people's descriptions of it, are not a valid object for study – rather the process by which it, and descriptions of it are constructed is what the sociologist should be interested in.

Language clearly has a key role here, as the medium in which descriptions and accounts are couched; and linguistic interaction, like all other interaction between persons and the social world, is taken as a putatively rule-governed accomplishment. People's accounts, to each other and to themselves, are a continuous procedure of glossing, by which the social world becomes a place, and a series of happenings, which make sense, and have meaning. This meaning itself is, of course, constantly negotiated and constructed; as is the significance and reference of utterances.

But, the problem with ethnomethodology from our point of view is that it notoriously neglects the ways in which people are *unequal* in the enterprise of constructing the life-world. It denies us the possibility of studying what constrains action, in favour of studying how people 'accomplish being constrained'. It cannot tell us why some individuals are in a position to change the rules, or break them without sanction while others are not. It cannot help us research how meanings become relatively fixed, or disrupted. It cannot tell us who has the power to fix meaning. From the point of view of our central problem in this paper – how we can relate people's accounts and descriptions to the way things are – for the ethnomethodologist it is clear that all we have are people's individual and negotiated accounts of how things are, and nothing more. We do not have access to any 'reality' against which to check these accounts; rather they are constitutive of the constructed reality which is the life-world. We are not licensed, then, by the ethnomethodological metaphysics, to find the apparent 'contradiction' in what Simone says puzzling at all; or even to identify it as a contradiction as such.

So far then we have argued against a theory which takes language to have a *sui generis* independent existence and structure which is determinant of the reality which confronts actors; and against an alternative which takes it that actors use language to gloss and *ad hoc* an essentially illusory but comforting pseudo-reality. We have also rejected the positivist position that people's talk and accounts are neither here nor there because reality is an independently existing series of objective facts *simpliciter*. It follows that we reject any account of 'contradictions' (as exemplified in Simone's talk about being a slag) as either unimportant variations – the expression of two different but equally valid 'glosses' of reality – or simply predetermined 'ideological' assertions (produced by false consciousness or alienation in a man-made language). So how are we to explain the significance of remarks like Simone's?

The practice of talk: 'contradiction abandoned'

Simone: They're cunts, it's disgusting, I don't agree with it at all.
Janette: I agree, I don't agree with it neither.
Sheryl: Same here.
EF: Why not? why don't you agree with it?
Fatima: It's dirty.
Janette: It's just.
Sheryl: It's terrible, they shouldn't be doing it.

EF: So you mean that you *don't* agree with the argument that cos god created men and women that means that homosexuality is wrong?
Janette: Oh no, I think to myself that if they want to go their way they can go their way.
(YP0402 13)

Janette: That's what gets me they beat up their kids and get about six months, especially the mothers right cos, you know in the [local paper] there was this women she picks up her baby and hit his head on the bannister, and it was just born, it was most probably three months and she was most probably just giving it milk still and it was hungry still so she picked it up right and she goes it was just after feeding and she hit it across the bannister and it died. You get soppy ones right who leave d'you know metal baths, you know in some parts of

London they ain't got a bathroom, she put the metal thingy on the gas ring and put the baby in it and left it in the boiling water, I think that it's bloody true and I d'you know cot deaths I think most of them are already . . .

Fatima: Most of them do that you know, the reason is right, they're killed by their mothers.

Joanne: --- she was about six months older than me it was her first child and she died when she was about ten months, and then they wouldn't have a baby, they wouldn't have another one for three years cos they feared what would happen

Paulina: when you've baby-sat, have you ever gone like this, and looked at it, and thought 'Is it breathing?'

Janette: Yeah, my mother used to say that.

Sheryl: God yeah, with a baby you can't see it breathing.

(YP1102 14)

At first sight, the data obtained from the discussions with the youth club group was a mass of contradictions like those exemplified above. Sometimes these were extremely stark, with the same girls offering two contradictory opinions in the space of only a few seconds, as when Janette opines that lesbianism is 'terrible' and so on, and that 'they shouldn't be doing it', and then says that people can do what they like. Sometimes people would just retreat from strongly expressed opinions – as when there was general assent to the idea that cot death babies are largely murder victims, followed by a general assent to the idea that this is not the case and that, on the contrary, cot death is a real and terrifying possibility for parents of young babies.

There were several possible ways to interpret these apparent contradictions in what the girls said about many subjects. The first possibility is that their presence in the transcripts is a result of the imperfect nature of the research method: using a standardized questionnaire, for example, which elicited one answer and one only to any particular question, would have revealed the girls' true attitudes or opinions on the topics. The second possibility, connected with the first, is that while one of Janette's verbalized opinions about lesbianism is her true opinion, the other is false; and it would be possible to put the mistake (of using a research method which failed to elicit true opinion) right by a process of checking back. That is, we should ask her the question again and get a 'proper' answer.

Many points can be made about the project of eliciting 'attitudes' or 'beliefs' or 'opinions' altogether; and the evidence of this data can be interpreted as showing that, far from having qualms about not having designed a precise attitude measuring instrument and administering that to the girls, we should be satisfied that such a procedure would have been quite misleading. After all, the evidence of this discussion is that the girls don't have one, unitary and consistent 'attitude' to lesbianism, or 'belief' about cot death and baby battering. Clearly, a standardized questionnaire would have forced them into constructing a single answer to each question, but in practice, in the real world, they work with a multiplicity of beliefs and attitudes. So the third possible interpretation of these contradictions is that the girls have lots of attitudes and beliefs, and not surprisingly they come into conflict with one another.

But there is yet another possibility. These utterances don't actually sound like doxastic propositions (that is, statements to the general truth of which Simone is committed) at all. To say that Simone *believes* that lesbians 'are cunts', or that Janette's discourse about baby battering could simply be translated into a set of attitudinal statements, is quite inappropriate. These passages are passages of *discourse* which is structured according to conventions. They, and others like them in the transcripts, are striking for their adherence to the respective conventions of generic ways of talking, or discoursing, about things. The first half of the extract about lesbianism, for example, reminds us of nothing more than the populist authoritarianism of the tabloids, with its categories of 'pollution', otherness, sub-humanity and so on. In the second half, the talk has switched to another set of conventions – that of liberalism, with its emphasis on the freedom of the individual, privacy in sexual matters, rationality, etcetera. The second extract exhibits a very similar change.

What determines which set of conventions are used: and what determines what changes are made? There are several factors: in the case of the discussion on lesbianism the researcher had intervened and introduced the notion of *arguments* for or against certain stances, for example. Because of her power in the group the girls had been forced into a specific mode of discourse, which we might call liberal. However, the discourse that is, so to speak, spontaneously triggered by the word 'lesbian' is that of the tabloid press. Note, however, that the girls are quite at home in the liberal discourse featuring rationality, and argument. This group, in fact, have an extremely varied experience and exposure to contrasting ways of talking. They are members of a youth project which emphasizes discussion and small-group work, anti-sexist and anti-racist activity and discussion, and political and community activity and talk about these as such. That is, they are used to and confident with the mode of discourse of the discussion group, which has a feminist and anti-racist content. The youth work practice also emphasizes what we might call liberalism too, though: co-operative modes of talk, a certain tolerance for people who disagree – within the limits set by anti-sexist and anti-racist work, an emphasis on reason and argument. But there are other linguistic practices which are important in the girls' culture – 'slagging off' (which conflicts with the 'discussion group' discourse favoured in the club), 'chit-chatting' and so on.

There is an extremely important issue for cultural and ethnographic studies highlighted here. The range of ways of talking used by these girls is peculiar to them. They are local linguistic practices, and we cannot attribute them to 'working class', or 'Black British', or 'feminine' culture. Of course, we may discover that some of them are shared by other groups of teenage girls. However, we cannot postulate a unified 'culture' which shapes and moulds the people born into it. Instead, these data give us evidence that there is a plurality of concrete practices in any society, and various people will participate in a variety of them. Neither conventional positivist research, with its emphasis on individuals' and groups' social action; nor ethnomethodology with its emphasis on actors as creators of their world, can adequately treat these issues. Social researchers must pay much closer attention to the questions of *what practices there are*, and *who participates in which*.

We can compare the linguistic practices of these working class and mainly black girls with those of the public school girls who are upper class and all white. These girls also had a multiplicity of ways of talking – but in this case the main contrast was between a traditional (Whiggish) kind of conservatism, and a liberal kind of feminism. Thus:

Fiona: What I hate about being a girl is that at dinner parties the men stay and drink port, and all the women have to leave the table and go and sit together and talk about babies and children.

Clare: Oh no, but I like that. The women must want to talk

about those sorts of things, and its good that they can be together.
Fiona: Yes but then the men talk about serious things, like politics and things when the women have gone. Well I don't mind them talking about serious things, but they should talk with us about serious things too.
Clare: Oh I like it, it's traditional.
(PSA3 5)

Here the disagreement is between group members rather than switches in tone in the group as a whole. But here is another example:

Candida: I hate the nouveau riche *far more* than I hate the middle classes.
(laughter)
Candida: They look down on the lower classes far more than we do. I mean, the character of a person isn't to do with class, it's to do with upbringing; the nouveau people are such snobs.
EF: How do you define a nouveau person?
Candida: They go to Tunisia for their holidays, they're really pretentious, we hate pretention – they buy all their furniture new, from Harrods; they don't own land.
Fiona: But social class doesn't make what people are like.
Cressida: Yes, no, social class determines what people are like, it does.
Fiona: But everyone's pretentious, our class is worse; but you can't talk about class, you can't generalise.
(PSA6 2)

In this discussion (which continued for a long time) this group of girls veered between the view that social class as such is irrelevant, and that a person's character, tastes and so on are determined by other factors, such as her individual upbringing, education, and friends, and the view that class is a meaningful and useful category in this sort of discussion. For some girls these two views cannot be prised apart. Fiona particularly in this extract veers between acknowledging 'our class' and denying its significance. But they all have a conception of class as a *birthright*, as rooted in tradition and culture. There is no trace of such a conceptualization in the talk of the working-class, or the middle-class comprehensive school girls;

and indeed a political theorist would associate such a conception of class with a particular sort of conservatism.

The public school girls had never taken part in a girls' discussion group of the sort set up for the purposes of the fieldwork before. In order to encourage an atmosphere which would facilitate honest and intimate discussion of feminity and sexuality the sessions included group-work exercises designed to encourage clarity of expression and listening skills, self-disclosure, and critical analysis. These games and exercises were taken from resources aimed at youth workers and teachers. So for example we played communication games, variations on the 'Truth' parlour game, and discussed film, television and fiction at length. In the early sessions the public school girls were sometimes bewildered and silenced by some of these games; for example they were asked to write down five or six words which described themselves. The tape recording of that session reveals that they found this an incredibly difficult thing to do – they couldn't think of any words, they didn't know any, and so on. After half a dozen sessions the upper sixth girls organized a games session themselves, during which we played extremely sophisticated communication and self-disclosure games (Frazer lent them her resource materials to help them plan this). By the end of our work together they didn't bat an eye-lid if it was suggested that a girl who had been talking about her very difficult relationship with her step-father asked someone to role-play him so that the rest of us could help her work out exactly how she felt about him.

These girls were acquiring and using a brand-new way of talking: they were learning the conventions of the consciousness-raising group. And, they were learning the uses to which this way of talking could be put; and learning that it gave them a new perspective on the world and on their lives. The youth club girls already knew this way of talking. Actually, as Janette's remarks at the head of this paper show, how to behave and what to say in the context of a girls' discussion group is practically like knowing a script. She goes on:

Janette: No cos even when we go on a weekend away you know you can't think of something to write, even the boys put it down – you know 'I am afraid that someone's going to laugh at me . . .'

Simone: But the boys don't want anyone to know they write it.

EF: Are you saying you're just putting it . . .?

Janette: I would.
Simone: No, I would think they mean it.
(YP0402 9)

All the girls were very interested in this question of what they were telling the researcher, and enjoyed discussions in which they had to shift into a supervenient mode, and reflect upon their own discourse. They all made perceptive remarks about the ways the data was being *constructed*:

Kate: Oh no, we're telling you the truth, definitely; this is a typical kind of conversation we have all the time.
Annabelle: (laughs)
EF: What's going on? what are you laughing at?
Annabelle: Oh no, I can't tell *you*, it's something I couldn't say to you.
(PSB 3 appendix)

Jemima: Well, for a start you're here, and we know what you are talking to us about. We never sit down and have this much time anywhere on our hands to talk about the things we do here – so that affects it.
(PSA 4 appendix 1)

There are two points to make here. To begin with, this sort of supervenient discourse in which you reflect upon what you are saying, is also a style of discourse which has to be learned. When and where it is appropriate to use it is also something to be learned – there are many contexts in which it is quite inappropriate to begin an enquiry into what one is really saying and what one means. Second, Janette's remarks might give a researcher a sharp pang of dismay – if it is really the case that people abide by the conventions of the context, and allow that to determine what is said, then what is the point of doing research at all? To return to the question which is at the centre of this paper – is it beginning to look as though the relation between what a person says and how things really are with them is entirely random, because what is said depends on what it is appropriate to say? In response to this we argue two things. First that the process by which people learn and know what to say must become a crucial object of the researcher's enquiry. And secondly, that we should be alive to the possibility that 'how things are with people' is not an objective and quite determinate state of affairs, but is itself at least partially constructed by how they say things are.

To say, then, that one thinks that lesbianism is 'disgusting' and to say that lesbians should be allowed to pursue their own personal and private pleasures, is not a *contradiction* in the sense in which social researchers often find this kind of statement problematic. Uttering these two 'opinions' within seconds or minutes is like the socio-linguistic phenomenon of code-switching (cf. Blom and Gumperz 1972). We have chosen to refer to the contrasting and alternative ways of talking that is revealed in this data as *discourse registers* – another metaphorically borrowed term from socio-linguistics.[2] There are appropriate and inappropriate discourse registers for any particular social context, so the use of a register is subject to norms and rules and sanctions, which have to be learned by members.

This analysis raises various implications for researchers. Who or what determines or fixes the rules governing code-switches? In the examples we have discussed in this paper the researcher, who was in a dual role of quasi-youth worker and researcher, had the power to determine what counted as an acceptable discourse register, so could impose a 'liberal' or 'feminist' register, the register of the discussion group, on the girls. The register of populist authoritarianism, and the tone of the tabloid press, was quite unacceptable in context and the youth club girls perfectly well knew this. Similarly, it is clear that the kind of discussion about sexuality, about which the groups were organized, and which relied on the conventions of the discussion group to enable it to occur at all, would have been quite unacceptable to, say, the staff and headteacher of the public school; or indeed among a group of girls reading about the latest baby-battering outrage, or sacked lesbian teacher, in the local newspaper. This raises a crucial issue in the sociology of knowledge – or rather, the social distribution of knowledge, which is not quite the same thing. How is it determined that upper-class young women do not have access to the register of feminism, while they do have access to a crucial register which the working-class girls don't learn – that of the formal debate? A connected issue is what determines the prestige and acceptability of a particular register. For example, the norms of a feminist discussion group, with its emphasis on co-operation, listening skills, self-disclosure and so on, are disvalued, and even reviled in the world at large.

Finally, there are implications here not just for social researchers but for all those engaged in political struggle. The question of what discourse registers exist, how they are valued, and who has access to them is less a question of cultural *difference* than one of *inequality*. The issues thrown up by this are complex, however.

Recent work in the sociology of language has shown how various groups are materially disadvantaged because they do not speak 'the language of power' whether this is defined as a particular linguistic variety: for example, standard English (cf. Gumperz 1982; Labov 1982), or as the language of important public or institutional domains: for example, the language of the courtroom (Harris 1984) or of important community rituals (Keenan 1974). In other words, a person who lacks either the ability or the opportunity to use the 'language of power' should be seen as suffering from a serious social deprivation, to the extent that she does not feel at ease in a range of crucial linguistic encounters (because she has not mastered the 'correct' way of talking). Such a person is excluded from the processes of society, and thereby rendered powerless to control or change those processes.

In our opinion, the concept of a language (or languages) of power has proved useful in focusing many current debates about the politics of language. But for the purposes of our discussion, which has a primarily feminist perspective, we would like to introduce the slightly different concept: languages of *liberation*. A 'language of power' is normally powerful simply by virtue of its association with currently powerful speakers, and not because of any intrinsic value; (hence the problem of whether to insist on access to powerful language for disadvantaged groups (Mukherjee 1986; Crowley, forthcoming)). A language of liberation, in contrast, is liberating by virtue of the *meanings* it makes available – meanings which are either illegitimate or at best unarticulated in competing discourse registers.

The 'feminist way of talking' is one example of a 'language of liberation', and as we have shown there are groups of women to whom it is still an unfamiliar language – notably the most economically privileged group of young women in this study, women who operate easily in the traditional 'language of power' (standard English, reasoned argument, formal debate, and so on). We would regard the unfamiliarity of upper-class public school girls with feminist ways of talking as a material disadvantage which requires some analysis. Researchers must attend to the structures which deprive some people of the opportunity to speak in particular ways, and to the concrete practices whereby people learn, or else are prevented from learning, the ways of talking that will empower and liberate them.

Notes

1 All data quoted were collected by Frazer for a study of teenage girls' ideas about and experience of femininity. Seven discussion groups met over an extended period during the school year 1985–6. They were as follows:

i) One group from an inner London youth project; 14–16 years; racially mixed (Afro-Caribbean, Turkish, white).
Parents' occupations include: kitchen assistants, factory worker, cleaners, part-time shop assistant, van driver.

ii) & iii) Two fourth form groups from an Oxfordshire single sex comprehensive; fourteen years; one included one Afro-Caribbean girl, otherwise white.

iv) One upper sixth form group from the same school; seventeen years; included one black African girl, rest white.
Parents' occupations include: secretaries, plumber, police officer, nurses, master butcher, midwife, cabinet maker, night porter.

v) One third form group from an Oxfordshire Headmistresses' Conference girls' public school; thirteen years, all white.

vii) One upper sixth group; seventeen years; all white.
Parents' occupations include: landowners, stud managers, managing directors, stock broker, army officer.

Letters and figures in brackets are references to transcripts: YP – youth project group; PSA – public school upper sixth; PSB – public school lower sixth. Further figures and letters refer to meeting date or number, and transcript page number.

2 The term 'discourse register' will bear more detailed explanation. When linguists use the term 'register' they normally allude to a range of co-occurring formal features characterizing particular fields of discourse (for instance, 'scientific English' is marked by the use of a specialized lexicon, of the passive voice, of embedded clauses, etcetera). Clearly the language of 'feminist discussion' or 'tabloid reporting' might also manifest distinctive formal qualities; but we are more interested in the range of meanings and underlying assumptions which inform these particular contexts. There is a connection between our notion of meanings/assumptions and the Foucaultian notion of 'discursive practice' or the term 'discourse' as used by discourse theorists. Hence we label our cluster of meanings and assumptions within particular contexts 'discourse registers'.

References

Ardener, Edwin, (1975), 'Belief and the problem of women' in S. Ardener, (ed.), *Perceiving Women*, Dent.

Ardener, Shirley, (1978), *Defining Females*, New York: John Wiley.

Barthes, Roland, (1956), *Mythologies*, excerpted in Susan Sontag (ed.), *Barthes: selected writings*, Fontana (1983).

Berger, Peter and Luckmann, Thomas, (1966), *The Social Construction of Reality*, Garden City: Doubleday.

Blom, P. and Gumperz, J., (1972), 'Social Meaning in linguistic structure', in J. Gumperz and D. Hymes (eds), *Directions in Sociolinguistics: the Ethnography of Speaking*, New York: Academic Press.
Cameron, Deborah, (1985), *Feminism and Linguistic Theory*, Macmillan.
Crowley, Tony, (forthcoming), *The Politics of Discourse 1840–1987*, Macmillan.
Elster, Jon, (1983), *Sour Grapes: studies in the subversion of rationality*, Cambridge: Cambridge University Press.
Festinger, Leon, (1957), *A Theory of Cognitive Dissonance*, New York: Row Peterson.
Frazer, Elizabeth, (1988), 'Talking about Femininity: the Concept of Ideology on Trial', Oxford University, (unpublished).
Garfinkel, Harold, (1967), *Studies in Ethnomethodology*, Englewood Cliffs NJ: Prentice Hall.
Gumperz, J., (1982), *Discourse Strategies*, Cambridge: Cambridge University Press.
Harris, S., (1984), 'Questions as a mode of control in magistrates' courts', *International Journal of the Sociology of Language*, 49.
Husserl, E., (1970), *The Crisis of European Sciences and Transcendental Phenomenology*, Evanston: Northwestern University Press.
Keenan, E.O., (1974), 'Norm makers, norm breakers: uses of speech by men and women in a Malagasy community', in Richard Bauman and Joel Sherzer (eds), *Explorations in the Ethnography of Speaking*, Cambridge: Cambridge University Press.
Labov, W., (1982), 'Objectivity and Commitment in Linguistic Science: The Case of the Black English Trial in Ann Arbor', *Language in Society* 11.
Lees, Sue, (1986), *Losing Out: sexuality and adolescent girls*, Hutchinson.
Moi, Toril, (1985), *Sexual/Textual Politics: Feminist Literary Theory*, Methuen.
Mukherjee, Tuku, (1986), 'ESL: The New Empire', unpublished mimeo.
Schutz, A. and Luckmann, Thomas, (1973), *The Structure of the Life World*, Evanston: Northwest University Press.
Spender, Dale, (1980), *Man Made Language*, Routledge & Kegan Paul.
Thompson, John B., (1984), *Studies in the Theory of Ideology*, Cambridge: Polity Press.
Wilson, Deirdre, (1978), 'Sexual Codes and Conduct: a study of teenage girls', in Carol Smart and Barry Smart (eds), *Women Sexuality and Social Control*, Routledge & Kegan Paul.
Whorf, B.L., (1965), *Language, Thought and Reality*, Massachussets: MIT Press.

Debating styles in a Rwandan co-operative: reflections on language, policy and gender

Johan Pottier

Introduction

The independent state of Rwanda inherited a culture marked by ethnic supremacy and male dominance. Since independence, some progress towards social equality has been made: dominance by one ethnic group has been abolished, at least in official rhetoric, while steps to incorporate women in the development process have been taken by the *Ministère de la Jeunesse et de la Coopération*. In spite of these positive moves, obstacles do remain, as ACORD (a London-based consortium of non-governmental organizations) has experienced in its development programme. ACORD is particularly concerned that women do not usually 'attend public meetings of the sort organised through the programme . . .'. Hence, 'women find it difficult to respond to new avenues'. ACORD has now proposed 'to extend . . . research work to look at more appropriate ways of reaching women' (ACORD 1987: ch. 3). The present article offers insight into this formidable task, with reference to a vegetable-producing co-operative in Butare, Rwanda's third largest town. I monitored its activities over a period of six months, between February and August 1986.

The co-operative, which I call CoopaduPeuple, holds bi-weekly, sometimes weekly debates. Contrary to its general organization, which underlines the thesis that 'work, in and of itself, is not a significant predictor' of equality in status and life opportunities (Blumberg 1981: 73), the debates themselves show that members – the vast majority being women – aim to bring about positive changes within the country's dominant ideology. *Coopérateurs* are critical of stereotyped views on the relationship between initiative, authority and gender, and engage in open debate to express and shape their views on production, work-sharing, progress and equality. Debates are lengthy, lively, and no argument is ever won or lost without struggle.

CoopaduPeuple receives attention from regional as well as national bureaucrats. At the regional level, this attention takes the form of technical advice, clarification of directives, and assistance with book-keeping. I shall restrict myself to interactions with regional (town-based) bureaucrats, but will discuss the relationship with national bureaucracy in a future article.

My experience of CoopaduPeuple suggests that the Rwandan tradition which defines objective logic as a male domain is being subjected to change. The challenge amounts to a reappraisal of the relationship between the pursuit of knowledge (i.e. development) and what Sutton *et al.* have termed 'the social authorship of ideas' (Sutton *et al.* 1975: 582). But the long-term outcome of this reappraisal remains uncertain. Recent progress made within CoopaduPeuple, especially since the election of a woman vice-president, may still turn out to be little more than token achievement. I shall demonstrate, in this respect, that there is a notable contrast in the ways in which the major organizational problem (settling debts) is defined by rank-and-file members on the one hand, and by outsiders in authority on the other. The possibility of mere token achievement is offset, however, by the tone and quality of the general debates – a quality which highlights that language is not just expressive of experience, but may in fact help constitute that experience. The debates reveal an internal cultural discourse, in which language is used not as an instrument for reproducing tradition but as a resource for change (Grillo *et al.* 1987: 294; also Miller and Swift 1977: 137). *Coopérateurs* are concerned about 'what' is being said in public debate; they are equally preoccupied with styles of presentation, with 'how' things are said. The importance of public debate for the implementation of policy in Rwanda has been stressed (Dupriez and de Leener 1983: 106; ACORD 1987), but never documented.

Through reconstructing the ways in which *coopérateurs* use language in debate, I hope to show how policy is internally negotiated. My focus is on the power of innovative speech, as used by ordinary members, which I shall set against the declining acceptability of formalized, authoritative speech – the mode adopted by CoopaduPeuple's leadership. Leaders, mostly men, convey their thinking in a style associated with past cultural patterns and norms. The rank-and-file perceive such norms, quite rightly, as conducive to idiosyncratic behaviour, mismanagement, and a policy which discriminates on grounds of gender. The generation of 'debts' is known to result from this. Norms that uphold inequality are now attacked by members who strive for social justice. Attention to language use, during general debates, is an integral part of their struggle.

Case material

1. Debts and dividends

CoopaduPeuple started in 1983, when town councillors amalgamated six smaller units, all of which had met, but never exceeded, the minimum requirement of ten members. The merger, the authorities believed, would be productive and enable producers better to reach Butare's central market.

CoopaduPeuple, which also runs a bread project, did not know any serious production problems in 1986, but its members (totalling some 75) invested a huge amount of their time and energy, while still awaiting their first cash rewards some three-and-a-half years after the merger. The problem of how members could be rewarded – an issue bound up with a complex local network of credits and debts – was the subject of many a debate, both in committee meetings and in those attended by all members. Key figures in the committee are its president, the secretary and the treasurer. The first two are men, the treasurer a woman. I shall refer to the treasurer as *trésorière*. When I started visiting CoopaduPeuple, the committee consisted of four men and two women, in spite of the fact that the workforce was predominantly female. A few months later, in the wake of bureaucratic pressures from the capital, two more women were elected to sit on the committee: one as a councillor, the other as vice-president.

My assistant and I were not the only outsiders who attended meetings, but we attended without fail. Other visitors who turned up from time to time were local bureaucrats (*encadreurs*, agronomists) or students from a nearby *Ecole Sociale*, a secondary school for young women who aspire to enter the social services. I start my sketches with a meeting at which three students and their teacher, Mrs Victorina (pseudonym), addressed a full assembly on the subject of the *coopérateurs*' ever-increasing debts. Mrs Victorina has significant responsibilities in Butare's social administration, in addition to her teaching. She is the co-operative's most important contact inside the town bureaucracy. Her students had monitored the co-operative's financial crisis over the past two years.

Victorina's opening speech touched on the nature of existing debts, which derive mainly from the accumulation of unsold produce. (There were also a few cases of arrears in paying back money borrowed from the co-operative's central fund, *La Caisse*.) In the absence of proper storage facilities, vegetables and bread need to be sold in one day, which often proves impossible. Produce not sold on the day is then either consumed in the homes of individual pedlars (whose teams rotate) or distributed on credit terms ('as a debt') to relatives, neighbours or friends. In either case, the produce is unlikely to be paid for, which causes members to go into debt. After opening the debate, Victorina asked her students to read out all recorded debts. This was a sensitive but well-conducted business. At the end of the meeting, Victorina gave guidelines for improving the everyday running of CoopaduPeuple.

It was a fine psychological move when the teacher-administrator started off by discussing the case of the *encadreur* who had vanished with a substantial amount of co-operative money. She gave details, together with a subtle reminder of what everyone suspected, i.e. that the president of CoopaduPeuple had been implicated in the fraud. She then stressed:

> It is not enough to make the *encadreur* pay up. All who belong to this cooperative have to pay back the money they owe CoopaduPeuple; whether for bread or vegetables. Also, those responsible for the money entrusted [when peddling] . . . must pay back or make the others pay [i.e. those who received 'as a debt'].

Victorina also referred to one member who had quitted the co-operative, leaving 'the greatest debt of all time'. She urged everyone to take care, but said she understood that some people disputed the debts recorded in their names. At this point, one older woman, Lucy, interjected: 'that kind of money, the leaders eat it and then claim we haven't paid them.'

Coopérateurs showed patience as individual names and debts were read out. The open session, which followed, was more animated. It started with a direct accusation, when Lucy reiterated: 'we always give [money] to the president, and perhaps he eats it, and he does not write down the *amafranga* [francs] he receives'. Turning round to face the president, who stood behind her, Victorina queried: 'Do you record the money people hand in?'

Embarrassed, president Remera (pseudonym) ignored her question, turning instead to the old man Rwamasasu. (The old man had been told his debt was 600F for bread and 95F for vegetables. 125F = £1.) When Rwamasasu asserted he had paid, the president retaliated: 'If you cannot remember your debt, I shall clarify it for you.' But Rwamasasu remained calm: 'That I am not asking you; that can be discussed later. You may first reply to questions [Victorina] has asked.'

Victorina seized upon the opportunity: 'You hide that you have eaten the money of this co-operative?' Adding strength to her query, she used the proverb: 'eating is pleasant; reimbursing is tasteless' (*kulya biralyoha, kwishyura bikabiha*). By making it clear that eating is 'tasty' and having debts 'distasteful', Victorina voiced her opinion that 'debts' could not be the same as 'food': debts had to be paid back. The possible interchangeability of the two terms – the idea that one needs to have debts in order to eat – had been a popular topic in recent discussion. Le Rigolo (nickname), a spirited young man, would return to this point later on, proposing that some debts be considered remuneration for years of hard work.

Victorina cautioned: 'you must take care with that co-operative money. You have to settle your debts and must avoid having them.' Le Rigolo intervened, bringing the discussion back to that sore issue that it is the leaders, *les supérieurs*, who have the heavier debts, and that ordinary members may well wish to follow that example. His proverb was to the point: 'He who steals with a baby on the back, is he not teaching that baby how to become a thief?' The imagery conformed to the popular rhetoric in which co-operative leaders are equated with parents (see section 2). Le Rigolo clarified:

> If the leaders help themselves to co-operative money, then members will need to do likewise. And they [the leaders] have the greatest debts. In all the debts [read out to us], the people who have the most are those who form the council of leaders (*inama y'ubutegetsi*). Because even that which has been written down, they are only the known debts. And that which you [Victorina] do not know about, it is numerous.

Remera gave in: 'I am the president and I have a debt. I admit this. But you should only look at that which concerns yourself, because you do not know how I am going to settle this debt.'

Dropping his authoritarian stance, he alluded to the possibility that his debts could be settled soon.

Appreciating this sign of goodwill, Le Rigolo spoke 'nice' words: 'Before they ask our members to pay back the debts, it is necessary that our superiors give the example.' Victorina, however, came to the president's rescue, more or less repeating what he had said: 'you should only look at the debt which concerns you; for even should others fail to settle their accounts, they will pay up before the law, and be punished.'

At this point, Lucy reminded everyone, with her usual gusto, of the more immediate problem: that their president had a habit of forgetting to record the money members paid in. She said she had definitely paid her debts and that the three students from the *Ecole Sociale* had been present at the time. The president agreed: 'Yes, I now remember.' The students took the records and crossed out her debt of 600F. Lucy then confronted president Remera: 'You will justify that!'

In turn, another member addressed the need for 'remuneration', explaining that it was virtually impossible not to have debts: 'For instance, food that is not sold, what can we do with it, if it cannot be sold on credit terms?' Victorina's reply indicated that 'debts' could still be considered 'remuneration'. She proposed that any produce, vegetables or bread, left unsold at the end of the day, be distributed among members:

> All produce, you must return it, because when you give it to someone outside the cooperative, or when you take it all for yourself, you know it will never be paid for. You must return [the produce] for distribution among the members, so that everybody receives a share.

But Victorina stood firm that anyone currently in debt had to pay up. Looking certain people straight in the eyes, she told them:

> I do not know how you can progress (lit., go forward) when everyone wants to eat alone [i.e. grab] that which is made for all. Also, in order to make your co-operative go forward, you need to understand that you must work together, so that you can have a profit together.

Quick-witted Lucy did not like being eyed at: 'You look at me as if I am the one who has eaten all the money.' Laughter followed.

It was lunch-time now, and hot. Victorina asked for a hands-up count and separated the members 'with' from those 'without' debts. Only a dozen women had no debts. Expressing her deep regret, Victorina proposed that the co-operative continue only with members who had no debts, including those who intended to settle them soon. The words of the teacher-administrator touched hearts: small token sums were paid into the kitty. One woman paid 20F on behalf of a younger brother.

To indicate she meant business, Victorina threatened to fold up the bread project, which had already been halted, temporarily, because of an outbreak of dysentery. She also threatened to drop the proposal for a fish-farming project, and to abandon the idea of a separate shop (*boutiki*) for CoopaduPeuple. To give members some idea of what they were about to forgo, Victorina explained how fish-ponds can be exploited on a co-operative basis, and assured everyone of her dearest wish to see bread-making continue. She took her leave, summarizing major points: that everyone, whether *supérieur* or ordinary member, should only think of his or her debt, and not point the finger at someone with larger debts who happens to be 'someone [big] in our co-operative'. To show her concern was genuine, Victorina stepped down to the level of the common people, asking: 'Do you think I am here for nothing? I have left a sick child at home and I do not even know whether I shall find it better or worse.' It was as if Victorina had reminded the workers of that 'real world' one must never forget about.

Victorina then proposed to hold a further meeting to sort out the alleged debts. People, she said, could come with their own notes – showing dates and amounts – for comparison with the president's records. She repeated how sad it would be if people were forced to leave the co-operative: 'Imagine that someone with a debt of only 200F would be shown the door! . . . That would cause shame; that would be exaggerated.'

Mrs Victorina had impressed her audience. No-one would have disputed this. Somehow, however, young Rigolo decided to fill in the bottom line, proclaiming: 'Should anyone place money next to me, I could show you what it means to eat *amafranga*.' His equally shrewd friend, sitting next to him, followed this up with a fitting proverb: 'A husband who has no debts, he is no longer a husband.' That was the heart of the matter! The problem of debt repayments could not be separated from the power husbands wield over wives. Victorina had merely called for goodwill on the part of (mainly women) *coopérateurs*, she had not addressed the underlying problem of gender.

Shortly after the meeting, the *trésorière*, at that time the more influential woman on the committee, told me:

> The husbands are messing up our project. Ever since the departure of the expatriate woman teacher who launched our bread scheme (when bread-making was independent of CoopaduPeuple) and the subsequent appointment of the *encadreur* (who embezzled funds), husbands have been a nuisance. Without husbands our co-operative would do well.

The women's ambition, she clarified, was to see two separate projects: one for women, one for men. Women could bake bread, men could grow crops. 'Or if this fails,' she added, 'we want to see the men go out of the project. The women are quite prepared to pay the men for doing the nightwatch (*zamu*) service.'

2. *Co-operation and imagery*

How women experience their involvement in CoopaduPeuple is clearly stated in the above passage. Many were the times during my research when the *trésorière*'s wish for a women-only co-operative was echoed by others. It also transpired that women only rarely distinguish between 'leaders' and 'husbands'. The reason is that the idea of a co-operative is solidly based on the model of husband-wife co-operation. I shall now decribe that model, as it emerged in group discussions.

The model revealed itself one Saturday morning (several months after the meeting described above) when I encountered six workers doing the 'extra day' (*umubyizi*). Doing *umubyizi* is one way of making up for not attending on the usual day the co-operative gathering. Also present that morning were the *trésorière* and the president. I told the two *supérieurs* that I was impressed with what I saw: the two sexes weeding side by side! This is common practice in CoopaduPeuple. I recalled scenes from previous fieldwork in Mambwe country, Zambia (Pottier 1988), and put it to my hosts that Mambwe people considered weeding an activity 'shaming' for men. My remark sparked off some comments:

> President: Everyone works according to the law, especially in co-operatives, there are no differences. Nowadays, in Rwanda, even women may join the army.
>
> Me: And in the home? Are there any differences in how men and women work?
>
> President: This depends on how husband and wife get on. Yes, there are tasks for husbands – thatching and fencing houses. Except for those, all others are carried out by either the man or his wife. Have you not yet seen husbands cook or sweep the courtyard?

There was more to this issue. As the president expressed it on a later occasion: 'Of course, the women too need help (with the bread project). For example: the men who cut the firewood and who take the bread out of the oven.' When the expatriate teacher was still around, the women brought their wood and kneaded the dough themselves. They also handled the oven. After the teacher's departure, and the incorporation of the bread project into CoopaduPeuple, the committee (men) argued that such activities (wood cutting, removing bread) required 'force' and would be undertaken by male members.

I was not getting very far with my conversation on gender-specific tasks, so I changed course. Via my interpreter, I tried the following:

> Every member of the co-operative, man or woman, is involved in community work during at least two and often three full mornings a week. For instance, *umuganda* (for the civil authorities) on a Tuesday; co-operative field work on a Thursday and, occasionally, an extra morning for making bread. Devoting so many mornings to communal labour, does this not hamper the work at home?

I was careful not to refer to women's labour *per se*. Women do outnumber men (by a 6:1 ratio), but as much labour time was required from individual men as from women. The president's reply was 'a beauty': 'Once you involve yourself in a co-operative, you must obey its laws in the manner that a wife must obey the laws her husband imposes.'

Guessing my interest in the matter, the *trésorière* switched promptly to explaining how the teams involved in bread-making co-ordinated their activities. She judged the gender issue rather sensitive in Remera's presence. When I did press somewhat, the *trésorière* gave a stereotype answer, indicating how the extra workload was not that serious a problem:

> For instance, if a woman has a child that is not yet attending school, and she knows that tomorrow she will work for the cooperative, that woman will do her cooking before going to sleep. In the morning she rises early, washes her hands and shows her children the food they will eat in her absence. That way the children keep themselves busy until she returns.

As the conversation developed, I became aware that the five women weeders had stopped work. Only the man continued. I found the sight of one man doing the weeding and five women posing on their hoes, pretending not to follow our conversation, quite delightful. The oldest woman, Lucy (again), then left her companions and walked over to join us. Hiding behind the *trésorière*, out of the president's sight, Lucy called out: 'Three mornings a week? . . . Yes, they torment me a lot!'

Remera, dismayed, ordered her to come forward: 'Explain yourself in front of us.' This was not a friendly invitation. Lucy emerged, laughed, said 'ha', and returned to her companions. Inwardly amused, her co-workers rebuked: 'How dare you? Once you are engaged in a business, you must finish it!' Many meanings were implied: you battle on, whether in weeding or in marriage, or even in this wretched co-operative.

The language of 'family life' permeates the rhetoric and ethos of all co-operative work. There were examples of this in every debate I attended. One of the more telling moments came at the end of the campaign to elect a woman vice-president, when a student from the *Ecole Sociale* decided to do some 'sensitization'. She asked: 'It has been a long time now since we started working with you, but I have yet to ask you something which concerns your cooperative. Could someone tell me what exactly is "the co-operative"?'

Pauline, the older of the three candidates (having just been defeated in the election) offered her thoughts: 'The co-operative, it is to work together well, just like husband and wife work together to ensure that their home progresses and that there are no personal profits (*ubulyamirane*).' Pauline's statement, which met with the students' approval, referred to *how things should be* (at home and in the co-operative), but was quite a departure from the president's own view ('a wife must obey'), which referred *to how things actually were*. The term *ubulyamirane* belongs to the language of sexual intimacy: 'profits' are made when the pleasure of one partner is at the expense of that of the other. Within a true co-operative, personal gain is inappropriate, since members must 'link their wood with the same cord'.

The 'family' metaphor is also used, for example, when the president addresses members as *banyamulyango*, i.e. people of the same family. Such a greeting implies responsibilities and solidarity. However, in one of his more agitated outbursts, of which there were many, Remera became exceptionally explicit: 'The superiors must punish. They have laid down the laws and members have accepted them. This is how it is within a co-operative: no pity! Punish! He who refuses punishment, he divorces with the family (*aciye ukubili n'umulyango*).'

With some exceptions, Rwanda's *supérieurs* are not over-concerned about policy calls for social equality. On the contrary, the old premise that 'a sense of corporate solidarity [can] be achieved in the midst of inequality' (Lemarchand 1977: 68) survives the day. Looking back at work by Macquet, Lemarchand makes the following observation:

> 'The king was a divine and paternal figure,' as Macquet reminds us, 'and this association helped create a feeling among the inhabitants of the country of belonging to an entirety that offered certain analogies to the family' (Macquet 1961: 152). But this was by no means a family of equals. (Lemarchand 1977: 68)

As several of the above statements make clear, the Rwandan family itself is also far from being a unit of equals. Many of the debts referred to by *coopérateurs* are directly related to husbands who harass wives to get the cash earned from peddling.

Something of the average man's attitude towards women showed up on the day bread-making resumed. Remera 'praised' the women in his co-operative as 'most valiant of warriors' (*abantu b'intwali cyane*): beings who do not suffer from *umusa* (the desire for heavy drinking); chosen people who have no debts, who take no bribes and have no *inenge* (moral/physical faults). Men, in contrast, the president said, wasted resources 'because of their stomachs that are very long'. However, almost within the same breath, he picked on two women who, rather obviously,

disapproved of his tongue-in-cheek flattery. He called them 'cows that are here merely to gaze at people with their eyes'.

The material in this section indicates that change along gender lines will take time. When women's work is valued positively, women are cast into the role of superior men ('valiant warriors') – a linguistic manoeuvre which also exists in English (Miller and Swift 1977: 142).

3. Gender and justice: excerpts from an open debate

More was revealed about the nature of debts, and the tension they generate, in that same meeting. The debate dealt with the problem of whether debts could be cancelled through expending labour. Among the 'actors' were Mafuta and Sarah, two very vocal Tutsi women (whose names are fictitious). Other participants were committee member Jerome (pseudonym), a man I shall refer to as Accountant (one of several men who head a team of women bread-makers), and three leaders: the president, the *trésorière* and the secretary.

The following excerpts from the debate, which went on for over two hours, show that global ideas about social justice, including gender equality, are indeed beginning to filter through. Moreover, some men lend support to the new ways of thinking, at least within the context of the co-operative.

When the debate opened it became clear that the committee had modified Victorina's policy proposal that members pay to cancel debts. A distinction was being made between 'vegetable' and 'bread' debts; only the latter needed to be repaid. The former could be settled through *umubyizi* (working 'the extra day'), at the rate of 100F per session.

Accountant: Those people with debts from selling vegetables, are they allowed to come and work [to erase the debts]?
President: Yes, indeed.
Jerome: What matters is that they come and work.
President: This is how it should be.
Sarah (disagreeing): They must pay up! Why has the law changed? Up to now you have said that those with debts will pay.
President (firm): Now it is finished, the discussion is dead. I refuse to go on discussing the same issues.

Mafuta: Long discussions? . . . Why? We women, you are going to lend us some money?

President (justifying his formal, 'set speech' approach): Yes, it is normal for people to engage in discussion, but their thoughts are never the same. *C'est vrai*!

Jerome (addressing the two women): 'What are you talking about? The work done (*umubyizi*) will yield and, eventually, will produce that money.

Mafuta & Sarah (moving on to a related issue): No, we cannot accept. You [the committee] will pay us [for years of devoted work] and we shall depart (i.e. leave for good). You lend us the money. Do we not work?'

All debts, the two women argued, had to be paid for. Should this not be acceptable, then the women too would want to have debts, would want to receive something. Mafuta and Sarah thus pressed for a loan, which they considered a fitting recompense.

President (expanding on his ideas): I rule that he who has a debt-in-the-vegetables or he who has borrowed from the Savings Bank (*Caisse d'Epargne*), he will work a day's work (*umubyizi*) starting at 7 a.m.

Jerome: And then the money we shall find it in that day's work!

President: Yes. But the debts from bread peddling, they must . . .

Sarah (interrupting): So, you will lend us, won't you?

President: What?

Sarah: Yes, you will lend us?

President (feigning authority): You, could you stop talking, your problem has been considered. You, my old dear, I am begging you the peace and tell me if you do not want it.

Mafuta & Sarah: We all cultivate here. The money that goes into the *Caisse*, we have worked for it. (Referring to a basket full of sweet potatoes, they asked): How much money can we find in there?

President: On this question I beg you the peace. Look, the roads are there [i.e. you may join, you may leave]. (Then, addressing husbands): What do the women want from me? I can see, they prevent me doing my work, those women.

Mafuta: What stops men paying off their debts? Once a man has been told, he knows how much he is in debt.

President (courteous): Be quiet, Giver of Life (*Ceceka*, *Mubyeyi*).

If this question saddens you, (don't blame me,) I am not the foundation of this cooperative. There are others, they have ranks, you will ask them. But do not shout amongst the members.

Mafuta (insisting on informal speech): Really, you are going to eat us.

Sarah: We are hoping for an agreeable understanding. Make them pay!

President (rude): You, I am asking you to shut up (*kuziba*) [as opposed to *gucececka*, which is polite]. Leave me in peace.

Sarah (unrelenting): Why are you trying to stop me? I too have laboured! So, are you paying me, and then I leave?

President (horrified): That one, if she does not want the peace, could she let us carry on with the programme?

Accountant: Yes, carry on with your programme, don't let the women talk.

Sarah: Pay me and I leave.

President (polite): You wish to be paid and then you will leave?

Sarah: Yes, come on, be quick.

President (demogogic again): You, the people gathered here, do you accept this?

Sarah (challenging the president's style): Come on, pay me for the five years that I have spent.

President (to Secretary): Are you recording that woman's words?

Sarah: Are you saying that people should be punished for speaking the truth?

President (to Secretary): Are you writing the words?' (Then, unable to control his anger, and trying desperately to emphasise his position as leader (whose words, by definition, must not be challenged)): I have no need of your truth!

Mafuta & Sarah (with forceful irony): What is all this? Look, he is writing! Could it be the money he is going to give? Anything else?

Jerome (with a change of heart?): No, if they so wish, we pay them and they can go.

Mafuta & Sarah (ignoring Jerome): Because you know that it is you, our superiors, who have many debts. Is this why you agree (amongst yourselves)?

(Silence)

Mafuta: No, you may all go home now. We shall see later.

Sarah: What is he writing? . . . That those who have borrowed money, their money increases nothing for us. That he who borrowed that money, afterwards, he will work there (in the fields) and I too will work there. Why? (Why such injustice?) Committee members must cease lending (from the *Caisse*), and may those who have borrowed pay back.

President: No, old dear, you listen. That money must be paid back following the method [of *umubyizi*] for those who cannot find that money.

Sarah (addressing all men): Ha! Anyone is capable (of finding that money) so long as he has built a home.

President (feeling the pressure): How much has been borrowed up to now?

Mafuta & Sarah: No-one has missed that opportunity!

President (angry): You, be quiet! You are saying that no-one has missed out? Are all people the same, then?

Mafuta: Everyone must reimburse. He who has a debt should know how to pay back. (At this point, the women had clearly succeeded in turning the tables. Addressing the president, Mafuta went on, politely): You too, be quiet (*ceceka*!), no-one has missed the opportunity. When people know they cannot find money, that's when they borrow. Otherwise, they don't.

President: The worst thing would be to let this happen again! From now on we must find every means to make the money return. The worst thing would be to lend money yet again.

Mafuta: You, president, you will be unable to pay back and you are now looking for that [way-out] which is simple.

Secretary (keen to 'kill' the debate): Mafuta, please let us finish our assembly. Your problem, we shall come back to it.

Sarah: You cannot ask us to remain quiet. You cannot make it a secret because you are men. You lent that money.

Here I must point out that Mafuta had in fact only just arrived! She had come to the meeting, but had not joined the *coopérateurs* for work that morning.

The president queried: *Niko* [You], Mafuta, you have come to cause disorder, while coming from where?

Mafuta: Let me create disorder then. I am speaking about the money I have worked for.

A husband: *Allez*! Sit down, I have had enough of your talk. And quick, or else, go away.

President (to the husband): Are you also implicated? Do you too want to be paid? Do you want your reward? Let all those who want their recompense agree that this is what they want. *Kabisa*! (Swahili: That's it!).

Torso (nickname, recently married, age-mate of Le Rigolo): Aha! Well, with your permission, you may add me to your list. And I shall never come back.

Mafuta & Sarah: Because the leaders have many debts, they say they are going to cultivate.

President: He who has a debt must cultivate for it.

Mafuta & Sarah: This is what we object to. Reimburse us and we shall go. All those years! It's not nothing.

President: Do not let this problem come back. My friends, this problem I refuse it.

The president threw his biro down, angrily, but made no impression.

Mafuta: If you wish, you may throw it 20 times or even 30, I am not going to remain silent.

(Later)

Mafuta: Do we (women and all other ordinary members), do we not cultivate? And does the money you lend, does it not come from the cooperative's savings?

Mafuta implied that whereas everyone cultivates, the superiors lend only to a few selected people/men. Feeling the pinch, the president now changed direction and, resorting to common logic, tried to defend his policy.

President: Look at that field over there. It is ready to be worked again, thanks to *umubyizi*. Absolutely! So, be quiet, be assured that our money will come back.

Jerome (spelling out the logic): For instance, the beans that we will now plant, will they not produce? And will we not see money in them?

Mafuta (not impressed): Have you, the president, paid up? Is this not the reason why you favour the rule that debtors pay through working extra days?

President: Why do you indulge in quarrels? And why do others support members who quarrel?

Jerome (philosophical, to president): Have you heard the people who go along with those quarrels? They are many . . .

President: Yes, if they find the situation is now impossible, look, then there are the *encadreur* of the *Commune* and the *encadreur* of the *Préfecture* (who can be consulted). Those who dislike my policy can follow the road and ask them whether my policy is possible or impossible. The authorities will tell us what they decide . . . But I am asking those women to stop talking.

In this particular debate, president Remera was unable to maintain the formal, dogmatic approach ('set speech') usually adopted by people in authority. He had to face the fact that the autocratic style of local leadership, which does not tolerate counter argumentation by people of lower status, was deemed inappropriate within the context of a co-operative. His words were being challenged by people without rank – something he and other committee men were not accustomed to. Remera had modelled his position on that of the traditional hill chief, whose views and arguments could not be opposed by commoners. On other occasions too, especially in meetings involving the entire co-operative, the setting had provided the ideal platform for challenging formal oratoric styles.

The leaders of CoopaduPeuple, as harbingers of the development message, aspired to be orators who, in Parkin's words, adapt 'very quickly to the changing demands and responses of audiences, [by] alternating between set and innovative speech', the latter being a style conducive to discussion and questioning (Parkin 1984: 349). The rank-and-file, however, expressed decreasing tolerance of the set style and a growing preference for innovative, question-conducive speech.

Conclusion

CoopaduPeuple has many committed people, mostly women, who persevere against the odds. From the point of view of gender, the constraints are many: there is still no proportional representation within the committee (in spite of the mentioned election); members find it difficult to control credit arrangements, and husbands (as Remera put it) have 'long stomachs' that crave for cash. 'Eating money' is common among committee members.

The case material I have reconstructed shows how *coopérateurs* perceive these adverse circumstances. Mismanagement, gender-related tensions, the spirit of co-operation, and the dire need for cash rewards, are among the issues regularly aired in group discussion. It was only with regard to gender relations that some progress seemed to have been made during the six months that I attended the debates. The involvement of female students and staff from the local *Ecole Sociale*, the election of a woman vice-president, and the unabated attack on idiosyncratic policy-making, indicate that the workforce of CoopaduPeuple is fighting inequality with some confidence and some success. However, there could be victims (when I left, it was unclear whether or not Mafuta had been expelled) and the reported election could still have been a case of token representation.

On the other hand, the debates give rise to some moderate optimism, since they provide a forum for challenging established cultural convention. This convention demands of resource-poor people, women and men, that they refrain from pursuing genuine knowledge or material success; aspirations that run counter to 'the natural order' (Crépeau 1985; Pottier 1986a, 1986b). Rwanda's co-operative movement, as I experienced it, constitutes a new, powerful challenge – a force which has arrived to stay.

This became particularly apparent when the rank-and-file formulated its own version of what was going wrong. Whereas leaders and outsiders (regional bureaucrats) defined problems solely in terms of finance (the need to settle 'debts' and the problem of securing a regular clientele), the workers themselves, through some of the more vocal members, went further and exposed the socio-structural imbalances that underly these debts. Through being clever with words, by forcing their president to shift from formal to informal style, these more vocal members undermined cultural stereotypes (the language of the dominant ideology) and worked towards instilling some change in the self-perception of fellow members. In doing so, they drew inspiration and strength from the poorly understood (but presumed sympathetic) support which the movement enjoys in higher bureaucratic circles, a theme I shall discuss elsewhere.

Planners who take the plight of the deprived at heart need to pay attention both to the content of local debates and to the styles used for expressing ideas or criticisms. Effective intervention, whether direct or reliant on the NGO style, depends on persuasion, which in turn demands familiarity, for instance, with formalized ways of stifling debate (Bloch 1975: 15), with forms of discourse that carry legitimacy, and with the practice of switching between modes of expression, especially between formal and innovative speech – a technique which lends individual speakers a certain creative capacity (Parkin 1984: 349). My case material shows that local actors are conscious of the restrictions imposed by formalized speech and that they know of ways to impose the informal, more innovative mode. Through persevering with the informal mode, ordinary members are able to challenge customary practices and norms. This perseverance (especially effective in the debate involving Mafuta and Sarah) goes some way towards showing that language does indeed assist in the construction of social reality. The members of CoopaduPeuple use language, often proverbs, to break with cultural patterns of the past.

Acknowledgement

The research on which this paper is based was made possible through grants, thankfully received, from the Economic and Social Research Council (ESRC, England) and the Overseas Development Administration (ODA). I also thank the British Academy and the School of Oriental and African Studies for supporting my participation in the conference on 'Understanding Global Food Problems', Aquinas College, Grand Rapids, Michigan (April 1987), at which this paper was discussed. But my greatest 'debt' is to my research assistant, Louis Ruzindana.

Bibliography

Acord, (1987), *Rwanda's Solution: The Search for Rural Employment*, London: Acord.

Bloch, M. (ed.), (1975), *Political Language and Oratory in Traditional Society*, London: Academic Press.

Blumberg, R.L., (1981), 'Females, Farming and Food: Rural Development and Women's Participation in Agricultural Production Systems', in B.C. Lewis (ed.), *Invisible Farmers: Women and the Crisis in Agriculture*, Agency for International Development, Washington, DC: Office of Women in Development, pp. 24–102.

Crépeau, P., (1985), *Parole et Sagesse*, Butare: Institut National de Recherche Scientifique.

Dupriez, H. and de Leener, Ph., (1983), *Agriculture Tropicale en Milieu Paysan Africain*, Paris: L'Harmattan.

Grillo, R.D. *et al.*, (1987), 'Anthropology, Linguistics and Language', in J. Lyons, R. Coates, M. Deuchar and G. Gazdar (eds), *New Horizons in Linguistics* 2, London: Penguin, pp. 268–95.

Lemarchand, R., (1977), 'Rwanda', in R. Lemarchand (ed.), *African Kingship in Perspective: Political Change and Modernization in Monarchial Settings*, London: Frank Cass.

Macquet, J. (1961), *The Premise of Inequality in Rwanda*, London: International African Institute.

Miller, C. and Swift, K., (1977), *Women and Words*, London: Victor Gollancz Ltd.

Parkin, D., (1984), 'Political Language', *Annual Review of Anthropology* 13: 345–65.

Pottier, J., (1986a), 'The politics of famine prevention: ecology, regional production and food complementarity in Western Rwanda', *African Affairs* 85 (339): 207–37.

Pottier, J., (1986b), 'La parole est à deux personnes: knowledge, ignorance and power in the context of urban agriculture in Rwanda', paper presented at the EIDOS conference on 'Local Knowledge and Systems of Ignorance', SOAS, December.

Pottier, J., (1988), *Migrants No More: Settlement and Survival in Mambwe Villages, Zambia*, Manchester: Manchester University Press, for the International African Institute.

Sutton, C. *et al.*, (1975), 'Women, Knowledge and Power', in R. Rohrlich-Leavitt (ed.), *Women Cross-Culturally: Challenge and Change*, The Hague: Mouton.

The politics of naming among the Giriama

David Parkin

First man: Who are you?
Traveller: I am Karisa son of Muramba son of Mweni.
First man: Ah! So you are of the MwaMweni clan. Then we are brothers-in-law, for my sister was married by a MwaMweni. Where do you come from?
Traveller: I come from Kaloleni, near Madebe's place.
Second man: My grandchild, the daughter of my son, was married to a man they call Musela.
Traveller: Yes, I know him. He is BiCharo, . . . that is Kahindi Ngumbao.

This is the kind of exchange that typically occurs between strangers among a people called the Giriama, who live in the immediate hinterland of the coast of Kenya. The Giriama are an African Bantu-speaking group numbering over a hundred thousand people, among whom I have done fieldwork for various periods since 1966. Paradoxically, the longer the period of fieldwork the more intractable appear to be the problems of cultural translation.

The little encounter given above is an example. It appears to be an English translation of a meeting between strangers. Yet what is really needed for an understanding of it is a cultural translation of the society's naming system. Without that, we are reduced to guesswork. Names are no mere labels. They inform discourse and can be as much a part of its creation of surplus meaning as are metaphors.

I will not attempt immediately to make sense of this exchange of names except to say that it contains a wide variety denoting clanship, occupation, personality, and personal identity, through a mixture of what we might call orthodox and informal or nicknames. It is in fact a simple exchange. Much more complicated ones have the characteristics of a language game which builds on shifting themes. They play with the possibilities of defining people and groups as more information is brought in. As with all games there is a competitive edge in the claims made: is the newcomer's clan one that the speaker marries into, are his contacts influential, and what is his own status?

There is an enormous anthropological literature on the study of peoples' naming systems. Lévi-Strauss's early structuralist accounts, to which I return in my conclusion, have been among the most influential (1966), and have themselves been based on still earlier ones. This is not the place to survey that and the subsequent voluminous literature, except to argue that the play of power in naming systems has been largely neglected. Naming may be a form of 'entitling', by which authority is conferred both on the receiver and donor of the name, or of objectification by which, through the choice of a particular name, the namer secures control over the named. In such situations it sometimes happens that persons anticipate such consequences by choosing or controlling the choice of their own names.

I emphasize these aspects of power and control in this essay. I try to show how among a people of coastal Kenya, called the Giriama, the naming system sets up an opposition between 'active' and 'passive' members of society, which paradigmatically also underwrites other distinctions: between active men and passive women in general, but also more specifically among men between those who are deemed active and passive, and in rare instances between active and passive women. 'Active' is here taken to refer to the capacity to influence events in a publicly visible manner, while passive denotes a lack of that capacity. This is the Giriama view, which does not lose sight of the parallel irony: that, through witchcraft and the use of medicine, those who appear passive may well be the most powerful unacknowledged movers of events, though admittedly this is regarded as applying almost entirely to men only. Naming among the Giriama, then, articulates the micro-politics of interpersonal relations. It thus provides a yardstick by which persons are measured and so provides them with a platform for more conventional political advancement.

The distinction between active men and passive women in the realm of naming clearly has implications for other gender relations. Men's patrilineal clan names are visible markers of their entitlement to property inherited from agnates and also to men's prior right to arbitrate on such related matters as the inheritance of the widows of deceased clan-mates, while women's names make no reference to clanship nor, therefore, to transmissible property and politico-judicial rights. This is not to say that women are without such rights, though they do indeed have fewer of them. However, while the jural status of a man can visibly be gauged from his names, that of a woman is most evident through the identity of her father or husband. Nevertheless, beyond the formality of such rules are hidden achievements to which both men and women aspire and which sometimes surface in the names by which they are known.

I have so far avoided referring to the category 'personal name'. This is a difficult enough notion even in Western discourse, where it may as much refer to, say, dynastic genealogy, nationhood, or religious demands (e.g. saints' names) as to the identity of a particular person. In Africa as elsewhere, as various writings have shown (Beattie 1980; Dieterlen 1973; Carrithers *et al.* 1986), the idea of a discrete and sharply separable person entrusted autonomously with his/her own fate is rare and revealed as a Western fiction. By personal name, therefore, I refer to one that is regarded as mainly the property of a particular person (a proper name) but may also be seen as deriving from a grandparent, some of whose qualities may go with it. Among the Giriama, also, all names, including those which we might wish to regard as personal, are seen as complementing each other and forming a system for marking life cycle phases, a system that the Giriama view as operating in large part over and above particular individual wishes.

There is, nevertheless, an area of naming, reasonably translated as nicknaming, which does catch individuals in the act, so they speak, either of carving out their own identities or, through the efforts of friends, relatives and neighbours, being sculpted by others. Among the Giriama, then, a few men, and in rare cases women, attempt to determine their own destinies or those of others, and, in doing so, seek new names that play a part in shaping these destinies and capacities.

A cross-cultural understanding of personal names must include, for example, New Guinea 'sorrow names' (Strathern 1970), Penan death names and friendship names (Needham 1954; 1971), avoidance names, descent names, teknonyms, and many others, variously subject to rules of award, transmission, and withdrawal, and involving many people in different duties and rights (e.g. Barnes 1982). While these are seen to be rule-based in the societies concerned, it is a matter for investigation as to whether and to what extent notions of self and person include at least in part the idea of autonomous agency. Among the Giriama, the area I have called nicknaming is that where individuals joust, so to speak, with the rules, by circumventing them and revealing how difficult it is to put them into practice: to call someone by a nickname is to subvert the authority of those who originally conferred, say, the clan name.

This opposition between rules and subversion has echoes of that between rule-governed society and innovative individual. Both are fictions. Thus the concept of rule presupposes constancy, yet rules in fact change all the time. Similarly, the concept of rational individual assumes a self-determining agent, whereas in fact so-called individual accomplishments are often rationalized fantasies of plans that went wrong or were never made in the first place. But in Western thinking the believed tension between society as a compulsive force and the individual as pitted against it is no less strongly felt and creates movement in each.

Giving a person a name or names is part of this tension, which can be read in various ways. From a structuralist perspective such names may be seen as mediating the contradiction between our being produced by society and therefore without individuality, and yet at the same time as able to speak about society and ourselves within it. From a post-structuralist perspective, giving someone a name draws on the tension between professed rules and facile individual fantasy and threatens to dissolve the distinction between them. That is to say, there is a point at which an increasingly unpopular naming rule may be defended by fewer and fewer people, by in fact no more than a few individuals, while yet other individuals propagate the use of their own variously coined names. This appears to have happened with regard to the now almost obsolete clan naming rules among such other Kenyan peoples as the Digo and Kikuyu, and even, some Girima claim, among their Mijikenda neighbours, the Jibana, Chonyi, and Kambe, and may I suppose occur eventually among the Giriama themselves.

When asked, the Giriama I spoke to first distinguished *three* kinds of names for men: clan, personal, and teknonym (based on, first, an eldest child's and, then, eldest grandchild's names), and *two* for women, who do not have clan names. Through further conversation an additional set of names emerged which are clearly regarded as less formal and which are variously translated as those of 'boasting', 'drinking', and 'self-awarded', and are almost solely the preserve of men. To some extent they overlap with the English notion of nickname. In this way, the Giriama do make an overall distinction between orthodox and informal or nicknames.

Orthodox names

1. Clan name (*dzina ra mbari* or *dzina ra ndani* – literally inside name). The clan name is given by men shortly after birth at a special ceremony. It belongs to the generation of grandparents, which I discuss in detail below.
2. Personal name (*dzina ra ku-gerwa* – the given name, or the less common *dzina ra sare*). This is chosen by the mother at birth, and is normally also that of a grandparent.

Christian and Muslim names assume similar status, with the European baptismal name called *dzina ra dini* or *dzina ra KiKristo*, and the Muslim one known as *dzina ra Kiislamu*.
3. Teknonym (*dzina ra mwana* – child name – *dzina ra mudzukulu* – grandchild name).

Informal or nickname

Less common term is *dzina ra kudzirava*, and more specific terms are: *dzina ra kudzigamba* – boasting name
dzina ra uchi – drinking name
dzina ra kudzigera/kudzipa – self-awarded name
dzina ra mahukano – insult name, often referring to ethnic origin and used at funerals, for instance, as well as between friends, and denoting ethnic joking relations.

Though orthodox names are given or assumed according to set rules over which the person named has no choice, the informal names are in a sense competed for: sometimes they are imposed by others and the named person may be unable to resist them, but sometimes they are encouraged and even promoted in the first place by him (rarely her). They are produced by the cut and thrust of combative personalities and are not subject to rules, or at least not explicit ones. There are other terms used to describe such informal names, as I have indicated above, just as there are names which are semi-formal but not identified in any consistent way. For example, after a succession of children's deaths in a family, a new-born baby may be named (usually in Swahili rather than Giriama), say, 'trouble' (*tabu*) or 'offering' (*sadaka*), with the intention, in the first case, of appearing to devalue the child in order to deter evil spirits wishing to harm and appropriate it, and, in the second, in order to appease such spirits. Such cases increased markedly over two decades in one area of accelerated economic complexity in which I worked.

The distinction between formal and informal names is undoubtedly blurred on occasion and over time but does reflect a clash between personal styles and the explicit social rules. Older linguistic usage would refer to it as a field of rule-governed creativity, in that key elders try to enforce the rules which are therefore constraining, while the inventors of new names try to make them stick. As with so many apparently trivial areas of contestation, the field becomes politically significant as a way in which traditional authorities incorporate new sources of influence and break the rules they might at other times defend: traditional authority is seen to be fallible (or not) and innovators effective (or not).

Let me now go on to show how, through the use of orthodox names, people attempt to place others within set relationships of clanship, sub-clanship, generation, age, gender, and by extension, marriage and affinity. I want then to show how this sets a scene for challenge and counter-challenge to people's thinking about power and its distribution.

The fantasy of rules: Giriama clan names

I regard the rules as fantasy since only some of them operate for some of the people some of the time. Elders sometimes speak of them as would a positivist objectifying material laws of reality, an ordering which clearly suits administrative and judicial thinking, but an ordering more believed in than practised. For neither they nor anyone can predict who will actually be known throughout or during part of his life by his clan name, nor to what extent and how often. Given the wide variety of name types, each person is made up of a shifting bundle of them, in the use of which we may glimpse both some operation of the rules and yet no consistent pattern.

The Giriama are the largest of nine self-recognized sub-groups, each with similar customs whose minor differences have internal importance for the overall grouping known nowadays as the Mijikenda.

For Giriama boys there is a naming ceremony. At this ceremony, carried out before he is a year old, the boy is given his clan name (*dzina ra mbari*) by a paternal grandfather. Girls do not receive clan names.

Giriama society, like other Mijikenda sub-groups, is neatly divided into sections (*mbari*), six in the case of Giriama, each of which is further divided into exogamous clans. Each exogamous clan (also called *mbari*) is normally divided into two sub-clans, each again called *mbari* or sometimes *lukolo*. Some clans have three sub-clans. Sub-clans are the units within which a man may inherit widows. Each sub-clan is called after the name of successive sons of the senior clan founder. The clan as a whole is divided into two named generations, one called the 'fathers' (*abiatu*, literally 'fathers of the people', or simply *baba*, 'fathers'), and the other called 'sons' (*ana*, literally 'children').

Each generation has (usually) six names, none of them occurring twice. The six names in each generation are ranked by birth order of their incumbents. Taking both generations, then, there are twelve names belonging to a particular clan, one set of six being senior to the other set, and each set internally ranked. A very small number of common names are found in other clans. Provided you know which names belong to which clans, a knowledge which key elders have, you can tell a man's clan by asking him his and his father's clan names. This is because the particular combination of, say, my name followed by my father's is not found in any other clan but my own. My father may in fact be of the generation called 'sons', but he is still my personal father and I am called X son of Y. That XY combination is unique to my clan.

The first six sons of a wife are given the six ranked names by birth order, so that you can tell which son is senior to whom. Seventh and successive sons of the same wife re-start the cycle, the seventh receiving the senior-most name, i.e. that of the first son, and so on. The sons of other co-wives are given the clan names in the same way.

At this point it may be helpful to outline the names of two separate clans (both of the Kidzini section), in order to summarize more clearly the way the system operates, or is ideally supposed to.

Overall, the sons of one man are ranked by birth-order and not by the marriages of their mothers. Thus, the first sons of each of two co-wives will share the same clan name of, say, Baya, but the son who was born first is senior, even if his mother was the second co-wife to be married. In fact, in everyday reference and address no two living sons of a man are likely to be known by the same clan name: the junior, i.e. second-born, is the one most likely to be

'Fathers'' generation:

1. Mweni (the first man of the senior generation; the clan is named after him)
2. Masha (ku-masha = to surprise someone)
3. Thoya
4. Baya
5. Nyule
6. Ziwao

'Sons'' generation:

1. Muramba* (mulamba? = a little black bird which leads the morning singing)
2. Maitha**
3. Tsofwa (ku-tsoha = to serve out drink, therefore passive = ku-tsofwa)
4. Taura
5. Bokole (paw-paw fruit which is yellow with ripeness)
6. Kumbatha

* The senior sub-clan is called Mwa Mweni amwa *Muramba*
** The junior sub-clan is called Mwa Mweni amwa *Maitha*
A third sub-clan would be called Mwa Mweni amwa *Tsofwa*

Since 'new' names will be added to successively differentiated sub-clans, they will in time assume the nominal appearance of distinct whole clans and may undergo their own internal differentiation.

Names of the Mwa-Baya-Mwaro clan

'Fathers'	*'Sons'*
1. Baya	1. Yaa
2. Mangi	2. Mweri
3. Jefwa	3. Mwaro
4. Mure	4. Kitunga
5. Nghoka	5. Mwanyule
6. Chogga	6. Wara

Figure 1 Names of the Mwa-Mweni clan

known by a non-clan name. At this level of everyday usage, then, the six clan names may be distributed by birth-order among the six sons of different co-wives. Let us say that one wife has the first son. He will be known as Baya. Then a second wife has three sons before the first wife has her second. The second and third sons of this second wife could then be known in everyday reference and address by the second- and third-ranked names, Mangi and Jefwa. Then, perhaps, a third wife has five sons before either of the other two wives produces a fourth or fifth son. This third wife's fourth and fifth sons will be known by the fourth- and fifth-ranked names, Mure and Nghoka. A fourth wife would need to produce six sons before the other wives produced a sixth, in order that her sixth son be known on an everyday basis as Chogga, the sixth-ranked name. In this fictitious case, each clan name of the generation would be in regular use for no more than one son in the family.

Although this spreading out of clan names in everyday usage already departs from the folk theory of naming, it is itself no more than a tendency. Quite often, at this quotidian level, only one or two sons in a family may be regularly addressed and referred to by their clan names, usually the senior-most.

Why should people seem to shy away from using clan names a great deal in daily communication? It is true that cutting down on the number of clan names for same-birth-order sons of different wives, or for first and seventh sons of a single wife, does avoid the confusion that might result from different sons of the same homestead being called or addressed by the same name. Nevertheless, everyone knows that a male must have his own particular clan name, even if it is not the name by which he is normally known. His clan name is in such cases kept in store, so to speak, for use on special occasions. In other words, Giriama males all receive or inherit clan names shortly after birth, but only a few of them are regularly known by such names.

Though hidden, however, clan names are not forgotten. Indeed, their socio-political significance is sustained by three main occasions on which men bring these names out of storage, though the extent to which they do so is largely their own responsibility.

First, a younger man may approach a 'nationally' respected elder for information about Giriama traditions, including its naming system, and perhaps membership in a secret society and its oathing procedures. A few such elders live in the Giriama traditional capital, the *Kaya*. The younger man, who may well be middle-aged, first offers the elder some palm wine. The elder will ask for the younger man's clan name and those of his forebears up to five generations. A possible response might be, in the case of the Mweni clan, 'My name is Mweni, son of Muramba, son of Thoya, son of Kumbatha, son of Masha . . .'. The number of possible sequences is colossal. The point of the question is said to be to ensure that the younger man is truly a Giriama in the father's line. Personal names and the names of forefathers' wives may also be asked for as part of the check, if the elder happens to have some knowledge of the particular line, but it is not expected that these forefathers' wives will be only Giriama: it is recognized that through inter-marriage they can be from any of the nine Mijikenda sub-groups or, rarely, from some other ethnic group.

The elders of some other Mijikenda sub-groups also insist on comparable confirmations of patrilineal ethnic 'purity' (which is more problematic among those like the Duruma and, formerly, Rabai and to some extent once matrilineal Digo, who recognize a limited form of double descent). The knowledge of these key elders is certainly not fossilized but is used in organizing modern political movements. In the past it was surrounded by tremendous secrecy and is still jealously preserved, though a combination in recent years of tourists and researchers willing to pay for information, is causing its dispersal. The younger man's recitation of clan names is said to be a means of identification, but would seem also to be half of a symbolic symmetry: the younger supplicant brings out clan names which are often effectively hidden from everyday knowledge: while the elder, in exchange, gives out secret ritual and other knowledge, including more details of the wider clan system and its names. The clan names do not, however, as with neighbouring Muslim Swahili names, take on a special, ritual, religious or mystical halo, a point to which I return at the end of this essay.

A second occasion on which a man may have to use his clan name is while travelling in other parts of Giriamaland. In passing a homestead he will greet and then, since he is a stranger, be asked about his home and clan name, and that of his father and grandfather. The questioner will reciprocate by giving details of his own clanship. He may go further and rapidly trace personally known kinship links with the stranger. Even if he cannot do this, he is likely to be able to work out from the stranger's clan name and clanship some classificatory kinship and affinal links. There are only some twenty-odd exogamous clans among the Giriama, and so, in the classificatory sense, almost everyone is related to each other by any number of ways. Giriama strangers can thus immediately create an impression of relatedness and even amity which either of them may try to build on if he wishes. This exchange of clan names is of course a politeness formula. But its importance is considerable among a people who travel frequently, seeking casual or permanent wage employment, herbal medicines native to a particular region or famous traditional doctors, or as petty traders. On the basis of the structural tie that the exchange of clan names creates, people can set up a personally instrumental relationship.

Third, knowing about clan names enables a person to try and structure relationships at funerals, whose social significance is considerable among the Giriama (see Parkin 1972: 77–86). Affines of the deceased should come in large number to his or her funeral. They should also invite their affines, who should also invite theirs. This customary use of serial affinity is tied up with marriage obligations and is respected. It means that among the hundreds of people present at any funeral, there are many drawn from a distance who do not know each other personally. Stating one's clanship and having it authenticated by those who know, publicizes marriageable categories and profitable possibilities. There is a boasting game played at funerals for enjoyment which reflects this emergent structuring of the event. Those neighbours and strangers whose precise clanship status is unknown to each other, may, over their palm wine, test who is the most senior. To return to the lists of clan names I have given, a man, X, may proudly announce that his clan name is Thoya (i.e. a third senior member of the 'fathers'' generation of the Mweni clan), reasonably banking on the chance that his opponent is unlikely to top that grade of the senior generation. His opponent in the game, Y, may indeed not be able to do so, perhaps faring no better than the second ranked name (Mweri) of the 'sons'' generation of the Baya-Mwaro clan. But, at some time, Y will come up against opponents of the 'sons'' generation who have a lower name-grade than himself, and he may see the chance as worth taking. That said, one can hardly blame a man whose clan name is sixth-ranked of the 'sons'' generation for avoiding such tussles if he can. But there are possible compensations. Even if a man has to concede seniority regarding his own clan name, he can seek to soften the blow and, through the names of ancestors, try to claim genealogical if not generational seniority, by demonstrating his descent from an alleged senior lineal founder, whose name is highly ranked. This challenge has more effect within a clan where relative lineal seniority is easier to gauge, but can also be made between clans as opponents vie with each other in claims to originate from a more senior point in their respective sub-clan's formation.

As with the example of the traveller politely exchanging clan-names with the stranger, this game may not by itself alter events. But repeated many times between different people in the numerous small drinking groups that make up much of the male attendance at funerals, it provides a structure into which events are fitted and shaped.

To repeat, there are three occasions when a man may use his clan name, even though he may normally be known by some other name. The system of clan names is, then, like a grid in dark but shallow waters which, in their movements, momentarily reveal scattered glimpses of it. The structure is there but never visible in its entirety.

More recently, the clan name of a father or grandfather has, for a very few poeple, taken on the status of the English surname. It is a name you suffix to other names. It is a style and does not inhibit a man from revealing his own and forebear's names under the three circumstances I have described. Not surprisingly, it is also a style adopted by the very small number of educated women, who have professional status, as teachers for example, and do not have to marry. It is the inverse of the other 'Western' style of a few women who suffix their husband's clan name to their own. At least such women acquire a clan name in this way, and it is significant that these women usually stand apart from other women by virtue of their education or work. They, again, are inversely paralleled by the case of a man who suffixed the name of his mother, and who, as a prominent traditional doctor, also stood apart from other members of his own sex. The custom is uncommon though long established. A few men use both their father's clan name and mother's personal name while others switch between them, perhaps using the one to the exclusion of the other for long periods. In this way, clan names may re-appear or as easily disappear, and perhaps remain unused. Such situational usages hide the complex structure of clan names as a whole.

Let me now return to the question of why clan names should be buried, so to speak, in ordinary everyday discourse. The possibility of confusion is of course a good practical reason for not calling every man by his rightful clan name all the time. With a single clan consisting of thousands of men allocated only twelve names, there might need to be some further means of identification. But the reason for hiding the structure seems to go beyond this practical problem. For a start Giriama clan segments or sections are highly interspersed geographically. The cluster of twenty-six small homesteads in which I first lived includes people from twelve different clans, a half or so of all Giriama clans. Very few women even manage to produce six children. The people could, therefore, use many more clan names on an everyday basis before becoming confused as to who is being referred to. The people do not, so to speak, take up their full allocation of clan names. Many extended families include no more than one or two males in a generation who are commonly called by their clan names.

So, while there is indeed a practical limit as to how many males can be called by the same clan name (and who refer to each other as *somo*, namesake, and their mothers as *misomo*), the Giriama tendency to hide their clan names cannot be explained by this factor alone. I suggest that this tendency, and the corollary usage of a wide range of non-clan names, neatly denote the contrasting parameters by which Giriama men define themselves: clan names are reminders of the need to conform for the most part, while other names open up a sometimes non-conformist route to personal power and self-advancement.

An early European district officer who had worked among a number of Kenyan peoples, once referred to the Giriama in 1914 as 'democratic' and 'independent' by nature (Champion 1914), but in the disapproving sense of anarchic (Smith, 1981: 141), a view echoed by others since then and since independence. In fact 1914 was the year of the famous Giriama rebellion against the British (Brantley 1981), and so it would be surprising if Giriama did not appear to display characteristics which Champion, the district officer, evidently found unpalatable. Nevertheless, Giriama men do indeed nowadays sometimes justify non-conformity in the face of what others regard as moral rules. While rule-governed behaviour is expected, non-conformists may under some circumstances be re-described as strong and fearless. Thus, a young entrepreneur was condemned by elders for ignoring custom. But after succouring to a number of their 'needs', he was praised as a true Giriama warrior leading the people along the path to economic modernity. The Giriama view is that there are indeed times to rebel, and they are ready to cite their uprising against the British in 1914 as evidence of this. But this view in no way invalidates the strong Giriama conviction and faith in traditional legal and dispute settlement procedures, which are seen as the corner stones of Giriama identity and continuity.

Similarly, although it is always partially hidden, the structure of Giriama clan names provides a relatively unambiguous means of inclusion and exclusion. There is always the method of checking a man's clan and sub-group by asking for his clan names. The identity of infiltrators from other ethnic groups is easily located in this way, and, even if their descendants are eventually accepted as Giriama persons as a result of long residence in a Giriama area, their foreign origin is always remembered.

In fact a number of Giriama clans are of non-Giriama origin, a fact well recognized by Giriama themselves, and, if preservation of clan and ethnic boundaries and purity were of such great concern to Giriama, then we might expect the clan names to be used more regularly and openly. But the ecological changes and frequent and rapid population movements of the Mijikenda peoples as a whole have made it neither practicable nor always useful to adhere strictly to boundaries and group membership. Unlike the Luo of Kenya, who, to use Evans-Pritchard's phrase, expanded southwards 'like a line of shunting trucks, each tribe driving out the one in front of it to seek compensation from one yet further in front' (1965: 209), the Mijikenda have for generations repeatedly moved north and south, east and west, and have alternately concentrated in and dispersed from small areas largely within the same region.

Under these conditions a flexible system of clan naming has been the most suitable: stored and so ready to be articulated in defence of shifting clan claims for territory or in marriage; yet not so insistently imposed that personal identities could not be given expression through other means than that of clanship. Nicknames are of course the most expressive of such alternative identities. Intermediary between them and clan names, however, are those which Giriama themselves regard as a separate type and which I call personal names, which belong to all Giriama, are not associated with particular clans, and so are less affected by customary rules of usage.

Personal names

In view of the use of the same cluster of personal names among all or most non-Muslim Mijikenda, it is in fact these rather than the lesser used clan names that might by themselves lead to confusion as to who in any grouping is being referred to, except that they are always qualified by some other name. These Mijikenda-wide names refer to roles, attributes, or events, well-known examples of which are: Karisa (the herder), Katana (child), Charo (journey, given to a child born while his father is away from home), Kazungu (European), Kahindi (Indian), Kasena (friend), Kaingu (cloud),

Kalume (male), Kadzomba (Swahili person), Chembe (named after the famous district officer, Champion, whom I have already referred to, but also, as a pun, meaning the head of an arrow), and many others. They are long-established names, yet their original coining can sometimes be clearly dated, and so they make up a second layer of permanency in the structure of names, somewhat below that of the even longer established clan names.

At this second level, also, are the names normally given to women. Some have clearly traceable meanings, e.g. Kadzo (beautiful one), Kache (girl), Kadii (a long time, referring either to a long gestation period or to a lengthy birth), Kahonzi (the pounder of maize), Kahaso (blessing or medicine), Kavumbi (prolonged rain), Kademu (rag), Karembo (prettiness), Kadale (brass beads), Kan(d)ze (outside), Kahunda (bridewealth), Ndzingo (back of the house, for a girl supposedly born there and in fact derived from the verb, to commit adultery), Mwaka (south or season), Dama (termite or possibly heifer, for which the term is *ndama*), Jumwa (restday or week), and so on.

Other women's names are like most men's names in lacking an easily traceable meaning, e.g. Nyevu, Maku, Mbodze, Monje, Sidi, Mbua, Kizi, and Mgundo. We may note that female names which have the prefix *ka*, expressing diminution, are more likely to have recognizable meaning than those that do not. Among men names prefixed by *ka* also carry clear meaning, as do most other men's personal names: Charo and Chembe (mentioned above), Kitsao (bullock), Kinda (young bird), Kenga (cheat), Kirao (feast), Mupati (wealthy), Ngumbao (hero, warrior), Ndago (thick, tough grass), and Chengo (new village). Indeed there are remarkably few men's non-clan names for which there is not a recognized meaning. People do not pretend to more than guess at the previous circumstances under which these meaningful men's and women's names were first coined. But they point to the invention of such names as an on-going process. These nicknames of the past now co-exist with clan names as the orthodox names of the present. The art of nicknaming continues, producing some names which will die with the person, if not beforehand, but others which catch on.

So, while clan names are formally and ceremoniously handed down relatively unchanged over the generations, other names are part of a public Mijikenda-wide artistic creativity which also stretches back generations. The line between established names and newly coined and therefore unique ones is marked by the use of the term *somo* to refer to or address someone with whom one shares a name, clan or non-clan, for which another term is *tsitwa*. According to Giriama, such namesakes are special friends because they share some indefinable quality that comes from names not simply labelling someone but being part of their human nature. Contrariwise, people with unique nicknames have correspondingly something unique in their personal make-up.

The easier traceability of meanings in men's non-clan names, compared with women's, suggests that there is a higher turnover of men's non-clan names. That is to say, more women's names have been used for longer periods and so have undergone phonological changes which have disguised their original meanings. Proportionally more men's non-clan names are being invented at any one time. This speculation would fit the ease with which men engage in banter about each other's names and reputations. Women, however much they also joke about other women's (and men's) personal attributes, are simply less likely to have the authority,in even an informal sense, to have these attributes inscribed as the person's name. It is an offence for men to discuss and re-name other men's women, and so, while it is true that a child's personal name is chosen by its mother, a new name for a woman is only likely to be invented when she is young on her father's authority, perhaps on the advice of a diviner treating the girl for a sickness requiring a new name.

Putting all this simply, men take a greater part than women in coining new names, and more new names are coined for men than women. Indeed, in so far as women provide their children at birth with personal names drawn from an existing pool, and given that these are often the names of a grandparent, it can be said that women reproduce the structure of names while men are more easily able to innovate within it. This is especially significant in view of the idea that by changing names persons may escape current misfortune or, to put the notion another way, can alter their character or destiny, concepts together translated by the term *mwenendo*, from the verb meaning to go or proceed. Preserving the Giriama metaphor, then, men are more easily able through name changes to alter direction in the course of life.

Informal and nicknames

At this point we can focus on the third level of Giriama names, that of pure inventiveness and context-specific meaning. There is some overlap in time between this third level and the second as I have explained. This third is the level of nicknames invented on the spot, or of names with meanings which directly refer to a situation, attribute, or problem, sometimes seriously, sometimes humourously. In this category, for instance, would be included the sorrow names found among the Wiru of New Guinea and other societies (Strathern 1970), as well as the nicknames which are puns on or statements about situations and persons.

Since this is the level of current tides and fashions, it is where foreign names are borrowed. European Christian names were first borrowed on any scale with the advent of the missions in the late nineteenth century (earlier elsewhere) and since then at an increasing rate, especially following Kenya's independence in 1963 and the expansion of education. Swahili Muslim names have only ever been used as a result of conversion to Islam. However, an increasing number of non-Muslim Giriama children have been given as names terms drawn from the Swahili language, e.g. *tabu* (male: trouble), *juma* (male: week), *matano* (male: five things), *sadaka* (female: offering, blessing, sacrifice), *nyanya* (female: grandmother), *bibi* (female: madame), etc., without being required to become Muslim. Some of these Swahili names (e.g. *Juma*, *Matano*) are even used by Muslim Swahili themselves who, after all, are also subject to changing fashions. But every Swahili has his or her Muslim name and most are regularly known by it. This was almost entirely the case among the Swahili-Digo community of fishermen among whom I worked, whose stress on Islam corresponded with their own desperate efforts to retain land and fishing rights in the face of government and entrepreneurial pressure to relinquish them.

At this third level of borrowed, invented, and context-specific names, we can also place the change of name that a person, especially a child, may undergo if he or she has been sick. I have mentioned the example of a child's name that was altered to *tabu* (trouble, see above) in an attempt, the father said, to deceive the spirits into thinking that nothing would be gained by possessing this particular child for they would get nothing but trouble from it.

At this level, too, are the nicknames invented by a man himself, or by others for him, to denote a personal quality or the circumstances of birth. There is a continuum from those names which are imposed to those which are invented by the named person for himself. Somewhere in between are the collusive games in which persons encourage some kind of nickname and try to shape its connotations.

Imposed nicknames often have an ironic quality. A young boy-child would wander off on his own, quite unlike other children and was called *kachimbizi*, from the verb *ku-chimbira*, to run away. The intended pun is that the verb and name are normally used of women who have a habit of running away from husbands, especially older men, and have to be returned to them. They are not without sympathy, even among some men, for there are many who regard it as perfectly natural that a young woman should seek to escape a much older husband. The ambivalently regarded failings of young adult women are thus laid lightly on the shoulders of a young boy who, even when he becomes a man, will still be known by the name, a continuing oblique reminder of some of the problems of marriage. An old man was known as *Mizigo*, meaning heavy loads. When younger he had many troubes, or perhaps gave his parents anxiety, and so was always heavily burdened or a burden to others. A man born when there was plenty of cattle and grain is called *katembe*, meaning rich. Less benignly, non-Muslims refer to a woman Swahili shop-owner as *Mama sikudai*, meaning 'Don't I have a claim on you', i.e. 'Don't you owe me something?', and to another Swahili Muslim as *Kapiga Mbifu*, ('He cries tightness', with *mbifu* referring to something, like an old coconut, that has dried out and become hard), because he holds back from paying those who work for him, whining that he is without money at the time. Neither of the two Muslims accept these nicknames and are each respectfully referred to by other Muslims by their formal names of Khaddiya Omar and Mzee Awadhi.

With these two exceptions, which clearly arose from tense ethnic-economic relations, nicknames are not invented and used without the knowledge of the adult to whom they apply. They are in fact spontaneously coined, or so it seems, at an informal gathering such as a dance, or when drinking or talking in small groups. The recipient is expected to take them in good humour, and usually does. But he has the right, so to speak, to denounce them. He may engage in counter-banter and thereby suggest alternatives. To the extent that a name becomes acceptable and so endures, the bearer of it has co-operated in its creation. He has publicly accepted that definition of his personality. Some men, and very occasionally women, go further than merely co-operating. They collude and encourage. They may even invent and publicize their own names. A young tourist guide who acts as one who has travelled far, seen much, and is a generous provider of palm wine, became known as *Musela*, meaning sailor, and is the person referred to at the beginning of this essay. A certain Giriama traditional doctor first introduces himself to strangers by his personal and clan names, but then asks them to seek him out in his home area by the name of *Mwiya*, thorn. This has the connotation of power through penetration, which is a quality ascribed both to effective medicine and to vengeful witchcraft. *Mwiya*, the doctor, does indeed warn of his dangerous anger if provoked, and at the same time advertises his curative skills. In the same combative mood, a man who has for most of his life been known by the orthodox Christian and clan names of Samson Ngumbao Mugandi, and who, as a church preacher, gave Christian names to his sons, took on the name *Zhaatu*, meaning 'coming from people' and referring to his claim in a family land dispute to be the senior-most of four grandparents and, as such, the lawful head of the family. More humourously an old woman became known as *Hawe Kadzo Kinyee*. The first of these simply means grandmother and may be used of older women generally, the second is a common personal name for a woman, while the last, the nickname, has the connotation of sexual promiscuity (for both men and women). The woman has grandchildren of her own and is a strong, authoritarian figure who jokes daringly with men, and much enjoys the allusions in the nickname.

Some cases of self-naming become particularly celebrated. A famous chief of Kaloleni died in 1965 after sixteen years of considerable popularity (Parkin 1974: 160–5). He played life the people's way, not the way of colonial government. He held fine feasts, drank palm wine as well as any man, managed to collect taxes without antagonizing people, was not above a little illegal ivory trading, had many wives and kept many cattle, and settled disputes using oaths in the traditional manner. Before becoming such a popular chief, he had coined for himself the name *Kidugwa*, which means hard fighter or competitor. He had already marked out the dominance of his character. Much later, in 1966, a young witch-finder who went on to become famous nationally, cultivated the name of *Kajiwe*, meaning little rock or something of enduring strength (Parkin 1968).

The judicious use of a mixture of orthodox and nicknames frequently defines an otherwise ambiguous social situation. For instance, a younger man, whom I came to know well during my first period among the Giriama in 1966, prided himself on his fearlessness. He joked with and insulted chiefs and headmen, yet stopped short of visibly incurring their wrath. Early on in fieldwork, when other people in and around my homestead were unsure as to how to address me, he called my wife *Hawe*, grandmother but also used by a man of his brother's wife. People were embarrassed: were he and I, then, no more than peers? Was I no higher in status than that? Dare he address my wife in that way? His judgement seemed sound, and anyway there was no alternative. I joked back and my status was settled. We were peers. He called himself in Swahili *Siogopi hata Ulaya*, which means 'I fear nothing, not even Europe(ans)'. The name was shortened to *Siogopi*, 'I fear nothing', and became widely used.

At one end, then, of the Giriama nicknaming continuum, people use names to shape the identities of others, including children. At the other end, men carve out their own identities. In the middle, men are offered nicknames which, through their responses, they accept or reject.

It is notable that passive nicknaming is of children and docile adults, while self-nicknaming is seen as a vigorous assertion of manhood through such motifs as fighting, drunkenness, and fearlessness. In between are men who respond to and even negotiate but do not initiate their own nicknames. Significantly such men-in-the-middle may even, through their names, be ambivalently likened to females while clearly remaining men: it was sometimes remarked that the old man, *Mizigo*, carried burdens just as a woman does, but had the strength of a man to endure them.

It is also notable that nicknaming is neither an attempt simply to label human qualities nor only to create them. It involves aspects of both and is best seen as an on-going process of human definition. A person is both what others make him and also what he makes himself and, from the Giriama viewpoint, the shifting and sometimes negotiable line between the two is a fact of human existence. Thus, manhood in the abstract may mean assertiveness but it is up to a man himself either to insist on his own manhood by inventing an appropriate nickname for himself, risking ridicule if his bluff is called, or not to take this chance and instead wait and see how others define him, and how much he can shift this definition in his favour.

Moreover, the continuum from passive to active nicknaming represents that from non-manhood to manhood. Non-manhood rather than womanhood is here the opposite of manhood: male children can in later life reverse nicknames given them when young; and even the few women who become 'like men' may be nicknamed, as in the example given above, though this is rare. Non-manhood is thus an area of indeterminacy waiting to be defined according to a combination of factors: whether the person is male or female, of thrusting or retiring disposition, and able to earn the respect and liking of those around him or her. Gender provides the clearest tendencies. Young girls may be nicknamed but not normally women, nor do women invent their own nicknames. Men on the other hand are given the chance to name their own degree of manhood, if necessary by subverting existing definitions or supplementing clan and other names.

There is an interesting meta-level parallel. The three naming levels which I outlined earlier (clan names, established non-clan or personal names and new names, including nicknames), also represent a continuum from passive to active definitions of self. That is to say, persons do not choose their clan names which can never be changed. Neither do persons choose their established non-clan names, but at least these may fall into disuse by propagating a new name, especially a nickname, the choice of which the person may sometimes influence or control. Thus, just as within the field of nicknaming there is movement between its active and passive modes, so there is comparable movement within the wider Giriama naming system.

Naming and gender

Since it is men much more than women who can move along from the passive to active modes, the naming system is really depicting a male struggle to escape the constraints of a definition of self imposed by others. Nicknames and personal names enable men to break away from the strictures of clan identity imposed by clan names, which nevertheless remain ineradicable and situationally retrievable although less used in everyday discourse. Men's assertiveness of the *Siogopi* type is the culimination of a journey beginning with the temporary subordination of clanship and finishing with the celebration of self-determining manhood. In other words male assertiveness is placed over and above clanship. The paradox is that clanship is only perpetuated by males among the Giriama and is in other respects regarded as being a very male phenomenon. But clanship is collective manhood, as evidenced in the male arbitration and ritual groups of which it is formed. By subordinating it partially through the use of nicknames and the public withdrawal of clan names, men create the indeterminate arena to which I referred where they can joust and assert themselves as unique individuals, only raising the obligations of clanship periodically and in a secondary manner. Individualism among Giriama men is thus a gradation. Its weakest representation is a man's clan name, for by this is connoted powerfully sanctioned collective obligations. Its strongest representation is the nickname invented by a man himself and foisted, so to speak, on an admiring public. In between is the personal name shared with at least some other Giriama and other Mijikenda or the nickname which has been given to a man with his consent. A Giriama man's repertoire of names is therefore within his range of possible selves, though names are not the only forms of self-identification and construction. But names are important both as markers of qualities and as constitutive of them. What differentiates men from each other is not the unique nature of a particular combination of selves, but more the possibilities for self-expansion and redefinition that each creates. What is striking about Giriama views of human nature is that it is labile and not fixed, as evidenced in the dynamic concept of *mwenendo* to denote what we would translate together as character, destiny, and even ambition. On the whole men regard this as a desirable quality in themselves but as threatening in women, a view not normally shared by women, as far as I can judge.

It is with regard to the use of teknonyms that gender distinctions are at their minimum. Only close kin and friends are entitled to address people by them. Even kinship terms can, like clan names, be used between persons of limited acquaintance who are nevertheless related classificatorily. Like clan names, however, teknonyms are rule-governed and cannot be freely chosen. Indeed, since they denote the honourable status of parent or grandparent, there would be no point in wishing to alter them. The implication in teknonymy that the birth of a child or grandchild ushers in the death of the parent or grandchild is not taken negatively, as is apparently the case in some other societies. Like clan names also, teknonyms are completely at odds with the energy and artistry that goes into creating nicknames: they are part of a person's movement through life stages and not inventively applied to him or her.

At the birth of their first child, whether a boy or a girl, the physical father and mother become known as, say, *BiKadzo* (formerly *AbiKadzo*) and *Mikadzo*, meaning father of *Kadzo* (a girl) and mother of *Kadzo*. With the birth of their first grandchild, the teknonym changes: the words for grandfather and grandmother are *tsawe* and *hawe*, and so the teknonyms referring to a (female) grandchild called *Kache* are *TsoKache* and *HaweKache*. The formula is exactly the same for boys. It is in fact an offence not to address friends or close kin by a teknonym if they have one. Teknonyms are constitutive not only of the persons named by them but also of those who use them in address, for the practice presupposes not just kinship and amity but also that all involved should be or become parents and grandparents, and that the unfortunate exceptions are victims, usually of others' witchcraft. Both teknonymy and clan names mark generational continuity. The first is used in households and close interaction. But the second, clan names, act most effectively in linking strangers wishing to locate their relatedness as well as in reproducing the alternate generations of particular clans which are geographically widely dispersed throughout Giriama country.

Terms of address among kin are too complex to be discussed here but involve the use of either teknonyms or kinship terms. The Giriama kinship terminology is of the wide-flung, open-ended Hawaian type and so, as I have mentioned, most Giriama can find at least some classificatory affinal or kinship link with each other, which will be used in mutual address should they become well acquainted. For those who already know each other well, such kinship or teknonymic terms of address are so normal that they may rarely actually call each other by their personal or other names. There is a logic to this. Given that their names are an aspect of a person's store of possible selves, it is inappropriate or at least risky for those closest to the person to use them to their face. This would be like deciding on the person's behalf which self was appropriate, and, since this might not accord with the bearer's own choice on that occasion, might lead to resentment.

It is among associates who are known but outside this close network that personal and nicknames are used. These are people who are intermediary between strangers and family and both compete and co-operate with each other, sometimes intermarrying. They include unmarried friends and kinship peers who use these names but switch to teknonyms when they become parents. The fighting or competitiveness comes before the intermarrying, however, and so it is these who argue over definitions of selfhood. These are public and therefore political battles and act as preludes and accompaniments to seeking office in, say, the local district council, the local branch of the ruling political party, the co-operative administration, or in a traditional society.

Those men and women who have come to use teknonyms with each other, on the other hand, tend to avoid the possibility of coming into conflict. Politically they have thereby set up something of a neutral zone in the more openly visible political battle for the names that most appropriately reflect men's views of themselves and their policies. This passive, teknonymous domain, with its accompanying use also of kinship terms of endearment and address, fits paradigmatically with the position of women who rarely experience name changes except through teknonymy: their possible selves are allocated according to predictable stages of the life-cycle. Only by subverting their primary domestic roles as wives, mothers, and marriageable daughters can women break out from the cycle: the equivalent of male escape from the generational constraints of clanship. Giriama men state that it is 'wilful' women who are most often possessed by spirits. They also recognize that it is 'wilful' women who, if they are not possessed, may run off to Mombasa or other towns and become Swahili-speaking Muslims. Men claim to regard spirit possession as the better alternative and worth tolerating.

Those few women who do run off, live independently, and assume the status of Muslim Swahili, necessarily take on a new name as well as religion and life-style. They take the name conferred on them by their adopted Islamic community. The name will probably be one of a limited number of religious names, and once assumed, is non-negotiable. In this respect, though they have switched from Giriama to Swahili status, these women have entered an equally structured set of roles. The difference is that their behaviour and identity are now seen to be subject to religious authority rather than that of clanship. But at least they are no different from Swahili men in this respect and so achieve some parity of status. This is not to say that Swahili male and female roles are not sharply distinguished, nor that in all respects women have equal status. It is just that the use of relatively fixed religious names to the exclusion of others applies to both men and women and is seen by the people themselves to represent their common subjection as individuals to the will of God. Of course, individuals can still make their distinctive impression on the world through trade, business, politics, or, in the case of men, religious office. But in doing so, they do not normally use their names as a way of building up, altering, or re-shuffling a repertoire of different possible selves, as do Giriama men.

The use of names in this way among Giriama men not only distinguishes them from Swahili men and women, it also distinguishes Giriama men from Giriama women, whose name repertoire is small and relatively fixed like that of the Swahili. Pushed to the level of an hypothesis, these differences suggest that where personal names (here including nicknames) can be changed and re-combined in different ways, people are likely to see themselves as individually closer to controlling much of their own destiny (regardless of whether they in fact do so), but that where names are fixed and non-negotiable some greater agency is seen as in control: in the case of Giriama women that greater agency is their menfolk, including the witches among them who afflict their children and health; for Swahili men and women it is their God. The significant contrast here regarding names is not that between Giriama and Swahili, but that between Giriama men who are more likely to see personal name changes as a means of social and political advancement, and Giriama women and Swahili men and women together who are less able to regard name changes in this way.

Personal naming in any society makes up some kind of language game. Among Giriama men this is complex and is a form of active reflexivity through which men may change themselves through statements about themselves. Among their less advantaged womenfolk, and among Swahili Muslims, for whom Islamic names have an important religious if not sacred quality, change is less acceptable, and nicknames have little of the assertiveness of Giriama males. Here the language game is more one of passive reflexivity through which persons maintain rather than attempt to alter themselves. The distinction suggests that language games differ from each other not only in terms of their logical complexity but also as instruments of power and subordination.

Let me conclude on this point by asking how far a naming system can be explained, following Lévi-Strauss, in terms of its logical coherence, as against the strategic uses to which it is put by individuals. Let me then ask whether this distinction between logic and strategy is here tenable.

Conclusion

Lévi-Strauss does in fact touch on the question of subordination in his discussion of proper or personal names. He points out that among the Penan, studied by Needham, it is in fact only children who are known by their proper names (or autonyms), and even then only until an ascendant dies, at which point a child is known by that dead relative's name, called a necronym. When another relative dies the child is then known by that person's name, another necronym. This use of successive necronyms occurs until he or she becomes a parent and so becomes teknonymously known by his/her own child's name (Lévi-Strauss 1966: 191–5, based on Needham 1954). In other words his personal name is never used after early childhood. There are yet other aspects, but all point to the member of the community with the least power, the young child, as the only one to be known by its personal name.

At first there appear to be some elements of similarity with the Giriama naming system, in which teknonyms take over from personal names. Lacking clan names women are particularly affected, since they appear to lose their only distinctive characterization of self, their personal name, and to remain with nothing but a teknonym. But what in fact do they lose? For a start they are only known by their teknonyms among close associates. Other people continue to refer to them by their proper names, sometimes also as wife-of-so-and-so. Secondly, even their personal names are normally those of their father's own mother and classificatory mothers, in order of sibling birth seniority. One could say that they were not given much in the first place to express their exclusive selfhood.

Boys similarly are given clan names and sometimes even personal names after grandfathers, so much so that one must wonder how far we can even refer to the existence among the Giriama of personal names which are the sole property, so to speak, of any one individual, i.e. his/her proper name, and not already 'owned' by an ascendant. In fact, as I have explained, there are circumstances in which children may be given names which stress their personal distinctiveness (for instance, to ward off spirits). In other words personal or proper names do exist, but only as exceptions to the rules. Otherwise the orthodox names, as I have called them, either identify people with the alternate generations of grandparents and grandchildren, or distance them from the immediately adjacent ones of parents and children, in both cases fitting them into a system of relationships. Apart from the exceptions, then, all such names play a part in subordinating expressions of exclusive selfhood.

Out of the idea of exceptions to the rules is born that of the nickname, itself governed by at least implicit conventions. Self-made nicknames among the Giriama are the most likely creations of speech to reverse subordination. Lévi-Strauss's mention of nicknames is sparse. He equates them with descriptive names of the kind given, for instance, among the Tiwi, or to cattle among some African pastoral people. They are created anew each time for each individual, no two individuals having the same name (Lévi-Strauss 1966: 188, 206–9; see also Akinasso on the Yoruba 1981). But he only ever regards them as bestowed upon an individual by others, and not as created by that individual for himself, as is the case among certain Giriama. This is not surprising, for Lévi-Strauss's elegant account depends on the idea of an underlying classificatory logic fitting names and name-types in relation to each other, and so acting as a self-determining agent. The simple difference, however, between being named by others (whether or not we call those others a society or a logic) and naming oneself, presupposes conflicting agencies, and requires that we seek to understand the uncertain play of power in this conflict.

Early in the essay I raised the possibility that personal names mediate the contradiction between our being produced by society and yet able to speak creatively about society. I now suggest that this is based on an inappropriate dichotomy of individual and society. It is inappropriate in two ways.

First, the Giriama have ideas which indicate a gradation of individualism. At one extreme is the assertive Giriama self-nicknamer who marks himself out discretely enough to satisfy any amount of Western insistence on the autonomy of the individual. At the other is the Giriama man whose clan name is so used that he is identified with it and with his constituent sub-clan and so partially merges his selfhood with that of other clan members. There is no point along this continuum that we can say that we have arrived at *the* or *a* Giriama individual. Rather, an individual occupies at any one time a number of dispersed points along this continuum, the combination of which varies among individuals.

Second, the rule-based clan names and creative nicknames respectively echo the concepts of *langue* and *parole*, and so of society and the individual. But it is more to the *idea* of rules that the clan names appeal, for in fact only some Giriama men are regularly known by them, even though all have had them allocated. Rather like the famous French Grammar which voluminously consists of more exceptions to the rules than of rules themselves, the system of clan naming in practice allows for many 'ungrammatical' forms of usage. Inventiveness is not the sole prerogative of nicknaming. Persons use names in ingeniously novel combinations and dissolve any neat boundary between rule-based and rule-less behaviour, and so between social and individual innovation.

The names by which persons are known are not, then, allocated by rule-governed institutions but by persons in competition with each other. From our conventional perspective we might say that such politics of naming is inscribed in a people's ontology more directly than is the case, say, with the politics of land allocation. That is to say, naming someone does more than give them an identifiable label, it is part of their personal and social construction. Giving someone land rights, or withholding them, has supposedly a less direct role in their personal and social make-up. However, I believe this to be an error. In much of Africa, as in many other agricultural societies, land is indeed coterminous with social, political, and personal identity, and its bestowal or withdrawal does not simply re-define but re-constitutes persons and groups. Indeed, one could say the same about the politics of religion or of parenthood in societies where these were of fundamental concern. Systems of personal naming are certainly distinctive linguistically and encompass an immense variety. But as aspects of political process, they are like politics anywhere: the struggle for the right to determine human entitlement and even who is human.

References

Akinaso, F.N., (1980), 'The sociolinguistic basis of Yoruba personal names', *Anthropological Lingusitics*, 22: 275–304.

Barnes, R., (1982), 'Personal names and social classification', in D. Parkin (ed.), *Semantic Anthropology*, London: Academic Press.

Beattie, J., (1980), 'The self in traditional Africa', *Africa* 50: 313–20.

Brantley, C., (1981), *The Giriama and Colonial Resistance in Kenya, 1800–1920*, Berkeley: University of California Press.

Carrithers, M., Collins, S. and Lukes, S. (eds), (1986), *The Category of the Person*, Cambridge: Cambridge University Press.

Champion, A.M., (1914), *Memorandum: Labour Supply and the Giriama*, Nairobi: Kenya National Archives.
Dieterlen, G., (ed.), (1973), *La Notion de la Personne en Afrique Noire*, Paris: Edition du Centre Nationale de Recherche Scientifique.
Evans-Pritchard, E.E., (1965), 'Luo tribes and clans', in *The Position of Women in Primitive Society*, London: Faber.
Lévi-Strauss, C., (1966), (1962), *The Savage Mind*, London: Weidenfeld & Nicolson.
Needham, R., (1954), 'The system of teknonyms and death-names of the Penan', *Southwestern Journal of Anthropology* 10: 416–31.
Needham, R., (1971), 'Penan friendship names', in T. Beidelman (ed.), *The Translation of Culture*, London: Tavistock.
Parkin, D.J., (1968), 'Medicines and men of influence', *Man* 3: 424–39.
Parkin, D.J., (1972), *Palms, Wine and Witnesses*, San Francisco: Chandler.
Parkin, D.J., (1974), 'National independence and local tradition in a Kenya trading centre', *Bulletin of the School of Oriental and African Studies*, 37: 157–74.
Strathern, A., (1970), 'Wiru penthonyms', *Bijdragen tot de Taal-Land-, en Volkenkunde*, 126: 59–74.

The exploitation of linguistic mis-match: towards an ethnography of customs and manners

Maryon McDonald

Going native

The material and ideas presented in this paper draw on fieldwork carried out in Brittany in the late 1970s and early 1980s, a time of the hey-day of political counter-culture in France. I spent part of my time in the ranks of the Breton language movement, attending the movement's meetings and studying, demonstrating and learning Breton with its members; and part of my time in an agricultural area in central Finistère, among native Breton-speakers. The members of the Breton movement, many of them students and some of them qualified social scientists, did not feel that my fieldwork had properly begun until I had gone to the 'real' people, the native Breton-speaking peasants of Lower Brittany (on this, see McDonald 1987).

Anthropologists have similarly pursued 'real' people and 'native' languages, although they have often been uncritical of the structures of enthusiasm within which such a pursuit is carried out. I hope to give some indication in this paper of the problems that might be involved. A much fuller discussion of these issues, and of the material and ideas presented here, can be found in other words cited in the text (see especially McDonald 1982; 1989). At the same time, the following paragraphs might, I hope, suggest ways in which an ethnographic approach to language might positively develop.

It might be helpful, before launching into the main body of the paper, to draw out two relevant stages in the history of earlier anthropological approaches to language which are of special relevance for the material presented here. Firstly, we can take the early days of anthropology, from roughly 1850–1920. This period was marked by increased travel and empire, and a corresponding interest in other cultures. Linguistics was already established as a discipline, and when anthropologists bothered with language at all, they generally approached it from within the framework of 'Indo-European' linguistics which this discipline offered with authority. Within this framework, language and race were taken to be congruent, and even consubstantial, categories (see Henson 1974; McDonald 1986a). A clearly related assumption was that of links between a language and the mental capacities and cultural proclivities of its speakers. Languages, like people, were divided into two broad categories: civilized and primitive. The most obviously 'primitive' languages were those outside the 'Indo-European' categorization, and it was the languages of this latter category which provided the model of linguistic order. Reports regularly came in of how primitive languages were incapable of precision, lacked certain areas of vocabulary or had too many words where one would suffice, of how their vocabulary was slippery and unstable and their sounds indeterminate and wavering (see the citations, from nineteenth-century and early twentieth-century anthropologists, missionaries and linguistics, in Henson 1971 and 1974). Moreover, the natives themselves were restless, shifty, subject to their emotions, unpredictable and mysterious. It was not difficult to read the mis-matches of the linguistic and non-linguistic into each other, and to confirm the boundaries which civilization sought, in self-definition, to draw around itself.

I shall return to such mis-matches, and their interpretation, later in this paper. The second stage I want briefly to mention in the relationship of anthropology and language is that inaugurated by Malinowski, from roughly the 1920s onwards. Malinowski claimed anthropological fieldwork as his own invention, and is generally held to have been the first anthropologist to have advocated carrying out research, on the spot, through the 'native language' (see Henson 1974: chapter II). There are many features of Malinowski's insights into language which we might now regret, and we have moved, I think, towards rather different notions, if only at a simple technical level, of what learning, speaking and understanding a language involves. However, such points easily become smart criticism from a safe distance. We owe it to Malinowski that, within the British tradition, language and translation issues came within the ethnographic focus.

Much of what Malinowski inaugurated was refined, or sometimes displaced, by the work of American anthropologists (notably the insights of Boas, Sapir and Whorf) and more especially by the insights into language which derived, through structuralism, from the work of Ferdinand de Saussure (see Ardener (ed.) 1971). However, the main principle has continued of learning, and conducting fieldwork in, the native language. It has taken some time to realize that, in the social context in which the native language exists, its definition and its learning and use are not unproblematic, and that these issues are very much the stuff of ethnography as are the persuasiveness of pursuing a different language, and the values which constitute it. Through the French and Breton example, I want, in this paper, to make some attempt at an ethnography of language difference and its interpretation. Ideas about 'going native' must inevitably pose questions about in whose world and imagery the 'native' is constructed, and similarly ideas about learning a language must inevitably pose questions about whose definition and image of this language, or whose socio-language, we are learning and obeying.

France and Britain

This paper is largely about the interpretations of language difference in France, but in any anthropological account some comparison with the home situation is inevitable. In this case, comparison with Britain is instructive. The two contexts of Britain and France offer two worlds of very different political and linguistic sensibilities. Both France and Britain have some consciousness of being 'nations', and have ideas about national languages. The political units of 'nations' as we now know them, and related ideas about national languages, took their shape largely in the late eighteenth and nineteenth centuries. It was, in many ways, France which gave the model of the modern nation to the world, and which encouraged the map of Europe and the wider world to organize itself into these apparently objective and inalienable units of the natural order. Ideas about 'nation' and about national languages do not, however, easily translate between the very different units of Britain and France. For example, Frenchmen will readily discuss *La France* and declaim '*Vive la France*!' in a way which in Britain could easily – were 'Brittania' to allow it – seem to be melodrama or simple xenophobia (cf. D. Johnson 1986). However, what might feel, to the British, to be melodrama, xenophobia or perverse self-obsession is closer, in France, to a tradition of necessary self-consciousness. A good deal of political reflection in France has been concerned with the very existence of the French nation, and its history is one of insecurity and constitutional volatility in comparison with that of Great Britain. France has been occupied by foreign forces, enemies and allies, four times in the last two hundred years, and has tried to define its way, over the same period, through two monarchies, one consulate, two empires, five republics, one definitive revolution, the Paris Commune, the Vichy regime, and May 1968. Through this succession of external threat and internal upheaval, France and the Jacobin State gave to the world a model of directive centralization, and France has developed a strong tradition of preoccupation of the nation with itself (cf. McDonald 1989).

One result of all this is that, in the French context, *la nation* and *la France* are synonymous in a monopoly of the 'nation' which has no equivalent in Britain. Wales and Scotland, for example, can claim national status and have national institutions (including libraries, universities etc.) without spelling the end of civilization as we know it. In France, on the other hand, areas such as Brittany or the Basque country are, at best, 'regions' or constituent parts of the single nation. Any attempt to map on to the French situation the constituent units of Britain, and to elevate the regions to nations, no matter how folkloric the elevation might be, still smells in France of serious political sedition.

'Nation' and '*la nation*' do not easily translate then, the one into the other. Similarly, notions of national languages, their place and status, pose translational difficulties of more than a technical kind. The French Revolution of 1789 marks, in conventional historiography, the birth of the modern French nation, and it was also an event which inaugurated an unprecedented politicization of the French language. French national identity and the French language became inextricably linked, with ideas of French-for-all-citizens inherent in the ideas of liberty, equality and fraternity. The French language, through a national education system, became an important means by which the French nation was to be created, and it has regularly been called on, internally and externally, as the main means of national self-definition. There has been no comparable politicization of English in England or the British Isles, where comparable resources of self-definition were not required and where English was already the largely *de facto* language of the kingdom two hundred years before France and French were reborn in active synonymy in the 1789 Revolution.

The stories of English and of national identity have not been so neatly aligned (see McCrum *et al.* 1986). In France, the ideal of French-for-all became a fairly constant battle throughout the nineteenth century, and on into this century, with fears for the very existence of France amply confirmed by opposition from largely clerical, aristocratic and anti-republican supporters of regional languages. It has not been until relatively recent times – since the new self-consciously international context of the post-war years – that the cause of promoting any regional language has become respectable in national political debate in France, rather than being cast as dangerously reactionary or seditious. It is only since the 1960s and 1970s that the cause of a minority or regional language such as Breton has moved from being the property of political reaction to being the property of the political left. This move was influenced strongly by the events of May 1968, and by other events such as Algeria and Third World peasant movements, and it was a political shift which came about under, and in opposition to, a largely right-wing regime. Since the late 1960s and 1970s, many French intellectuals have found political excitement and mileage in attacking French and writing about Breton, and in a Republic which has, since its inception, made the French nation and the French language synonymous, there could be no better stick than a regional language, such as Breton, with which to beat the government and the Establishment on the head (cf. McDonald 1987: 127).

The modern Breton movement (or *Emsav* in Breton) is made up of many overlapping groups and societies, united, in public statement at least, in 'defence' of the Breton language. The modern movement is, in its dominant self-image, almost entirely left-wing, and its members well-educated, often to university level. Most members of the movement, or 'militants' in their own terminology, were themselves brought up in French, but they have generally learnt Breton and use it with some enthusiasm. For these Breton militants, as for many educated Frenchmen, Breton is now definitely a 'language'. Until recent times, it was only French which, in educated circles, was dignified with the title of 'language'; everything else was a *patois*, *idiome local* or *dialecte*. If Breton is a language, however, then it should, in the militants' view, be able to replace French. The result of such an ambition is a mis-match of socio-language between the militants' Breton language, which should ideally be used everywhere and for all purposes, and local use of Breton amongst native Breton-speakers. I shall return to this sociolinguistic mis-match in the last section of this paper.

The relationship between the militants and the native Breton-speakers whom they claim to represent, is an interesting and complex one, of which I can give only very brief glimpses here. A brief outline of a very common format of militant discussion meetings in Brittany might itself suggest some of the problems involved. Militants often meet, amongst themselves, to discuss the state and future of the Breton language. The discussion commonly laments the demise of Breton, and blame is laid largely on the French State. French national policies are said to have been deliberately designed to destroy Breton, and to have oppressed and traumatized the Breton people. Native Breton-speakers are said to be becoming difficult to find, especially in the locality (usually urban) of the meetings, and even when native-speakers can be found they will not converse freely in Breton with the militants. Native-speakers are, it is concluded, 'ashamed' of Breton. It will be necessary to 'conscientize' the Breton people, therefore, and also for the militants to promote Breton by using it themselves and by constructing their own Breton-speaking environment.

In the meantime, in the nearby countryside or sometimes in the same bar, native Breton-speakers might well be conversing in Breton amongst themselves, and the more so once the militants have ended their meeting and taken their well-educated and politically loaded presence elsewhere.

There are no official census figures giving the number of Breton-speakers, but 500,000 is the estimate most commonly given in militant literature. Although we do not have official figures, we do have some idea of the demographic shape of the Breton-speaking population. The most commonly presented picture is one of a constant retreat of the Celtic Breton language, retreating first before the invasions of the Romans and continuing right on up to the invasions of Chirac and Mitterand. However, while Breton continued to contract socially and geographically within the French political context of the nineteenth century, the classes and areas within which Breton was spoken grew in numerical size of population. It seems likely that the number of Breton-speakers reached its highest ever level in the twentieth century, just prior to the First World War. Most of these speakers were geographically concentrated, then as now, in western Brittany. After the First World War, Brittany's population, rather than rising as it had in the nineteenth century, began, like that of France more generally, to fall or remain at much the same level – this demographic alignment being itself an index of the more general and pervasive influence of metropolitan values in the regional countryside at this period (cf. E. Weber 1977). The number of Breton-speakers declined also due to the social and economic ambitions of parents who, aided by the schools, were bringing up their children in French. After the Second World War, Brittany participated in the more general 'population explosion' but this new population growth, largely among those living in or aiming for the towns and for the growing secondary and tertiary sectors of the post-war economy, was not in social or geographical sectors consistent with the transmission of Breton. We thus have a notional profile in which the number of Breton-speakers peaked in the period before the First World War, then began a steady decline, and has fallen off more sharply in the decades since the Second World War.

It is interesting that just when the native Breton-speaking population, concentrated in the peasantry of westernmost Brittany, was thus in demographic decline, both the Breton language and the peasant became ripe for revaluation. A romantic association of Breton, the peasant and the soil was already common in nineteenth-century clerical and aristocratic Breton nationalism. However, events of the 1960s, including both political changes and a notable shift of population in France from country to town, together with the influence of Third World peasant movements, helped firmly to implicate the peasant in the 'alternative' and politically leftist discourse of the modern urban intellectual. Brittany's population remained predominantly rural until the mid-1960s (later than the population of the rest of France) and the Breton-speaking peasant then quickly became a ready focus of intellectual interest, finding himself revalued in a vision of an 'alternative society' which the modern Breton movement has strongly espoused.

Political, economic and demographic differences between France and Britain have resulted in a very different situation in terms of both of the general majority contexts, and of the status and shape of the regional minorities inhabiting these contexts. In Britain, the Celtic minorities are numerically small, but are relatively well known on the international stage. In many ways, the political and literary reflection which, in Britain, could go into the construction of these minorities went, in France, into the existence of the French nation itself. At the same time, France has retained relatively large rural populations, speaking regional languages, and in these populations and their languages has been invested a powerfully persuasive political morality of opposition to centralization and the 'system'. In spite of the differences of context, there is nevertheless much in this political morality, as it is applied to the regional languages, which is common to the British context and to many other contexts in which cultural difference is found or asserted. It is to some of these common features of cultural difference, its construction or interpretation, that we turn in the next section.

Order and disorder

Anthropologists, in their study of other cultures, now tend to give priority to the conceptual worlds under study. Some features of these worlds may feel more concrete than others, but they are none the less conceptual for that. The cultural or conceptual worlds we study are all category-based, and modern anthropology has become, for many, the study of categories or classificatory systems in action, whether or not the classificatory systems in question find expression or backing in language (see the essays in Parkin (ed.) 1982). We know that when different cultures or classificatory systems come into contact, they do not match up neatly, and this mis-match or lack of fit readily leads to misunderstanding. This could happen when different modes of greeting meet each other (see Ardener 1982 on the shaking of 'hands' in Ibo and English) or when different modes of teasing behaviour are encountered, leading to a sense of impending violence (see Benson 1981:41 on such encounters in Brixton) or when a whole complex of mis-matches gives a heightened sense of threat, volatility and strangeness (see Husband (ed.) 1982 on customary European views of blacks). It is now well established in anthropology that one set of cultural practices, when observed or heard through the structures of another, can make its practitioners seem volatile, unpredictable, irrational, inconsistent, capricious, or even dangerous. This sense or location of disorder and uncertainty in the 'other' is very common in the drawing of us/them boundaries, whether in the boundary of civilized/barbarian or in nineteenth-century expressions of nations and their frontiers, or in the drawing of centre/periphery relations more generally (see Okely 1983 on relations between the sedentary majority society and the mobile Traveller-Gypsies). The apprehension of mis-match, or lack of fit, will be picked up particularly at an us/them boundary, evoking it, giving it expression, and empirical confirmation. There will commonly be a dominant discourse (or genre, or systematized way of talking about it) in which the mis-match will find expression, and in modern European thought that apprehension of indeterminacy easily becomes confirmation of a rational/irrational dichotomy, and of the various systematized versions of this, in 'reason/emotions', and so on, which the twin discourses of positivism and romanticism, accompanying the construction of nations and their peripheries, have left us in legacy (cf. McDonald 1988a; 1989). To take one example: the common image of the excitable, fun-loving, soulful, and sexy or passionate French held by the self-consciously rational English should, within this framework, come as no surprise. The self-consciously rational Englishman 'knows', within a now very common discourse of representation, that Frenchmen are emotional and passionate, and differences of verbal and body language, in which the French can appear to get very excited with their words and tone, and wave their arms about and, good heavens, kiss each other, readily confirm the imagery and its distribution between the two halves of the English/French pair (the us/them boundary operative in this instance). In a taxonomy of national self-definition, where nations define themselves in contra-distinction to other nations, the French readily reproduce versions of this imagery of themselves and turn it to virtue. When, however, metropolitan France turns its face not outwards to other nations, but inwards to its peripheries, it does not claim this imagery but attributes it instead to the margins and re-situates itself on the other side of the dichotomy, as structured centrality, or order and rationality.

The dualities involved in this imagery are not, I would stress, mere ideas floating in the ether, but a unity of theory and observation which has constructed the realities of national, racial, ethnic and gender differences, and the map of human knowledge, and much else besides. In this unity of theory and observation, or simultaneity of mis-match and its interpretation, can be found empirical proof that the French, say, are emotional, that women are irrational, that blacks are violent and sexy, that the Celts are other-wordly, that facts and values are indeed separate things, and so on and so on. At the same time, any half of these self-evocative dichotomies can be cast in positive or negative light. Being primitive and irrational might exclude one from rational government, but it does allow the attribution and assumption of poetry, spontaneity and down-to-earthness perhaps.

Relations between intellectuals and peasants, and between Paris and Brittany, have made great use of such imagery, in both its negative and positive expressions. In a negative light, educated France has commonly seen Brittany as close to the soil and natural, but thereby also primitive and dirty, as well as untrustworthy, potentially violent, emotional, and given to drink. The truth and proof of such perceptions have regularly been found in anything from the *chouan* revolts to differences in modes of drinking (see McDonald 1988b). At the local level within Brittany, however, the landed moral security of the peasantry has been able to find, within the same structures, moral disorder and uncertainty on its boundaries, casting intellectual newcomers in very similar colours (see McDonald 1989: chapter 14).

In more positive light, from nineteenth-century romanticism to modern, post-1960s opposition to the 'system', intellectuals have also pursued the Breton peasant as anything from the repository of religiosity and spirituality to the model of let-it-all-hang-out liberation. I want to turn now more specifically to the empirical proof of such realities that can be found, and has often been found, in the Breton language the Breton peasant speaks. It is the language, above all, which defines the modern, self-consciously 'Breton' identity of the militant intellectual, and he regularly looks to the peasant world for confirmation of the cultural difference which he himself seeks, and, within this, of the political morality which, for the movement, divides the Breton, in language and identity, from all things French.

Learning Breton is an important activity of the movement, and militants learn their Breton in schools and universities and outside mainstream education in classes which they themselves organize. I will give here two examples of linguistic commentary, interpreting syntactical and semantic mis-match, which regularly occurred in militant Breton classes and meetings, both at university level and outside it.

First of all, we can take the example of word-order in Breton. A strong moral and political position was commonly taken over this by militants, and the word-order in Breton regularly boasted as an important Celtic and distinctly un-French aspect of the language. Some explanation is needed to understand this question. For example, in French, the sentence *je vais à l'école* ('I go to (the) school'), begins with *je*, as does the English with 'I'. In Breton, however, there are several possibilities of word-order. The most 'neutral' statement, which would usually translate the French *je vais à l'école*, would begin with a verbal noun or infinitive, followed by a form of the verb 'to do', giving *mont a ran d'ar skol* (word-for-word, 'going I do to the school'). A translation following the french word-order, giving *me a ya d'ar skol* (word-for-word, 'me, I got to the school'), would usually draw attention to the subject, as in the French *moi, je vais à l'école*. If 'to the school' is put first, followed by a conjugated verb, this usually emphasizes where one is going, as in, for example, *d'ar skil ez an* (word-for-word, 'to the school I go'). These three possibilities, with their different emphases, might answer, respectively, the questions: 'What are you doing?' 'Who is going to (the) school?', and 'Where are you going?' Students were frequently warned against always putting the subject (for example, *me*) first, in imitation of French word-order. We were warned, indeed, against any tendency towards 'contamination' of Breton by French, syntactical or lexical.

The word-order pattern in Breton is usually explained as 'putting the most important idea first', and the whole 'Breton' world was commonly read into this, especially by younger, enthusiastic teachers and by students. It was said in one class that Breton-speakers spoke like this because they were 'direct', 'frank', 'spontaneous' and thought 'concretely'. 'Celts', it was said in this connection, had a 'well-known hatred of abstraction'. Having to think again about putting the subject first helped to 'deconstipate' the minds of learners, it was explained, 'liberating' them from the 'logical restraints of French': their minds were thus opened up to a different world in which *je*, for example, did not come first because Bretons were less concerned with the 'self' than with the 'community'. Breton contained within itself the structure of a 'different society'. Such views about the word-order of Breton are very common amongst enthusiasts, whether expressed orally or in print. When translated literally, word-for-word, the word-order of Breton can make it sound very curious and often poetic, in French as in English. For example, a poet might say *beau est ce livre* ('beautiful is this book') in French, although this word-order in Breton, as *brav eo al levr-man*, is a prosaic statement. None the less, many enthusiasts have, by literal translation, willingly found poetry, metaphor, allegory, and strong hints of philosophical and political subversion and revolution in the word-order of Breton, along with revelations of a truly Celtic and minority world (for some of these ideas in print, see Ozouf-Sohier 1970:7; Brekilien 1976:96–105; Servat 1979:85; CNB 1981:9). When read through the structures of French in this way, Breton conjures up and confirms a wonderful world of different relations, in which the syntactical becomes the social, and in which poet and dissenter alike see hope and liberation.

Negative images of savagery, deficit and disorder have here been replaced, within the same structures of interpretation, by poetry, revolution and the alternative society. In keeping with this, in Breton classes and meetings, militants do not use the term *merci*. Here we come to my second example. Many Breton-language courses and militant meetings are conducted in leisure hours or during holiday periods, and an atmosphere of holiday is common, with the very use of Breton tending to encourage the conviction that normal rules no longer apply. At meal-times on Breton-learning courses, some learners and teachers would regularly delight in throwing bread; on one occasion an enthusiast put his feet up on the dinner table. Through 'Breton' came a flurry of releases that ranged from a scorn of 'structure' and 'grammar' in the classes, to a flouting of conventional manners. On one occasion, when food was thrown and snatched at meal-time, it was explained that 'peasants do not say "thank-you", you see'. 'Breton does not have a word for *merci*', and politeness was all part of a 'bourgeois, French world'.

The question of *merci* (or 'thank-you') and its related politenesses is an interesting one. Both in Breton-language classes and outside them, militants sometimes live their synonymous opposition to the 'system', capitalism and French, and their image of the popular peasant world, by flouting normal manners. Food is not usually thrown or snatched by peasants in their own daily world, however, and such behaviour would be considered rude. The popular Breton-speaking world has, on the contrary, its own often strict politenesses (see Hélias 1975; 1977). My own experience with Breton-speaking peasantry suggests, however, how this misinterpretation by the militants might arise, with easy confirmation of the reality they live and pursue. Social eating in the peasant world, beyond the immediate family, is commonly part of a system of giving and repaying, with its own obligations and courtesies. It is usually only when something is given (food or otherwise) that is not part of the local system of reciprocation, that 'thank-you' is said, as *merci*. There is often reluctance to say *merci*, because it can imply acceptance of a debt to the giver, which the receiver has neither the means nor the intention of repaying appropriately: *merci* would, in this sense, close reciprocation. *Merci* is also used in the same routine sense that it has in the French-speaking world; as such, however, it is more commonly used by the women at village level, and also on special occasions, or with outsiders who are ambiguously placed in the local system of reciprocation.

The *merci* of local Breton-speakers is, therefore, rarer than the *merci* of the wider French world. The non-linguistic courtesies and obligations of peasant reciprocation do not find linguistic expression, and cannot be translated either linguistically or socially into the militant world, where no comparable system of reciprocation exists. The impression is readily formed, therefore, that 'peasants do not say "thank-you" ', and that, on this evidence, they live in a world of healthy rudeness and unaffected naturality. The exploitation of this mis-match by the militants, being 'Breton' in their meetings, brings feet on to the table, bread flying through the air, and turns a playful holiday world into serious political opposition and peasant authenticity.

Where is the 'language'?

I have said that militants of the Breton movement see Breton as a 'language', and they would like it to be used fully and officially. For the moment, however, the native Breton-speakers of Brittany have their own socio-language, their own complex proprieties of differential Breton and French-use (for details see McDonald 1982; 1986b; 1989). These properties do not match the linguistic ambitions of the militants, but, as I shall suggest in a moment, the militants have, within their own political epistemology and historiography, their own way of dealing with the mis-matches involved.

The values invested in French and those invested in Breton largely determine, for speakers and observers alike, what French or Breton is. We cannot somehow sweep away these values – whether they are the values of the French authorities or of the Breton militants or of native Breton-speaking peasants – and get to the language underneath, or get behind the obstacles, the interpretations, or the socio-linguistic evaluations, to find the language in its true or pristine form and value. The language does not exist external to the social context of its evaluation and use.

The language *is* the values invested in it, or the values woven into it by its speakers.

In some ways, the enthusiasms of minority language movements such as the Breton movement, and those of anthropologists, have been very similar, and in their shared enthusiasms lie both an interest in the 'native' language and the obstacles to an ethnography of language and language difference. The Breton movement's interest in the Breton language has, within their own evaluations of it, its own momentum and persuasiveness. The movement's focus on the Breton language, and the values within which that language and culture are defined, do not include, other than as aberrations or default, the manners, properties and aspirations of the native Breton-speaking population whose world the Breton movement would seem to be claiming to defend. If people do not speak Breton in all contexts this is, in the militant view, because they have been oppressed by the French nation-state, suffer from alienation, 'mental blocks' and complexes as a result, and are 'ashamed' of their language. This view is constructed in discursive independence of the world it purports to defend but, at the same time, can find ample confirmation of the alienation, complexes, shame, etc. which it sets forth. Since educated people such as those involved in the Breton movement can create around themselves a French-speaking context, this alone might seem to confirm both the disappearance of Breton and the 'shame' attached to Breton by its native-speakers. It is assumed that, were the native-speakers *not* ashamed or complexed in some way, then they would simply carry on in Breton. There is no space in this model for respect of the customary boundaries of which it is demanding transgression, or for the complex system of social proprieties into which are woven, at the popular level, the use of Breton and French. Breton can easily, within this system of proprieties, appear less formal, less posh, less polite, less prestigious or less sophisticated, and it might seem, on those grounds, that shame must, therefore, be attached. However, there is a more complicated distribution of moral pluses and minuses here, and if Breton can seem less formal, and so on, then it can also be more friendly and intimate. Such an image of Breton, although the mere obverse of apparent 'shame', is not difficult for militants to accept (as the earlier example of *merci* might suggest). In certain bars, in the fields, and among the men at some mixed gatherings, for instance, there might be contexts in which French is inappropriate. Popular sanctions, tacit or ribald, against the use of

French (if only surprise, or a sense that someone was angry, or the expectation of a joke, which an unexpected use of French might create) might be taken within the militant world to be simple confirmation of the right and natural way for Bretons to behave. When Bretons do *not* speak Breton, they are ashamed (and so on) and when they *do* speak Breton, they are still confirmation of the militants' views. If it is accepted, however, that there may be popular sanctions against French, it has to be accepted that there are also strong contextual sanctions against Breton. The contextual proprieties involved in each case cannot be understood independently, and together form a coherent system of values. The 'shame' which the Breton-learner may personally encounter among Breton-speakers is not quite what it seems. It is not shame of Breton, but shame of Breton in specific social contexts, part of which may be the educated learner himself. When the learner or militant is not there, Breton may again flourish, and will be without shame. The militant view of Breton identity is a very common one of national and minority identity alike, demanding the identification of a people with a particular language and culture. Militants focus on the language. Bretons not only have their language, however, they also have their manners.

References

Ardener, E. (ed.), (1971), *Social Anthropology and Language*, London: Tavistock.
Ardener, E., (1982), 'Social anthropology, language and reality', in D. Parkin (ed.), (1982).
Benson, S., (1981), *Ambiguous Ethnicity*, Cambridge University Press.
Brekilien, Y., (1976), *Le Breton. Langue Celtique*, Quimper: Nature et Bretagne.
CNB, (1981), 'La Langue Interdite . . .', in *Le Canard de Nantes a Brest*, no. 107–8.
Hélias, P.-J., (1975), *Le Cheval d'Orgueil*, Paris: Plon.
Hélias, P.-J., (1977), *Le Savoir-Vivre en Bretagne*, Chateaulin: Le Doare.
Henson, H., (1971), 'Early British Anthropologists and Language', in Ardener (ed.), (1971).
Henson, H., (1974), *British Social Anthropologists and Language*, Oxford: Clarendon Press.
Husband, L., (1982), *Race in Britain. Continuity and Change*, Hutchinson University Library.
Johnson, D., (1986), 'French identity: the historian's view', in J. Bridgford (ed.), *Image and Identity in France*, Association for the Study of Modern and Contemporary France.
McCrum, R., Crann, W. and MacNeil, R., (1986), *The Story of English*, London: Faber & Faber.
McDonald, M., (1982), 'Social Aspects of Language and Education in Brittany, France', D.Phil. thesis, University of Oxford.
McDonald, M., (1986a), 'Celtic Ethnic Kinship and the Problem of Being English', *Current Anthropology* 27 (4): 333–47.

McDonald, M., (1986b), 'Brittany: Politics and Women in a Minority World', in R. Ridd and H. Callaway (eds), *Caught Up In Conflict . . . Women's Responses to Political Strife*, London and New York: Macmillan.

McDonald, M., (1987), 'The politics of fieldwork in Brittany' in A. Jackson (ed.) (1987), *Anthropology at Home*, London and New York: Tavistock.

McDonald, M., (1988a), 'Stereotypes', paper presented to 'Identity' workshop, Department of Human Sciences, Oxford University, January.

McDonald, M., 1988b, 'Drinking and Identity in the West of France', paper presented to social anthropology research seminar at Oxford University and the LSE.

McDonald, M., (1989), '*We Are Not French*!' *Language, Culture and Identity in Brittany*, London and New York: Routledge.

Okely, J., (1982), *The Traveller Gypsies*, Cambridge University Press.

Ozouf-Sohier, M., (1970), 'Deux langues, deux cultures', *Le Pays Breton* 149:7.

Parkin, D., (1982), (ed.), *Semantic Anthropology*, London: Academic Press.

Servat, G., (1979), 'Une voix en avant, deux voix en arrière', in *Bretagnes, les chevaux d'espoir*, Special issue of *Autrement*, no. 19, Paris.

Weber, E., (1977), *Peasants into Frenchmen*, London: Chatto & Windus.

Language, power and linguistic minorities: the need for an alternative approach to bilingualism, language maintenance and shift

Marilyn Martin-Jones

Over the last thirty years, the sociolinguistic study of bilingualism among linguistic minorities has been dominated by two different research traditions: the first began with the work of Weinreich (1953) on *Languages in Contact* and was subsequently developed by Ferguson (1959) and, then, Fishman (1967 and 1972) during the 1960s and early 1970s. For those working within this tradition, the main concern was with accounting for the functional differentiation of languages in bilingual communities. The conceptual framework and the research procedures developed during this period still continue to be influential today. The second and more recent tradition is that associated with the work of Gumperz (1982) and Gal (1979). Within this second tradition, the emphasis is on the social and linguistic processes operating at the micro-level of social encounters and conversational interactions. The focus is on the individual bilingual, on the emblematic use of language and on change over time.

In this paper, I will present a critical evaluation of these two different approaches to the study of bilingualism among linguistic minorities. For the most part, I will be drawing on work related to the situations of regional minority languages in Europe. I will focus on the ways in which the conceptual framework developed within each of the two approaches reflects the influence of particular schools of thought in the social sciences and particular ways of thinking about social relations and social action. I will deal first with the notions of 'diglossia' (Ferguson 1959; Fishman 1967) and 'domains of language use' (Fishman 1972). I will show how these notions are derived from structuralist and functionalist views of language and society and I will outline the constraints that are inevitably imposed on the study of bilingualism by constructs developed within a structural-functional framework.

In the second part of my paper, I will then turn to work by Gal

(1979) and Gumperz (1982) which represents quite a different approach to bilingualism. They draw primarily on interpretative traditions within the social sciences and their focus is on the way in which individual bilinguals draw on the languages in their repertoire in face-to-face interactions with other bilinguals. This focus on individual patterns of language choice is coupled with the use of network analysis as a means of accounting for variation. Focusing primarily on the work of Gal (1979), I will compare this approach with that developed within a structural-functional framework. I will then go on to indicate what I see as the main limitations of this micro-interactionist approach.

In the final section, I will look at a third area of work on bilingualism among linguistic minorities which has not received the attention it deserves. Contributions in this area have come primarily from anthropologists, sociologists and linguists concerned with regional minority languages in Europe. I will argue that these studies demonstrate the need for an alternative agenda in sociolinguistic research on bilingualism among linguistic minorities and I will consider some of the issues that would need to be included on that agenda.

The structural-functional perspective

Weinreich (1953) was the first to approach the study of bilingualism from a structural-functional perspective. His particular concern was with the extent to which the functional differentiation of languages in contact situations could act as an impediment to what he called 'linguistic interference'. He also introduced the term 'domain of language use' to American sociolinguistics. The term had first been used by a German linguist, Schmidt-Rohr (1932), some twenty years beforehand. Weinreich noted that some attempts had been made to build taxonomies of language functions but hinted that these could only be improved upon as comparative evidence from language surveys in different bilingual communities became available.

A similar taxonomic approach to the description of language functions is evident in the diglossic models developed by Ferguson (1959) and Fishman (1967). In these models, a binary distinction is made between High (H) and Low (L) language varieties. The use of H and L varieties is seen as being governed by community norms of appropriacy, with the H variety being more appropriate for formal situations and the L variety being more appropriate for informal situations. The communicative functions of the languages varieties are thus represented as if they fell into a neat pattern of complementary distribution, with virtually no overlap. Ferguson says that, in diglossic situations, the functions of H and L varieties only overlap to a small extent.

Fishman (1967;1971 and 1972) was the only one to extend the diglossia concept to bilingual situations, so, in the remainder of this section, I will be referring primarily to his model of diglossia. The shortcomings of this model are particularly evident if we look at bilingualism among linguistic minorities. I would like to draw attention to four central problems. All four stem from the structural-functional view of society which underpins the diglossic framework.

The first derives from the way in which the language choices of individual bilinguals are characterized. They are seen as mere reflections of community-wide norms. Fishman (1972) uses the term 'choice' quite liberally in describing the language practices of individual bilinguals, however, the use of the term is hardly apt since the model actually denies the possibility of choice. All members of a bilingual community are seen as being constrained to 'proper usage' (1972: 435), with the languages in the community repertoire falling into a neat pattern of complementary distribution. As one researcher concerned with bilingualism among minorities has rightly observed: 'Complementary distribution of the co-existing languages virtually eliminates the possibility of random choice' (Eckert 1980: 1054).

There is no scope for dealing with individual or group variation within a structural-functional framework of this kind because of the emphasis on norms and consensus as central features of social relations and social activity. For researchers faced with the sociolinguistic realities of language use among linguistic minorities, the limitations of the consensus model are only too apparent. Among linguistic minorities everywhere, there are individuals and groups with divergent interests and allegiances which are associated with markedly different linguistic practices and language attitudes. It was sociolinguists working in situations characterized by this kind of diversity who first began to contest the concept of community implicit in the diglossia model. Gumperz, for example, argued that: 'The assumption that speech communities, defined as functionally integrated social systems with shared norms of evaluation, can actually be isolated, . . . [is] subject to serious question' (1982: 26).

The second and fundamental problem in Fishman's work also derives from structural-functional thinking. Power is treated as a secondary phenomenon while norms and values are seen as being the most basic features of social activity. Diglossia is characterized as a natural and common sense reality. No account is given of the social origins of the functional division of labour between the H and L languages. The model merely represents this division of labour as a natural form of social and linguistic order, thereby implicitly reinforcing the legitimization of the H language. Eckert demonstrates very clearly the inadequacies of the diglossic framework in her study of a Gascon-speaking community in Ariége. She says that, in this community, Gascon and French are not 'separate and equal' but 'separate and unequal' (1980: 1053). She illustrates her point with reference to the notion of appropriacy. She shows how constraints on the 'appropriate' use of Gascon are not accompanied by constraints on the use of French. It is only the minority language which is deemed to be 'trespassing' on the domains of the dominant language. As Eckert points out, severe social sanctions can operate to prevent a minority language from 'trespassing' in domains where the power of dominant social forces is vested. An excellent example of this is the widely documented nineteenth-century phenomenon of minority language children being physically punished at school for speaking their mother tongue.

The third problem with the diglossia model is the inadequacy of the notion of situation of language use. In the early formulation of the model, speech situations were differentiated in rather vague socio-psychological terms with reference to degrees of formality. Fishman attempted a number of refinements of this notion of situation of language use from a sociological point of view (1971 and 1972). Using the concept of 'domain' as a pivot, he tried to link the analysis of language use in face-to-face encounters with 'widespread cultural norms and expectations' (1972: 441) operating at the macro-level of social relations.

According to Fishman, 'domains are defined, regardless of their number, in terms of institutional contexts and their congruent behavioural co-occurrences' (ibid.). In other words, they are seen as broadly equivalent to the spheres of activity in which social life is organized and in terms of which society's members conceptualize their own individual activities. In his model, domains are differentiated according to the 'role relationships' which characterize them and according to other components like locale and topic. They are portrayed as abstract 'sociocultural constructs' rather than actual instances of language use and as part of a system of societal regularities underpinning actual speech event. However, Fishman did not address himself to the question of exactly what connections there might be between domains as abstract sociocultural constructs and actual speech events and their interpretation; or, between widespread cultural norms and expectations and the language choices of individual bilinguals.

Breitborde (1983) has attempted to explore these connections in a more explicit manner. Like Fishman, he argues that the nature of social encounters is primarily defined in terms of the social statuses (or role relationships) of those who are involved in them. He goes on to observe that, as social actors, we rarely present ourselves in terms of a single social status: He says: 'We interact with others with whom we are linked through a variety of relationships and, while certain statuses may be dominant in a particular situation, others are present for potential manipulation by us or others' (1983: 24).

Breitborde then proposes a means of accounting for the way in which social statuses are ordered within societal domains. Unfortunately, the solution he offers remains firmly situated within a structural-functional paradigm. He suggests that 'the degree of overlap between domains establishes which statuses are relevant in which situations, i.e. the structure of the macro-level determines the internal structure of social situations' (1983: 26–7).

As in Fishman's work, what we see here is a rather rigid and deterministic account of the way in which situations of language use come to be defined. Communicative interaction and code choice among bilinguals is seen as a mere reflex of macro-level statuses and structures.

Not surprisingly, attempts to apply a domain-type analysis in ethnographic observations of language use in bilingual minority communities have not met with much success. In her study of a Gaelic-speaking fishing community in Scotland, Dorian (1981) found that the use of Gaelic was broadly associated with three domains: home, religion and work. It was still predominantly used in the first two domains. However, in the work domain, there was considerable variation among speakers in their use of Gaelic and English. Patterns of language use reflected the identity of the interlocutors, the setting and the function of the interaction in subtle and multi-faceted ways. Of all these domain components, Dorian reported that the age and the identity of the interlocutor carried the most weight, often overriding setting in influencing language allocation.

Gal (1979) in her study of a minority Hungarian-speaking community in Oberwart, Austria, also found that the age and the identity of the interlocutor was most likely to influence a speaker's choice of Hungarian or German. Domain components such as topic or locale carried much less weight. As an ethnographer, she came to the following conclusion about the utility of domain analysis:

> A few weeks of observation in Oberwart made it clear that no single rule would account for all choices between languages. Statements to the effect that one language is used at home and another in school-work-street, would be too simplistic. (1979: 99)

The fourth problem with the diglossic framework is that it offers no means of explaining change over time. Within this static model, it is not possible to account for the social and linguistic processes involved in language retention and shift among bilingual minorities. Various modifications of the diglossia model have been attempted in order to accommodate bilingual settings where one language variety is beginning to be used for functions formally reserved for another. For example, Fasold (1984) uses the term 'leaky diglossia' to refer to situations such as these. However, attempts to make adjustments to the original diglossia framework only serve to highlight its deficiencies. The only way to account for change in patterns of language use is to attribute it to the breakdown of diglossia and of societal consensus regarding appropriacy of language allocation.

This is precisely the line of argument that Fishman resorts to in his characterization of situations of bilingualism without diglossia. He says that:

> Bilingualism without diglossia tends to be transitional . . . Without separate though complementary norms and values to establish and maintain functional separation of the speech varieties, that language or variety which is fortunate enough to be associated with the drift of social forces tends to displace the other(s). (1971: 298)

So, for Fishman, a fictitious stable bilingualism is the norm and the only acceptable form of social and linguistic order. Bilingualism without diglossia, on the other hand, is seen as a deviation from that norm and an inevitable phase in the shift to monolingualism.

Fishman's claims about bilingualism without diglossia have enjoyed much more attention than they deserve. They are based on a false set of premises: first, as I have already indicated, the notion that languages in a bilingual community fall into a neat pattern of complementary distribution is an overly simplistic one and clearly at odds with sociolinguistic realities. Empirical work conducted over the last ten years or so has demonstrated quite conclusively that language use among bilinguals is highly variable. Rapid and frequent codeswitching has been shown to be a characteristic feature of conversational interaction in situations of bilingualism with and without diglossia.

My second point follows on from this first one: if diglossia represents an idealization of actual communicative practices in bilingual communities, how then can its absence be claimed to be a predictor of language shift? The contrast in Fishman's model between an idealized, stable situation of bilingualism with diglossia and transitional bilingualism without diglossia, is, in my view, a spurious one.

Thirdly, the association of diglossia with a notion of stability is highly misleading. Ferguson (1959) was the first to identify stability as a feature of diglossia. It has even been suggested that diglossia can reinforce stability (Wexler 1971). This preoccupation with stability again reveals the influence of a structural-functional view of society. Most situations of bilingualism with or without diglossia are characterized by variation and change. Moreover, as Eckert (1980) has pointed out, diglossic situations can actually embody the source of change. Among linguistic minorities, the conflicts implicit in diglossia can constitute a significant factor in language shift to the dominant language. Eckert says:

> The functions of the standard language exist in opposition to those of the vernacular, and this opposition can operate as a powerful force of assimilation, by interacting with and reinforcing social evaluation of the domains in which the two languages are used. (1980: 1050)

She goes on to argue that, given certain configurations of

economic conditions and social inequality, minority languages may not be able to survive any type of diglossic situation.

In her work, Eckert gives us some pointers as to how a more dynamic, historical model of the relationship between dominant and minority languages should be formulated; one which offers a way of accounting for the processes of language retention and shift within linguistic minority communities. Her work is grounded in a different theoretical tradition, which incorporates a conflict perspective. I will discuss her views, along with those of others who have developed a similar approach to bilingualism in the third section of this paper.

The micro-interactionist perspective

Since the late 1970s, there has been a shift away from rather fruitless attempts to provide synchronic accounts of the norms governing 'stable patterns of choice'. The focus in more recent work such as that of Gal (1979) and Gumperz (1982) has been on variation and change over time. Gal's (1979) study of language shift among Hungarian speakers in Oberwart, Austria represented the first major step in this direction. In this study, Gal argues that the primary goal in investigating language shift among linguistic minorities should be to ascertain how change in patterns of allegiance actually takes place. This can only be achieved, she says, by focusing on social and linguistic processes operating at the micro-level of interaction.

The shift from macro- to micro-level studies of bilingualism reflects the increasing dissatisfaction among sociolinguists with the structural-functional view of the role of language in social life. As Gumperz puts it:

> There is a need for a social theory which accounts for the communicative functions of linguistic variability and for its relation to speakers' goals without reference to untestable functionalist assumptions about conformity or nonconformance to closed systems of norms. (1982: 29)

The alternative model of language use, proposed by Gumperz and applied by Gal in her study in Oberwart, draws heavily on the interpretative traditions within the social sciences, including symbolic interactionism, ethnomethodology and the work of Goffman. Gumperz's model has obvious attractions for linguists because it offers a rationale for observing language use at the level of face-to-face interactions. Central to the model is the premise that individuals express intentions and make choices in the context of their conversational interactions with others. Individual members of society are portrayed as active subjects who create their own meanings through strategic uses of language in context.

Sociolinguistic analyses of bilingualism based on this paradigm represent a considerable advance over those developed within a structural-functional framework. Individual bilinguals are seen as actively contributing to the definition and redefinition of the symbolic value of the languages within the community repertoire in the context of daily interaction, instead of passively observing idealized norms of language allocation. It is also possible to accommodate divergent patterns of allegiance and shift among members of the same community. The model can also account for change over time in patterns of language use since the emphasis is on process rather than structure.

However, there are still a number of major problems implicit in this approach to bilingualism among minorities. I will comment here on two related issues: (1) the way in which the linguistic choices of individual speakers are accounted for; and (2) the significance accorded to social network analysis. To illustrate my arguments, I will refer primarily to the study of language shift conducted by Gal (1979).

I turn first to the problem of accounting for individual language choices. The observational focus is on the individual. Concentrating on language use at the micro-level of individual interactions makes it possible to provide fine-grained and systematic descriptions of language use. However, problems arise when attempts are made to account for individual choices. Explanations are typically sought with reference to socio-psychological processes. However, in my view, this approach to the study of bilingual discourse over-emphasizes the freedom of choice speakers have in expressing their intentions. It also over-emphasizes the degree to which bilinguals can consciously monitor and control their use of language. Speakers are characterized as autonomous conversational participants who consciously opt to project messages about their social identity in accordance with their perceptions of the identity of their interlocutors. Individual cognitive strategies are emphasized at the expense of the social.

In Gal's study, for example, the focus is on the presentation of self through strategic patterns of language choice. She says that bilinguals in the minority Hungarian-speaking community in Oberwart either show a commitment to a peasant identity by using Hungarian or they opt to speak German, which has 'connotations that include prestige and pride in their social mobility and their worker status' (1979: 172). Gal never fully addresses herself to the question of what the source of these connotations of 'prestige' and 'pride' might be. Like other sociolinguists working within this paradigm, she sets out to provide a genuinely social account of language variation and change in a linguistic minority community. She aims to 'show how factors such as class, education, or sex enter into speakers' cognitive strategies and their linguistic choices during interaction' (1979: 13). However, because of the limitations of the conceptual framework she has adopted, Gal falls far short of these stated aims. In her analysis, she has no way of taking account of the social relations of inequality which lie behind the communicative strategies of individual bilinguals.

This brings me to the second related problem. One way in which Gal does attempt to introduce a social dimension to her analysis of the situation in Oberwart is by using the concept of social network. In doing so, she is employing a research procedure first introduced to sociolinguistics by Blom and Gumperz (1972). Social network analysis has now been widely adopted in recent sociolinguistic work despite the fact that anthropologists and sociologists have found it to be of only limited value.

In the seventies, sociolinguists working among heterogeneous populations were attracted to network analysis for much the same reasons as anthropologists working in urban settings in the sixties. It offered a way of focusing observations on the interactional links between people within a local area: men and women involved in regular face-to-face interaction with each other and engaging in the mutual exchange of rights and obligations. Involvement in close-knit networks came to be seen as a key factor in the development and reinforcement of communicative norms, conventions and values. Gumperz outlines the rationale for adopting the concept of network in sociolinguistic work as follows:

> Whenever networks of relationships reflect long-term interpersonal cooperation in the performance of regular tasks

> and the pursuit of shared goals, they favor the creation of behavioral routines and communicative conventions that become conventionally associated with and serve to mark component activities. (1982: 42)

Linguists who have used network analysis in studies of variation have, as in many of the earlier anthropological accounts, concentrated almost exclusively on the internal structure of networks. They have been concerned with factors such as network density and with the nature of the relationship between different members of a network. Various means of quantifying type and degree of network involvement have been devised. Correlations have then been established between network variables such as these and the patterns of language use observed for individual speakers.

In her study of Oberwart, Gal (1979) constructed an index of 'peasantness' based on the attributes associated with peasant status in the Hungarian-speaking community. The patterns of language choice for each of her thirty-two informants were then compared with their scores on the network index. She found that the use of Hungarian did indeed closely reflect degree of involvement in peasant networks (as measured by her index); while a preference for the use of German correlated closely with the range of urban-based social contacts that each speaker had.

The way in which Gal interprets these correlations suggests that she conceives of networks as independent dimensions of social organization capable of shaping social practice, albeit indirectly. She says that: 'Social networks do not influence language use directly but rather by shaping people's goals and their means of action' (1979: 15). Gal is not alone in assigning such significance to networks. There is growing confidence among sociolinguists that the concept of social network can be used to explain some patterns of linguistic variation. It has also been suggested that networks might provide a way of linking analyses of the patterns of language use of individual speakers with analyses of socio-historical processes operating at the 'macro'-level. This view comes over in Gal's study too. She argues that the connection between 'macro'-level forces and sociolinguistic processes operating at the level of face-to-face interaction can be characterized as follows:

> It is through their effects on the shape of social networks, on the status speakers want to claim, and on the cultural association

> between linguistic varieties and social groups that macro-sociological factors can influence the language choice of speakers in everyday interaction. (1979: 17)

Too much analytic weight is given here and elsewhere in Gal's work to the concept of network. As Grillo (1986) has pointed out networks are only of secondary significance in social explanation. He suggests that one useful way of conceptualizing them is as the 'ground on which people respond to, and manage, the pressures of change' (1986: 6).

In Gal's quantitative analysis of variation in the patterns of bilingual language use in Oberwart, age and gender also turned out to be important social variables. For example, among the younger informants in her study, the contrast in patterns of language choice between those with a peasant network and those with a predominantly urban network was much slighter than for those aged over 35. Age of the informant was thus more significant as a social variable than pattern of network involvement.

Ultimately, age, gender and network-related differences in patterns of language use in this and other linguistic minority communities need to be more fully explained with reference to developments taking place at the political and economic level, to the ideological impact of these developments and to concomitant shifts in social relations of inequality. Gal actually describes the political and economic history of Oberwart at some length and gives a well documented account of the way in which unequal relations of political and economic power have become established between the dominant German-speaking community and the increasingly marginalized Hungarian-speaking one. However, this account is merely presented as a historical backdrop to the study. No explicit linkages are made with the analysis of day-to-day patterns of language use because the model Gal is working with does not allow her to do so.

Beyond the limitations of current approaches

In more recent work, Gal (1983) has come to acknowledge the need to take fuller account of social and historical conditions in studies of bilingualism and language shift among linguistic minorities.[1] She outlines as follows the questions that still need to be addressed in this area of sociolinguistics:

> stability as well as change in usage patterns over time should be viewed as speakers' responses to large-scale social processes most often originating far outside their own communities: Among the crucial questions, then, are how should these processes be conceptualised; how do they come to effect speakers' conceptions of each language's connotations; and how do speakers actively incorporate these connotations in interaction strategies which allow others to interpret speakers' communicative intent? (1983: 65)

As I have shown, Gal focused primarily on the third question in her work in Oberwart. She also partially addressed the second question but did not go beyond a detailed description of the 'connotations' associated with Hungarian and German. She did not, in my view, pursue far enough the issue of how 'large-scale social processes' come to influence the 'connotations' of dominant and dominated languages. Throughout the Oberwart study, there are strong hints that she does, in fact, see the search for answers to the first question as being of vital importance. She has now stated this view more explicitly: 'A historically and materially based understanding of the relationship of domination, exploitation and conflict between emerging classes and ethnic groups within successive levels of political-economic organisation constitutes the foundation of an adequate theory' (1983: 66).

As I indicated in the introduction to this paper, there is a third area of work on bilingualism among linguistic minorities which has hitherto been rather overshadowed. But, it is in this work that the most interesting attempts have been made to address the first two questions posed above by Gal (1983). This work, has, for the most part been carried out by anthropologists, sociologists and sociolinguists concerned with indigenous minority languages in Europe. The main focus of this work has been on finding ways of incorporating a conflict perspective in the study of language use and language change among linguistic minorities. The social phenomena and social processes seen as primary by those working within this tradition are: (1) The ways in which divisions between linguistic groups are related to class divisions and to political and economic relations within the framework of the state; (2) the processes involved in the imposition of power and the reproduction of power relations; (3) the nature of conflicts and social struggles generated by relations of power.

The first studies of bilingualism to incorporate a conflict

perspective were those carried out by Catalan linguists working in Spain (Aracil 1965; Ninyoles 1969; Vallverdú 1970). This approach was subsequently adopted in research on varieties of Catalan and Occitan spoken in southern France (Bernardó and Rieu 1973; Couderc 1974; Eckert 1980; Gardy and Lafont 1981; Kremnitz 1981). The initial focus of the work of these two groups was on reinterpreting the notion of diglossia. By 1972, a Research Group on Diglossia had been set up at the University of Montpellier. The work of this Research Group and that of the Catalan Sociolinguistic Group has continued to draw on developments in conflict theory over the last twenty years.

In the British context, there are several researchers concerned with minority languages in the Celtic periphery who have also attempted to incorporate a conflict perspective in their work. Among them are Williams (1979, 1987) and Williams and Roberts (1982) in their work on Welsh; and McKinnon (1977, 1984) in his work on Scottish Gaelic in the Western Isles. Like their counterparts in Spain and France, those working in the British context are native speakers of the languages they are studying and have been actively involved in local language movements.

The term 'Sociolinguistics of the Periphery' (Lafont 1982: 92) has been coined to refer to this area of work on bilingualism among linguistic minorities. The term has two main connotations: (1) it emphasizes the need to situate the study of the sociolinguistic fortunes of indigenous minority languages within a centre-periphery model of political and economic relations (Hechter 1975); (2) it also highlights the concern of these researchers with the social impact of their work: they see their research as a means of contributing to the struggle for the rights of linguistic minorities.

As I indicated earlier, one of the main interests of those working within the sociolinguistics of the periphery has been with reformulating the notion of diglossia. The linguists working on Catalan and Occitan were the first to re-examine the concept as a societal phenomenon from a conflict perspective. In addition to describing the *what* and the *how* of the diglossic distribution of languages within a local population, they addressed the more fundamental questions of *why* the two languages within diglossia came to be functionally differentiated and *how* diglossia changes over time. They saw diglossia as a form of social and linguistic order which is brought into being when a standardized code is imposed in new institutional structures such as local government bureaucracy or state schooling. In her historical account of diglossia in the Pyrenees of Ariége, Eckert (1980) shows how the introduction of French through structures such as these eventually led to a massive shift away from Gascon, the local variety of Occitan. She concludes that:

> Diglossia does not arise; it is imposed from above in the form of an administrative, ritual or standard language. By virtue of its political and economic status, this language becomes requisite for access to power and mobility within the society. (1980: 1056)

Eckert does not deal explicitly with ideological power, but at several points in her study, she illustrates the pervasive influence of ideology in sustaining the dominance of French. This comes over most clearly in her account of the symbolic oppositions established between Gascon and French within the community: first, an 'inside/outside' opposition which eventually gave way to a 'private/public' opposition. This shift in the symbolic valuation of the two languages led to the rapid legitimization of French and, on the other hand, the devaluation of Gascon. Others working on the sociolinguistic history of varieties of Occitan have given ideology more weight in their analyses. Both Lafont (1977) and Gardy (1978) have documented the rise and spread of the term *patois* as a label for varieties of Occitan as these varieties became increasingly stigmatized. They show how the denigration of Occitan language varieties was a direct consequence of the codification of French. The Catalan linguists also drew attention to the role of ideology in the development of diglossia. For example, Ninyoles (1969), focused on the way in which the social devaluation of Catalan was gradually internalized by its speakers so that they came to view their own language abilities as inadequate. In a recent review of work on both Catalan and Occitan, Kremnitz (1981) concludes that this particular effect of ideology is at its most intense during the most advanced stages of language shift.

One of the ways in which ideology works is that social practices take on a commonsensical nature. This is especially true of linguistic practices. Speakers of minority languages can contribute to the legitimization of the dominant language or to the devaluation of the minority language without being aware of doing so. This point is emphasized by Gardy and Lafont (1981) in their discussion of French/Occitan diglossia. They say: 'The devaluation of the functions of the dominated language takes its course all the more easily because it is a hidden process' (1981: 77). The emphasis on the conscious choice of language as an 'act of identity' by those working within the interactionist tradition overlooks this crucial effect of ideology.

The sociolinguists of the periphery have also taken up another major theme of conflict theory: that is, the fact that the imposition of power generally takes place in conditions of struggle. Diglossia is thus seen as characterized by conflict rather than by complementarity. McKinnon (1977; 1984) employs the notions of power and solidarity to describe the symbolic value assigned to English and to Scottish Gaelic on the islands of Barra and Harris. According to McKinnon, the use of Gaelic often represents a form of protest against the intrusion of English in public life on these islands. He notes that the power/solidarity opposition between English and Scottish Gaelic that he observed in these Scottish communities is a more general phenomenon that has also been documented in other situations characterized by core/periphery relations of this sort:

> A local language functions as a vehicle for community social solidarity and an intrusive language as the language of power epitomised in the form of economic activity, administration and communications which core society establishes in the periphery. (1984: 495)

In their analysis of language policy developments in Wales, Williams and Roberts (1982) demonstrate how language conflicts are most directly manifested when political demands are made by minority groups for the extension of their language(s) into institutional contexts such as state education or the broadcast media. These demands can result in the granting of concessions to linguistic minority groups, although such concessions are often a ploy for retaining power.

The attempts that have been made so far to reinterpret the notion of diglossia from a conflict perspective have, I feel, proved to be quite fruitful. The work carried out within the sociolinguistics of the periphery offers a means of overcoming several of the problems inherent in the structural-functional model of diglossia. This work can provide much more fertile ground for developing future research on bilingualism among linguistic minorities than the work I described in the first two sections of this paper.

As I see it, there is one key way in which the sociolinguistics of the periphery still needs to be developed: much more attention needs to be given to accounting for actual linguistic practices in bilingual communities. Lafont began to move in this direction when he introduced the term: 'fonctionnements diglossiques' (1979) in his work on Occitan. The concept was, however, never fully defined. Kremnitz (1981) takes up the term again in his review of work on diglossia conducted from a conflict perspective. He acknowledges the contribution of the work conducted within this framework but calls for a shift of focus to the micro-level of 'fonctionnements diglossiques':

> Even within a relatively small society, 'fonctionnements diglossiques' could be very different in detail from what we consider diglossia to be. Diglossia is only the outcome of all these locutionary acts. In each communicative act, the relationship between interlocuters is governed by constraints of power, politeness, habit and by taboos and it is these that determine actual linguistic practices . . . it is only when we take account . . . of these micro-situations that we will arrive at more accurate descriptions of the overall situation. (1981: 72)

To my knowledge, there have not yet been any moves in the direction anticipated by Kremnitz in the early 1980s. A shift of focus to the micro-level is, I feel, inevitable if we are to understand more fully the complex and subtle ways in which language mediates social relations of inequality in minority communities. As I have shown, the work conducted within the sociolinguistics of the periphery has provided some answers to the first two questions posed by Gal (1983). The reinterpretation of diglossia from a conflict perspective has served to sharpen our understanding of the ways in which choices between languages are socially determined. It has also highlighted the ideological constraints operating in diglossic situations. A shift of focus to the study of linguistic practices at the micro-level would now enable us to gain insights into the ways in which individuals manage these constraints in the communicative cycles of daily life and in different institutional contexts. We would therefore begin to address the third question posed by Gal.

As a sociolinguistic dimension of the social order, diglossia is both constraining and enabling. While it is important to take account of the fact that the communicative resources that bilinguals draw on in their everyday discourse are socially determined, it is also important to emphasize that individual speakers do not just draw on these resources or follow communicative conventions in a mechanical fashion. Individual bilinguals in minority communities draw on the linguistic resources in their repertoire in strategic and creative ways. Language use among bilinguals is complex and variable and generally involves much more than a two-way choice of code. Communicative resources are combined and juxtaposed in subtle ways through code-mixing and code-switching. The activity of using resources in this way to meet the changing demands and contradictions of concrete social encounters is a creative one. In the sociolinguistics of the periphery, what is needed is a model which emphasizes the active and creative nature of social and linguistic practices, in keeping with the interactionist tradition espoused by Gal and Gumperz, while retaining the central theoretical premises of the conflict tradition.

If we are to move beyond the limitations of existing sociolinguistic accounts of bilingualism among linguistic minorities, I suggest that it will be along lines such as those that I have illustrated above. A multi-dimensional approach is clearly needed if we are seeking to provide adequate explanations of variation and change in minority language use and to account for the fact that the voices of some dominated groups endure and others give way to the voice of the dominant majority.

Ackowledgement

Invaluable comments on previous drafts of this paper have been received from Margaret Deuchar, Norman Fairclough and Joseph Gafaranga, Ralph Grillo and Robert LePage and Glyn Williams.

Notes

1 After this paper was written, two further theoretical contributions by Gal (1987; 1988) were published. In these two articles, Gal presents the case for adopting a new comparative approach to the study of minority bilingualism: one which would enable us to go beyond individual community level studies and gain more general insights and one which would provide explanations of the differences as well as the similarities observable across language groups. She insists that this approach would need to be grounded in what she refers to as 'a systemic view of political economy' (1987: 650) so as to take account of the historic position that different minority groups have come to occupy within a world economic system

characterized by unequal development and relations of dependency between core and peripheral regions. She also argues that without this systemic perspective, and without giving primacy to the economic basis of class and ethnic relations, it is impossible to achieve any general insights as to how diglossic relations of inequality come to be imposed, sustained or contested.

References

Aracil, Ll., (1965), 'Conflit linguistique et normalisation linguistique dans l'Europe nouvelle', Nancy and Valencia. Reprinted and translated into Catalan: 'Conflicte lingüistic i normalització lingüistica a l'Europa nova' *Papers de Sociolingüistica*, Barcelona: Edicions de la Magrana, (1982).

Bernardó, D. and Rieu, B., (1973), 'Conflit linguistique et revendications culturelles en Catalogne Nord', *Les Temps Modernes*, no. 324–325–326.

Blom, J.P. and Gumperz, J.J., (1972), 'Social meaning in linguistic structures: codeswitching in Norway', in J.J. Gumperz and G. Hymes (eds).

Brago, G. and Civelli, M., (eds), (1982), *Linguistic Problems and European Unity*, Milan: Franco Angeli Editore.

Breitborde, L.B., (1983), 'Levels of analysis in sociolinguistic explanation: bilingual code switching, social relations, and domain theory', in J. Fishman (ed.).

Couderc, Y., 1974, 'D'après Ninyoles, "Idioma i prejudici": Le problème linguistique en Occitanie', *Cahier* no. 1, Groupe de Recherches sur la Diglossie, Montpelier.

Dorian, N., (1981), *Language Death: The Life Cycle of a Scottish Gaelic Dialect*, Philadelphia: University of Pennsylvania Press.

Eckert, P., (1980), 'Diglossia: Separate and Unequal', *Linguistics* 18: 1053–64.

Fasold, R., (1984), *The Sociolinguistics of Society*, Oxford: Basil Blackwell.

Ferguson, C.A., (1959), 'Diglossia', *Word*, 15: 325–40.

Fishman, J.A., (1967), 'Bilingualism with and without diglossia: diglossia with and without bilingualism', *Journal of Social Issues*, 23: 29–38.

Fishman, J.A., (1971), *Advances in the Sociology of Language*, vol. 1, The Hague: Mouton.

Fishman, J.A., (1972), 'Domains and the relationship between micro- and macro-sociolinguistics', in J.J. Gumperz and D. Hymes (eds).

Fishman, J.A., (ed.), (1983), *Levels of Analysis in Sociolinguistic Explanation: International Journal of the Sociology of Language*, vol. 39.

Gal, S., (1979), *Language Shift: Social Determinants of Linguistic Change in Bilingual Austria*, New York: Academic Press.

Gal, S., (1983), 'Comment on article by L.B. Breitborde', in J. Fishman (ed.).

Gal, S., (1987), 'Codeswitching and consciousness in the European periphery', *American Ethnologist*, 14 (4): 637–53.

Gal, S., (1988), 'The political economy of code choice', in M. Heller (ed.).

Gardy, P., (1978), 'Les territoires de la langue', *Pluriel*, no. 16.

Gardy, P. and Lafont, R., (1981), 'Diglossie comme conflit: L'exemple occitan', *Langages* 61: 75–91.

Giles, H. and Saint-Jacques, B., (eds), (1979), *Language and Ethnic Relations*, Oxford: Pergamon.

Grillo, R., (1986), 'Social networks in Anthropology and Linguistics', paper presented to the Anthropology and Linguistics Workshop, University of Sussex, Autumn 1986.

Gumperz, J.J., (1982), *Discourse Strategies*, Cambridge University Press.

Gumperz, J.J. and Hymes, D. (eds), (1972), *Directions in Sociolinguistics: The Ethnography of Communication*, New York: Holt, Rinehart & Winston.
Hechter, M., (1975), *Internal Colonialism: The Celtic Fringe in British National Development 1536–1966*, Berkeley: University of California Press.
Heller, M., (ed.), *Codeswitching: Anthropological and Sociological Perspectives*, Berlin: Mouton de Gruyter.
Kremnitz, G., (1981), 'Du "bilinguisme" au "conflit linguistique"' *Langages*, 61; 63–73.
Lafont, R., (1977), 'Sobre el procés de patoisització', *Treballs de Sociolingüistica Catalana*, no. 1, Valencia.
Lafont, R., (1979), 'La diglossie en pays occitan, ou le réel occulte', *Bildung und Ausbildung in der Romania, Band II: Spachwissenschaft und Landeskunde*, Munich: Wilhelm Fink Verlag.
Lafont, R., (1982), 'Le discours idéologique dans l'enquête sur la diglossie' *Cahiers de Linguistique Social* no. 4–5, Proceedings of the Montpellier Colloquium on: 'Situations of Diglossia'.
Ninyoles, R.Ll., (1969), *Conflicte Lingüistica Valéncia*, Valencia: Eliseu Climent Editor.
McKinnon, K., (1977), *Language, Education and Social Processes in a Gaelic Community*, London: Routledge & Kegan Paul.
McKinnon, K., (1984), 'Power at the periphery: The language dimension – and the case of Gaelic Scotland', *Journal of Multilingual and Multicultural Development* 5 (6): 491–511.
Schmidt-Rohr, G., (1932), *Die Sprache als Bildnerin der Völker*, Jena.
Vallverdú, F., (1970), *Dues ilengües: Deus funcions*? Barcelona: Edicions 62.
Weinreich, U., (1953), *Languages in Contact*, (reprinted in 1968), The Hague: Mouton.
Wexler, P., (1971), 'Diglossia, language standardisation and purism', *Lingua*, 27: 330–54.
Williams, G., (1979), 'Language group allegiance and ethnic interaction', in H. Giles and B. Saint-Jacques (eds).
Williams, G., (ed.), (1987), *The Sociology of Welsh: International Journal of the Sociology of Language*, vol. 66.
Williams, G. and Roberts, C., (1982), 'Institutional Centralization and Linguistic Discrimination', in G. Braga and M. Civelli (eds).

Creole in the classroom: political grammars and educational vocabularies

Roger Hewitt

Introduction

The Caribbean Creoles spoken in the United Kingdom include French-based Creoles brought from islands such as Dominica and St Lucia but spoken by a relatively small number of British people, and the more widely spoken English-based Creoles of islands such as Jamaica, Trinidad, and Barbados. In the emigration from the Caribbean to the United Kingdom between the late 1940s and the mid 1960s Jamaica provided by far the largest numbers and has also been an increasingly important source of popular culture for many British people of Caribbean origin. This has contributed to the emergence of Jamaican Creole as the dominant Creole influence on the speech of young blacks born in Britain, regardless of parental provenance.

This paper will argue that a number of approaches have been made to the issue of the place of Creole in British education and that these have themselves been shaped by a range of political 'grammars' evident in educational debates over language since the 1960s. Many of these approaches, however, have paid little regard to the actual Creole-utilizing practices of the young people who are their object. On the basis of ethnographic evidence it is clear that the issue of the relationship between Creole use and 'ethnic identity' is not simple, and that a consistent subversion of simple notions of ethnicity is evident in the language of young inner-city blacks. Rather than existing as a cultural given, ethnicity functions much more as a political resource amongst other resources and is often strategically employed in everyday anti-racist struggle. The strategic use of Creole and the simultaneous development of a 'mixed', Creole-inflected London English – shared to varying degrees across racial and 'ethnic' boundaries – suggests that much of the political and educational debate is now misplaced. It also makes clear the need for a deconstruction of essential notions of 'ethnicity' which introduce politically contradictory elements into what were intended as liberatory educational strategies and positions.

Much of the confusion in debates concerning minority cultures is rooted in the political history of the notion that cultures are 'incommensurable'. Originating in the writings of Herder, the 'incommensurability' argument and the accompanying re-evaluation of both non-European and non-'high' cultures was articulated within Herder's essentially anarchistic critique of eighteenth-century autocratic power and its relation to dominated peoples (Barnard 1969; Clark 1955). Its reappearance in the anthropology of Boas and Benedict (Stocking 1974; Benedict 1935), however, involved its relocation in a new political context – that of the modern state – and in a pluralistic critique of the relations between majority and minority interests. Both Herderian and Boasian statements of cultural relativism perhaps obscured an underlying moral universalism, but their differing understandings of the state display a theoretical tension which is still starkly evident in contemporary debates around state education and the position of ethnic minorities and their languages. This tension emerges especially in the contrast between certain British anti-racist political stances that concern themselves with the role of the state in racial domination (Mullard 1982; Gilroy 1982; Sivanandan 1983) and the pluralistic notions of multiculturalism against which they are posed. The issue of Caribbean Creole, its use and position in the English educational system, is one in which this tension is clearly evident both at the level of theory and, in parallel form, in the patterns of language use themselves.

Political grammars and the place of Creole in education

The earliest British educational responses to the presence of Creole speakers were very different from the response to speakers of Asian languages. Where for the latter a whole new ESL infrastructure was created, children of Afro-Caribbean parents were not regarded as presenting a problem of this kind. Their mother-tongue was conceived by educationalists and many parents alike as English or as a dialect of English and the relevant language issue here was thought to be one of 'interference' by Creole in their written and spoken production of the language (Wight 1969;

Wight and Norris 1970). This initial item in the lexicon of educational responses to the presence of young Creole speakers – located in the deficit/deprivation discourse of the 1960s – was theoretically consistent with the traditionalist conservative political grammar associated with the view that Creole is bad or broken English; that the business of educational institutions is to promote high standards and that the presence of Creole or other dialects in the schools could only contribute to their decline. However, other variants of the same item – those in which a distinction was maintained between notions of 'correctness' in written and in oral discourse – seemed also to permit of their use in a second ideological context – one in which democracy rather than the maintenance of cultural continuity was the engine.

In practice the democratic thrust was constituted by two independent political grammars, one socialist and one liberal pluralist. In British educational circles between the late 1960s and mid 1970s the socialist grammar was notably visible, especially in the initiatives of a number of local education authorities – most prominently the Inner London Education Authority – where a conscious attempt was made to advance the prestige of dialect through classroom work and an emphasis on the 'validity' of oral forms. At the same time the impetus in the classroom was derived from a convergence of rapidly changing social conditions and a new generation of teachers who had felt the influence of educationalists such as James Britain, Harold Rosen and Douglas Barnes, academics who were attacking both the political and educational presuppositions of the traditional English language syllabus. A whole new vocabulary of practices was generated which was widely regarded as the unification of political and educational progress. Academic support for these practices came from many sources but particularly important was, of course, Labov's essay 'The Logic of Non-Standard English', which was widely read by English teachers and which was a contemporary restatement of the Boasian, neo-Herderian, thesis of the incommensurability of cultures (even if 'incommensurability' was transformed into 'equality' and an epistemologically important distinction blurred).

Despite the prominence of socialist thought and practice, by the mid 1970s and under the influence of such thought, liberal pluralism was establishing itself as the reasonable and more widely acceptable face of English language teaching. The areas of apparent agreement between liberal pluralists and socialists were many and much cross-fertilization of ideas and practices with respect to language in the classroom could take place while underlying contradictions were obscured in the detail of work at the 'chalk face'. Indeed, both might maintain that all languages are of equal validity; that there is no such thing as a 'primitive' natural language; that all languages should be treated with equal respect regardless of the social and economic circumstances of their bearers, and so on. It was primarily in the perceived theoretical contexts of these recognitions – one concerned with power and class defined in economic terms, the other concerned with merit and class conceived in cultural terms – that the fundamental differences lay. Thus the same broad vocabulary of classroom practices might be used in the expression of either grammar.

By the early 1980s the rhetoric of linguistic egalitarianism had become well established as integral to the common sense of English language education. It found concrete realization particularly in what became known as the 'repertoire approach' – an approach which emphasized the range of different kinds of language necessary for communicative competence and allowed non-standard varieties of English a place in that range. In the words of the Swann Report, this approach:

> now recognised as being particularly appropriate to West Indian children, is one that values all languages and dialects as an important part of the child's linguistic repertoire. The intention is not to change or replace any particular dialect but to develop a sharper awareness of and interest in the different language forms that a child can use, thus avoiding confusion between them. (HMSO 1985: 422)

On the basis that Creole is a dialect of English, therefore, there is a transformation into educational terms of the pluralist perspective in which British Afro-Caribbeans are seen as a 'dialect' of British society and underlying issues regarding class or race conflicts are excluded from the discourse.

The field of relevant political grammars is not, however, limited to the above. Despite the compromise between professional opinion and the educational priorities of the Conservative government, which produced the Swann Report's own conceptual multilingualism, a sustained attack on its content from the 'new right' followed its publication (Palmer 1986). Indeed, specifically with respect to language, a 'libertarian' conservative political grammar, largely replacing the traditionalist conservative one, was making itself apparent prior to and during the Rampton (HMSO 1981) and Swann Commissions' deliberations. This position, exemplified by Honey (1983), argues that it is a sociolinguistic fact that Creole is not the language of the state, the academy or the world of employment. 'Non-standard varieties' should be strenuously avoided if students are not to be encouraged to develop skills in an area which can only lead them into unfair disadvantage, 'in any crucial encounter outside his own immediate speech community' and especially in the job market place (ibid.: 20). Honey argues that, 'For schools to foster non-standard varieties of English is to place their pupils in a trap. To persuade such speakers that their particular non-standard variety of English is in no way inferior, nor less efficient for purposes of communication, but simply *different*, is to play a cruel trick.' With respect to political power Honey adds, 'Whether we like it or not the "language of the state" in Britain is Standard English [and] action which impairs the ability of any future citizen to communicate adequately in that medium is an act of political emasculation' (ibid.: 24).

We have, therefore, so far, four political grammars, two of which exclude any possibility of Creole in the classroom and two of which are consistent with some vocabulary of educational strategies involving Creole. It is also true to say that all four of the positions have been predominantly articulated by white commentators. Of the two remaining positions that have been most clearly articulated on this issue, both have been best put by black writers, one – deriving from a Marxist libertarian political grammar – would also translate into a strategic *avoidance* of Creole in the classroom, while the other – deriving from a black radical grammar – points to its inclusion. The former holds that capitalism's adaptability finds expression at the cultural level in various manoeuvres which neutralize by incorporation potential challenges to the hegemony of its dominant classes. The accommodation to Creole within the school curriculum represents just such a systemic response. For this reason, although the aims of multiculturalism may be interpreted within an anti-racist perspective and the explicit incorporation of Creole may *appear* to be part of anti-racist struggle, in fact the underlying political and economic reality is such that those who advocate Creole in the classroom are the unwitting dupes of the system and their educational practices serve above all to blunt what is for black youth a primary weapon of resistance. This position has been argued in different ways by black theorists Hazel Carby in her paper 'Multicultural Fictions' (n.d.) and by Maureen Stone (1981). Stone's position in fact also combines this with elements in the 'libertarian' conservative position in also seeking to speak for the putative concerns of (conservative) black parents.

In contrast, the black radical position asserts that a form of home colonialism exists in British education which, amongst numerous racist institutional practices, includes the systematic down-grading of Third World languages. With respect to Creole this involves failing to recognize it as a language in its own right and casting it instead as a 'dialect' with its implicit and sometimes explicit connotations of 'bad' or 'inferior' English. This denial of linguistic and cultural integrity and legitimacy is but part of the wider political and economic pattern of White domination of Black peoples, reflected in and partly constituted through, the educational system at the institutional level. Racism thus exists not only outside the context of educational settings as an ideology and as arrays of economic and political racial practices, but is actually enshrined in a Eurocentric curriculum, in racist pedagogical practices, in racialized disciplinary procedures, and in policies and rhetorics which are aimed at *concealing* the predominance of the underlying racism. It does this by paying lip service to 'cultural equality' in order to maintain the racial status quo. In this view, anti-racist practice within education should work on several fronts simultaneously, including the linguistic/cultural front, and contribute to the fight for justice and the transformation of Black/White power relations. It is within this context that an attention to Creole should be paid – a strong assertion of black cultural heritage within an anti-racist struggle (Dalphinis 1979; 1985; Wong 1986; Mullard 1980).

The vocabulary of practices made possible by the black radical grammar is somewhat different from either the socialist or liberal pluralist positions. The insistence, for example, that Creole should be treated not as a dialect of English but as a language in its own right, already logically removes it from its most common niche in the curriculum and implies a range of other locations such as Black Studies, Political Education, Social Studies or Language Awareness and even Modern Languages – although Creole's lack of a written tradition renders this last possibility unlikely. Nevertheless, such a view might imply the kind of practice for which Ian Hancock has argued in the Caribbean situation:

> Without a doubt, the study of creoles, and especially Caribbean creoles, should be made an integral part of the West Indian educational curriculum. Assignments in Creole should be given and graded just as rigorously as those given in English; and just as creolisms in English are corrected by the teacher, attention should also be brought to the intrusion of anglicisms into Creole. (Hancock 1984)

Within this group of three positions endorsing some form of attention to Creole in the classroom – the liberal pluralist with Creole as a community language/dialect; the socialist one in which Creole is one of the marginalized tongues of the working class; and the black radical, in which Creole is the historical language of Black struggle against White oppression – a fundamental confusion exists which derives from the apparent contradiction between claims that (1) Creole should be accorded an equal status with other languages in the education system and (2) that Creole is a language of political resistance.The first is a claim made to some fundamental principle and insofar as its justification is felt to be political rather than academic, the only context in which such a 'claim' can be made is a pluralist one, for both economic and race conflict theories render 'claims' of this sort merely symptomatic. The second, in which Creole is a 'language of resistance' with both an inward (community) and outward (social structure) face, is an argument that seems to point away from any context in which 'rights' are claimed and, indeed, away from formal incorporation in the education system at all. It is nevertheless common to find both assertions simultaneously made. Certainly both are present in socialist and Black radical presentations (Sutcliffe 1982; Wong 1986), while usually only the 'community' aspect is presented in liberal pluralist accounts (Edwards, 1979). In the latter case, however, not only are the implications of conflict interpretations avoided but conflict itself is regarded as a rectifiable malfunction in the pluralist order. Thus, writing of the potential role of sociolinguistics, Robert Le Page has commented: 'it is hoped that before long the subject we know as 'sociolinguistics' will be introduced as an O or A level subject. There is probably no discipline which deals with, and more effectively defuses, racial or class tension' (Le Page, 1981: 21–2).

Here, education, and by implication the state, are conceived of as disposed to benign influence and not, as in the other paradigms, implicated – albeit in challengeable ways – in the maintenance of various forms of domination. This split in the conceptualization of the state and the kind of national entity it implies, lies at the root of the 'community language'/'resistance language' divide and is a dichotomy already implicit in the shift from Herder's cultural politics to those of the early twentieth-century American anthropologists alluded to at the outset.

How relevant are these political grammars and educational vocabularies to the young people who are their ostensive object?

Adolescent Creole usage: some ethnographic evidence

The 'home language' of many British-born black adolescents is likely to be one of the Caribbean Creoles if their parents were born and raised in the Caribbean. However, Creoles differ internally and from one to another with respect to their continuity with English. Both class and geographical factors will influence the extent of Creole speech in the home. Furthermore, there may be internal familial differences in the extent of Creole usage – between husband and wife and between siblings, especially where some of the children were born and raised in the Caribbean while others were raised entirely in the UK. These divisions are sometimes re-enforced by lines of censure. Both parents may warn against the use of Creole by their children because of its association with low status and economic failure, and this may be enforced with respect to both boys and girls. An alternative pattern is where both parents discourage the use of Creole but the warning is only enforced by the mother or *against* the daughter. Inter-sibling censure also occurs between older siblings who were born and raised in the Caribbean and who feel it natural that they should speak Creole, and younger children, born and raised in the UK who, some claim, should only speak English. Thus even within families, Creole use in conversation is frequently asymmetrical, and 'home language' for many black adolescents will not refer to the Creole they speak but the Creole they hear.

Already, therefore, there are the domestic conditions for considerable differences between British-born youngsters with respect to their use and knowledge of Creole. Local demographic factors introduce further bases for variation and these may re-enforce domestic variation. The two areas of south London in which I conducted ethnographic field work from 1980 to 1983 and again in 1985[1] differed markedly with respect to the patterns of

Afro-Caribbean settlement, Area A being one in which ethnic minorities[2] from 'New Commonwealth and Pakistan' households constituted only 14 per cent of the population, of whom approximately 80 per cent were of Asian or East African origin, and Area B, where Afro-Caribbeans constituted over 25 per cent of the local population. Unlike the families of Asian and East African origin, the small Afro-Caribbean population of Area A had not settled in distinct areas but was widely scattered. Furthermore, the homes established in Area A often represented second or third moves away from initial settlement areas. Families were thus often more affluent than those of Area B – which *was* an initial settlement area – and also lacked a locally coherent Afro-Caribbean community grounded on neighbourhood. Indeed, British born black *girls* from Area A spoke remarkably little Creole and, despite pockets of friendship groups of young men in their late teens and early twenties many of whom had in fact grown up in the Caribbean, Creole speech amongst the majority of boys was very limited both with regard to frequency of use and competence with the language.

Area B, constituted by a cluster of four inner city wards, provided a different kind of context for domestic patterns of Creole use and non use. While Area A was predominantly *white*, Area B was predominantly *mixed*, with Afro-Caribbeans, whose settlement had actually started in the late 1940s, constituting something over 25 per cent of the total population and 40–50 per cent in some neighbourhoods. There were no significant numbers of members of other ethnic minorities. What was lacking from Area A in terms of a neighbourhood culture which could support whatever levels of Creole use were generated within the home – or which could even contradict the domestic trend by providing a stimulus to the use of what was proscribed – were better provided in Area B. Evidence from this area, therefore, may provide a better case for considering the pertinence of the educational arguments.

The steady growth of the Afro-Caribbean community in an area well-known since the nineteenth century for its working-class community and political networks, effected a replenishment and transformation of an area whose economy and population had been plummeting since the 1930s. By the early 1970s, black community organizations, churches and social clubs were well-established, and local shops and market stalls came to reflect Caribbean culinary tastes. As white social networks became dismantled and fragmented, black networks of kinship and association steadily established themselves. Thus an area that for geographical and historical reasons had always been socially well-defined and community conscious, retained something of its long-standing coherence partly as a *result* of the nature of its ethnic transformation.

Creole use in this area can be said to include the Jamaican and other Creoles employed by members of the older generations and younger people who had been born and mainly raised in the Caribbean, and the 'London Jamaican' employed to varying degrees of fluency by black British children of Caribbean parentage. Features of this Creole have been described by Sutcliffe (1982) and Sebba (1986), however, it is evident that, especially with regard to lexis, London Jamaican is a highly fluid, frequently changing speech form which draws on other urban British as well as Caribbean speech in a process of perpetual self-renewal. Particularly through its association with expressive urban oral genres such as rapping and toasting (Bones 1986a; 1986b) and the changing trends of urban youth, it has acquired a creativity which quickly renders any documentation of its form outdated.

An important feature of London Jamaican Creole is the extent to which it is used in code-switching, for while some black British adolescents employ London Jamaican in sustained dialogue, for many the more common practice is to move between a London English and London Jamaican for various strategic and stylistic purposes (see Sebba 1983a; Sebba and Wooton, 1984; Sutcliffe 1982; Hewitt 1986). The most subtle motivations for such code-switching practices remain, for the most part, unresearched. However, amongst some of the most common triggers were competitive relations of various kinds, from formal game and sporting ones to disagreements and argument. The *movement into* Creole appears to be more significant here than the sustaining of Creole use, and the question of interactants' command of the language may itself become salient at a different level, if indeed it ever becomes salient at all. I witnessed, for example, an argument between two sixteen year old boys in which, at the outset of the dispute, both moved from London English directly into Creole. As the argument became more heated, one vigorously sustained his Creole whilst the other – in apparent recognition of the seriousness of the argument – reverted to the London English which seemed to be his most natural, unforced and authentic voice. Both boys were British born and grew up on the same local council estate, yet, because of familial differences, Creole was for one of them the natural language of sustained serious argument, for the other it was not. For both, however, the level of initial disagreement had made the *switch* into Creole appropriate. Similar switches were triggered by references *to* competitive situations and often occurred within conversationally embedded narratives concerned with various domains of rivalry.

Another common trigger – especially if it occurred in conjunction with some form of competitive relation – was the mention of any aspect of black youth culture itself. The following exchanges, for example, show how Creole pronunciation is introduced to underline the kind of personal excellence that is part of the D.J. 'sound system' culture. The speakers are talking during a lunchbreak at a South London F.E. college.

Extract 1:

Girl: What do you do here?
Boy: 'A' level Maths, Statistics and Computer Science.
Girl: So you're a brain-box are ya?
Boy: Well I try to be.
Girl: [Laughs. Then, referring to a previously made offer by the boy to bring his sound system to 'play out' at a wedding:] You'll definitely play free?
Boy: Yeah, *jes' check me. Check me de date, right*?
Girl: Yeah, 'cos I heard your sound is . . .
Boy: *Yeah man, jes' write down de details, ya know*
Girl: . . . up to scratch.
Boy: What d'ya mean 'up to scratch'? *My soun' is A1 soun' system troughout de lan'; de fifth odin of Jah.*

Extract 2:

Boy (1): My sound's only been good for the last free years.
Boy (2): Why?
Boy (1): 'Cos that's when I get money, ennit. Before it used to be, um, Marshall thirty watt amplifier, a pre-amplifier, two eighteen inch boxes . . . an' a out o' date record box. But now *four 'tousan' five 'ondred watt, six quad boxes*.

In the first extract the boy moves into Creole pronunciation precisely to emphasize the superiority of his sound system over others. In the second, in which he describes his own previous equipment, which was poor and of low output, his pronunciation is purely that of local London English (e.g. the 'f' on 'free' where standard would have 'th' and Creole would have 't'). But when he boasts of his current system he moves into Creole pronunciation.

These kinds of switches, articulated around internal peer social relations, were, however, capable of extension to relations with those *outside* the peer group. In particular, with respect to the politics of Creole use, these strategic moves are also a feature of switches where conflicts with those in authority occur or are enacted in narrative – conflicts, for example with the police, with teachers, youth workers, employers, DHSS officers and so on – and often form part of interactions where power is contested. Here the dramatic structure of peer interactions provides a template which informs actual out-facing interactions as well as peer group narratives about such interactions. A form of figurative positional continuity is maintained and is grafted on to interactions where dominance relations obtain. In other words, a common peer group discursive structure is re-utilized in interactions that open onto social structure. In the majority of positionally differentiated exchanges between blacks and whites in institutional settings it is the whites who hold the dominant positions. It is not surprising that, either directly or in 'off record' asides (Brown and Levinson 1978), switches to Creole occur as an immediate form of resistance to the mundane face of racial domination. Most importantly, this resource for political challenge is available even to youngsters with minimal fluency in Creole and a limited range of Creole-utilizing discursive strategies.

Even without such obviously political linguistic practices, it has been argued (Brandt 1984; Gilroy and Lawrence, forthcoming; Hebdidge 1976) that the very existence of a generationally-specific Creole of this kind represents a resistive cultural strategy of black youth, produced within a particular political, economic and historical setting. Whatever the force of this argument, it is at least the case that *because* of the fairly specialized set of functions for which London Jamaican is most widely used – in contrast to the much broader functional base of the Creole of the older generations – and because of the congruence between the inward-facing, peer group aspect of usage and the outward-facing, oppositional aspect of Creole usage, the London Jamaican of black youth may be said to constitute an 'anti-language' (Halliday

1978) rather more than it can be said to constitute a 'community language' as that term is usually understood.

In this sense the 'language of resistance' argument concerning classroom practice does, indeed, seem more accurately to reflect what is actually occurring in the Creole usage of young blacks, even where London Jamaican may be taken up only infrequently into the arena of political contest and many of its uses may not be 'political' in any such direct sense. The Creoles of the older generations fit far more clearly into the concept of 'community languages' in which ethnicity constitutes the quality of a reproduced cultural life, than do the specialized urban tones of London Jamaican. For the latter, ethnicity is less dedicatedly 'lived' than *used* as an instrument of interactional power and also in daily political struggle. This in no sense detracts from the ability of other Creoles also to become instruments of struggle but it is to say that for London Jamaican Creole that register is especially evident.

There are, however, considerable complications to this state of affairs, not the least of which is that the very model of code-switching appears to recede from clarity when the particular London English which provides the alternate code is considered. Certainly the London English used by black adolescents clearly differed from 'London Jamaican' where pronunciation was concerned, and certainly strategic shifts to such pronunciation were readily apparent. But the English of many black youngsters also itself displayed evidence of Creole influence beyond those stretches that might be plainly treated as switches. Lexical and grammatical forms often entered in from Creole sources, although which forms, where they appeared, and how frequently, varied greatly from speaker to speaker. (A very similar situation is described by Hill and Hill (1986) in the case of Malinche Mexicano and Spanish.) Within the textual environment of Extracts (1) and (2) above, for example, the boasting which closed Extract (1) was followed by a reversion to London English pronunciation and contained the utterance: 'Tell 'er what my sound would do to her yard!' – where 'yard' is a Creole word meaning 'home'. Extract (2) is also followed by a return to London English but one where the Creole past tense marker 'di' (sometimes 'did') also appears: 'I had about a hundred an thirty watt. I used to have this [Trow? (amplifier)] as well, about a hundred watt, but that di' soon blow up!' Furthermore, while such Creole influences may have been more evident and highly focused (LePage 1975) in the speech of black youngsters, they were by no means restricted to black speakers but were to varying degrees evident also in the speech of white and ethnic minority youth other than Afro-Caribbean from the same localities. (For an account of both of the above mentioned items in the speech of white adolescents see Hewitt 1986: 152, 191.) This form of London English has been described as 'Black Cockney' (Sebba 1983b), Black London English (Sebba 1986) and more broadly as 'British Black English' (Sutcliffe 1984), although I have preferred to use the less specific term 'local multi-racial vernacular' and to leave to the investigation of individual cases the question of the extent and nature of Creole penetration (Hewitt 1986).

Especially with regard to this vernacular, an important difference between the experience of the parental generations (both black and white) and their children was that, whatever the home influence, neighbourhood and school friendship groups were very commonly racially mixed. Black and white children were born in the same neighbourhood, attended the same primary schools, grew up often in the same street-corner groups, and, despite common but not inevitable same-race *close friend* selection, were exposed to many identical peer-group influences. One linguistic consequence of this was that the historic strains of both Cockney and Creole had their impact on the speech of black and white alike, despite differences of degree. Thus while it is true that most locals could more or less accurately tell the race of an unseen adolescent speaker – where non-locals or at least those unfamiliar with inner-London speech might report knowing only that Cockney was being spoken – it was not the case that the London English of young blacks took on any specialized symbolic meaning of race or ethnicity. Neither was it manipulated or controlled for specific stylistic effects concerned with those aspects. Rather, it was itself the site of low-key, social-symbolic renovation, wherein ethnicity was, if anything, deconstructed and a new *ethnically mixed* 'community English' created from the fragments. It was in this context that the stressed switches to London Jamaican Creole entered in for specific interactive purposes inflecting the language in various ways relative to contextual constraints.

It is worth noting here that mixed language forms have often been produced by the tendency of the adolescent peer group to integrate divergent cultural inheritances through mechanisms apparently specific and interior to adolescent peer group social structure. These mechanisms translate externally guaranteed social elements into the terms of the internal ecology of peer relations. While similarly functioning mechanisms may be a feature of adult peer conversational interaction too (Hewitt, forthcoming), the 'we' of the adolescent peer group seems to have a special dominance and intensity where languages are involved, (as evidenced in the mixed forms reported in such studies as Parkin 1977; Blanc 1982; Jansen 1984). With respect to Area B, it was as though the friendship groups linguistically unpicked both black and white ethnicity and re-assembled its constituent parts in terms of the groups' own structures and needs.

There was, therefore, a two-way movement evident in the language use of black London adolescents in which a de-ethnicized, racially mixed local 'community' language was creatively established alongside a strategic, contextually variable use of Creole (and other markers of ethnicity) often employed as markers of *race* in the context of daily anti-racist struggle.

Political and educational implications

These trends in black adolescent language use provide in themselves something of a critique of the various arguments concerning classroom practices. Certainly there appears to be a clear contradiction between adolescent practice in which mixed forms are forged, and the Swann Report's desire for leading pupils to 'avoid confusion between' Creole and non-Creole forms, except where the distinction was itself strategically employed in code-switching practices. Furthermore, where Creole *was* strategically employed, it was not the relatively stable 'community language' Creole of the older generations that was involved, but much more commonly, the 'London Jamaican' anti-language of black youth. When this form is consciously used, the question of 'confusion' is far from educationally pertinent for its use is actually structured around the importance of its contrast with other forms.

What is, of course, implied by the Swann approach is the desire to enable youngsters to have a further choice of code which will include the prestige forms that are privileged by contexts of public examinations, some employment requirements, and further and higher education. To attempt to describe the meaning of such choices purely within the pluralist terms of 'appropriate' language use, is, however, to leave out of the educational process important non-linguistic information about why and how some languages are associated more with the registers of power and cultural authority than others.

By contrast, both the socialist and Black radical perspectives do include an account of language which takes the dimension of power as fundamental. However, where notions of language and 'ethnic identity' are overplayed in their rhetorics – albeit within the transformed terms of 'Roots' politics – they unwittingly come to share those same logical premises from which nationalistic conservative views of the inseparability of cultural and political coherence are derived. In so doing they slide towards culturalism and fail to take up the opportunity of unambiguously arguing for 'Justice' (Mullard 1984) as a truer source of political/national coherence. In this way they allow themselves to attract many of the same arguments that are aimed at the cultural pluralists by the 'new right'.

Not only is the 'cultural roots' strand liable to be implicated in a contradictory political strategy, it is also at odds with the subtleties of the street usage of young blacks for whom the well-defined form of 'identity' envisaged is actually *avoided* more often than it is embraced. Furthermore, where it *is* embraced it appears to be as a resource amongst other resources in a complex urban context where *race* is a quotidian issue of considerable salience, while 'ethnic identity' is not. Thus it seems that in approaching the political *context* of Creole language use, insufficient attention has been paid to the implications of the actual Creole utilizing practices of young blacks and to the dynamic which dissolves and subverts 'ethnicity' in the same environment as that in which 'ethnicity' is strategically mobilized as part of anti-racist struggle. Here again, the work of Hill and Hill provides important echoes, when they contrast the Mexicano 'purists' who seek to reconstitute the solidarity of the community through a language purged of Spanish influence, with those users of the 'mixed' code who take up the full range of symbolic resources offered by a language redolent with the resistive possibilities of multi-vocal speech (Hill and Hill *op.cit.*: 400–1).

What is not contradicted by black adolescent Creole usage is, however, the argument for situating the study of Creole and other languages within the broad domain of social and political education. Neither is the practice of 'legitimating' the 'community' Creoles of the older black generations contradictory as part of the important *pastoral* climate within which learning takes place. Freed from simplistic claims concerning 'ethnic identity' and young black people, both practices are quite consistent with non-deterministic political analyses which see the school as an arena of potential challenge to prevailing racisms and other instruments of inequality and injustice.

Nevertheless, if any direct *political* lessons concerning educational language policies and the Creole of young blacks are to be drawn, they may well reside more in their deconstruction of ethnicity in language and the possibility of deconstructing the terms within which dominated peoples are drawn falsely to represent themselves. Perhaps the point for educational activists is to lay bare not the tactical issue of language rights, but the structures of domination which evoke and pre-structure the terms of the debate and the available positions within it. This is to avoid a different kind of 'language trap' to the one John Honey had in mind. This is the trap of arguing about the specific rules of entry into a club when what is really desired is an assault on the power of those who do the rule-making. It is, perhaps, as a result of *this* trap that the structures of political argument over minority languages remain almost tediously constant across the world. Minority/majority language rights debates seem to assume suspiciously similar forms whether in Hawaii, Scandanavia, England or California. This may have more to do with the structure of power than it has to do with the structure of communities or the structure of languages. Indeed, both 'education' and 'language' tend to become political constructions under conditions of intense domination and contest far in excess of their constructed quality at other times. One might assume that at a time when the 'national curriculum' is being pushed to the fore, these issues will continue to be locked into precisely these reiterative terms, and invitations to the folk-ghetto of ethnic identity will remain warmly open. In such circumstances, the need for deconstructing the arguments for all 'ethnicities' is especially acute.

Notes

1 This research was made possible by generous grants from the Nuffield Foundation and the Leverhulme Trust respectively.

2 The two areas referred to here are decribed in detail in Hewitt (1986).

References

Barnard, F. M. (ed.), (1969), *J. G. Herder on social and political culture*, Oxford: Clarendon Press.
Benedict, R., (1935), *Patterns of culture*, London: Faber & Faber.
Blanc, M., (1982), 'Social networks and multilingual behaviour: the Atlantic Provinces Project', paper given at the 4th Sociolinguistics Symposium, University of Sheffield.
Bones, J., (1986a), 'Language and Rastafari', in D. Sutcliffe and A. Wong (eds), *The language of the Black experience*, Oxford: Basil Blackwell, pp. 37–51.
Bones, J., (1986b), 'Reggae Deejaying and Jamaican Afro-Lingua', in D. Sutcliffe and A. Wong (eds), *The language of the Black experience*, Oxford: Basil Blackwell, pp. 52–68.
Brandt, G., (1984), 'British youth Caribbean Creole – the politics of resistance', paper given at the conference on languages without a written tradition and their role in education, Thames Polytechnic, 31 August–3 September.
Brown, P. and Levinson, S., (1978), 'Politeness: some universals in language usage', in E. Goody (ed.), *Questions and politeness: strategies in social interaction*, Cambridge: Cambridge University Press.
Carby, H. (n.d.), 'Multicultural Fictions', stencilled occasional paper no. 58, Birmingham: Centre for Contemporary Cultural Studies.
Clark, R. jr., (1955), *Herder: his life and thought*, California: University of California Press.
Dalphinis, M., (1978), 'Approaches to the study of creole languages – the case for West African language interference', *The Black Liberator*, 1: 83–91.
Dalphinis, M., (1985), *Caribbean and African languages: social history, language, literature and education*, London: Karia Press.
Edwards, V.K., (1979), *The West Indian language issue in British schools: challenges and responses*, London: Routledge & Kegan Paul.
Gilroy, P., (1982), 'Steppin' out of babylon: race, class and autonomy', in *The empire strikes back*, Centre for Contemporary Cultural Studies, London: Hutchinson.
Gilroy, P. and Lawrence, E., (forthcoming), 'Two-tone Britain', in P. Cohen and H. Bains (eds), *Multiracist Britain*, Basingstoke: Macmillan.
Halliday, M. A. K., (1978), *Language as social semiotic*, London: Edward Arnold.
Hancock, I., (1984), 'Standardization and ethnic defence in emergent non-literate societies', paper given at conference on languages without a written tradition and their role in education, Thames Polytechnic, 31 August–3 September.
Hebdige, D., (1976), 'Reggae, rastas and rudies', in S. Hall and T. Jefferson (eds), *Resistance through rituals: youth sub-cultures in post-war Britain*, London: Hutchinson.
Hewitt, R., (1986), *White talk black talk: inter-racial friendship and communication amongst adolescents*, Cambridge: Cambridge University Press.
Hewitt, R., (forthcoming), 'The social relations of conversation', Adolescents and Language Use Working Papers, London: Sociological Research Unit, Institute of Education, University of London.
Hill, J. and Hill, K., (1986), *Speaking Mexicano: dynamics of syncretic language in central Mexico*, Tucson: University of Arizona Press.
HMSO, (1981), 'West Indian children in our schools', interim report of the committee of inquiry into the education of children from ethnic minority groups, London.
HMSO (1985), 'Education for all', the report of the committee of inquiry into the education of children from ethnic minority groups, London.
Honey, J., (1983), 'The language trap: race, class and the "standard English" issue

in British schools', London; National Council for Educational Standards, Kay-Shuttleworth Papers on Education, no. 3.

Jansen, T., (1984), 'A language of Sophiatown and Soweto', in M. Sebba and L. Todd (eds), *York Papers in Linguistics 11: Papers from the York creole conference*, York: Department of Language, University of York.

Le Page, R., (1975), 'Projection, focussing, diffusion', stencilled paper, York: Department of Language, University of York.

Le Page, R., (1981), *Caribbean connections in the classroom*, London: Mary Glasgow Language Trust.

Mullard, C. (1980), 'Racism in society and schools: history, policy and practice', Occasional Paper no. 1, London: Centre for Multicultural Education, University of London Institute of Education.

Mullard, C. (1982), 'Multiracial education in Britain: from assimilation to cultural pluralism', in J. Tierney (ed.), *Race, migration and schooling*, Sussex: Holt.

Mullard, C. (1984), *Anti-racist education: the three o's*, London: NAME.

Palmer, F., (1986), *Anti-racism: an assault on education and value*, London: Sherwood Press.

Parkin, D., (1977), 'Emergent and stabilised multi-lingualism: polyethnic peer groups in urban Kenya', in H. Giles (ed.), *Language, ethnicity and intergroup relations*, London: Academic Press.

Sebba, M., (1983a), 'Code-switching as a conversational strategy', stencilled paper tabled at York Creole Conference, University of York.

Sebba, M., (1983b), 'Language change among Afro-Caribbeans in London', stencilled paper, York: Department of Language, University of York.

Sebba, M., (1986), London Jamaican and Black London English, in D. Sutcliffe and A. Wong (eds), *The language of the Black Experience*, Oxford: Basil Blackwell, pp. 149–67.

Sebba, M. and Wooton, T., (1984), 'Codeswitching as a conversational strategy', paper presented at 5th Sociolinguistics Symposium, University of Liverpool.

Sivanandan, A., (1983), *A different hunger*, London: Pluto Press.

Stocking, G. W. jr., (1974), *The shaping of American anthropology, 1883–1911: a Franz Boas reader*, New York: Basic Books.

Stone, M., (1981), *The education of the black child in Britain: the myth of multiracial education*, London: Fontana Paperback.

Sutcliffe, D., (1982), *British Black English*, Oxford: Basil Blackwell.

Sutcliffe, D., (1984), 'British Black English and West Indian Creoles', in P. Trudgill (ed.), *Language in the British Isles*, Cambridge: Cambridge University Press.

Wight, J., (1969), 'Teaching English to West Indian children', *English for Immigrants* 2 (2).

Wight, J. and Norris, R., (1970), *Teaching English to West Indian children: the research stage of the project*, Schools Council Working paper 29, London: Evans/Methuen Educational.

Wong, A., (1986), 'Creole as a language of power and solidarity', in D. Sutcliffe and A. Wong (eds), *The language of the Black experience*, Oxford: Basil Blackwell, pp. 109–22.

'Janus-faced signs' – the political language of a Soviet minority before *Glasnost*'

Caroline Humphrey

It is not easy to discover the political attitudes of minority peoples of the USSR in the pre-*glasnost*' period. Any such idea as we must approach it, as it appears in speech or writing, cannot be fully understood on its own, since it exists in a context consisting of the domain of possible concepts. 'Possible concepts' include memories, ideas expressed in dialects or the vocabulary of special groups, latent and about-to-be-formulated notions, and ideas which cannot be stated in given political circumstances. It is from the domain of possible concepts and the evaluation attached to them that we can perceive the resonance of the political vocabulary which is actually used. The paper discusses the emergence of new political ideas among the Buryat and their fate in the twentieth century – a story which is necessarily incomplete, not only because of the distance of the subject from ourselves[1] but also because all that is available to us for study, language as actually employed, is necessarily ambiguous and open to interpretation.

A proposal to study ideas by means of analysis of the political vocabulary entails some obvious methodological problems. The first is the lack of any generally accepted theory, in either linguistics or philosophy, of the relation between words and consciousness. It would clearly be mistaken, as Skinner has pointed out (1980: 562–78), simply to equate the word and the concept, since it cannot be a necessary condition of someone thinking along certain lines that s/he already possess a corresponding and accepted linguistic term. Furthermore, in the case of certain highly general terms, such as *being* or *infinity*, used with perfect consistency by an entire community, it might be possible to show that there are no concepts which answer to their agreed usages. However, Skinner concluded that, while there can be no single formula for the relationship between concepts and words, we can assume for practical purposes that 'the possession of a concept will at least *standardly* be signalled by the employment of a corresponding term. As long as we bear in mind that "standardly" means neither necessarily nor sufficiently, I think we may legitimately proceed' (1980: 564).

This formulation seems preferable to the position on this subject of the early 'materialist' semiologists such as Voloshinov. Voloshinov (1973: 10–15) argued that consciousness itself can only come about by means of some kind of semiotic material. Anything which represents, depicts, or stands for something outside itself is a sign. We can remain neutral on his bald statement, 'consciousness itself can arise and become a viable fact only in the material embodiment of signs', which would appear to deny the possibility of deliberate invention of terms, but still find valuable many of his other ideas. In particular, let us pause on the idea that 'reality reflected in sign is not merely reflected but *refracted*'. For Voloshinov it is because signs are subject to ideological evaluation that they may distort reality. This insight of Voloshinov's, an advance at least on Saussure, is attached by him to the notion of the class struggle.

> How is this refraction of existence in the ideological sign determined? By an intersecting of differently oriented social interests within one and the same sign community, i.e. by the class struggle. This social multi-accentuality of the sign is a very crucial aspect. By and large it is by this intersecting of accents that the sign maintains its vitality and dynamism and capacity for further development. . . . The very same thing that makes the ideological sign vital and mutable is also, however, that which makes it a refracting and distorting medium. The ruling class strives to impart a supra-class, eternal character to the ideological sign, to extinguish or drive inward the struggle between social value judgements which occurs in it, to make the sign uni-accentual. (1973: 23)

A similar point has been developed sociologically by Bourdieu and Bloch, without, however, focusing on Voloshinov's idea that any sign is always actually a focus for different evaluations. There are problems with Voloshinov, though: we may accept his idea of the ideological conflict over evaluations without agreeing that *this* alone is what gives rise to the 'refraction of existence' of the sign. The 'refraction of existence', or the body of myths and beliefs which seem to us to misrepresent the world, has never been shown to be linked entirely and systematically with the intersection of social interests within a community. This is not to say that ethnographical studies, particularly in fact those of relatively simple classless societies, have not been able to demonstrate a close correspondence between the interests of social divisions (e.g. those between the sexes) and a significant part of the symbolic content and structure of the cosmology, but they have never explained the whole of the 'misrepresentation' nor its general motivation. (To explain, for example, even a primitive cosmology such as that of the Nuer or the Barasana should we not also look at the struggle between given social forms and 'nature' (the environment as perceived), or at relations with other societies as Lévi-Strauss has pointed out, and in more complex cases at attitudes to ethnicity, and the interaction with perceived past states of this same society?)

If we must decouple Voloshinov's causal link between 'multi-accentuality' and the 'refraction of existence' this is not to deny the importance of both of these ideas. However, in my view it is necessary to unhinge yet another of the connections in his causal thinking, the explanation of 'multi-accentuality' of the sign by the class-struggle. As this study will demonstrate, some classes, if classes are defined by politico-economic position, may incorporate a far greater internal diversity of evaluations than others, which may be characterized by something like unanimity. In other words, it is not simply class which produces divergent 'accents', though class may have this function. In the case of the Buryat, pre-Soviet political cultures, of radically non-European kinds, have been far more important than class. For peoples like the Buryat the Soviet state did in fact operate, as it was intended to, on non-class lines, drawing into its arenas and functions virtually anyone prepared to engage in the official political discourse along the correct 'line'. The line, frequently subject to abrupt change, was the product of specific political circumstances in eastern Siberia, and it was maintained by repression and terror. This meant, as the twenties and thirties progressed, the sloughing off of sections of the population, as indigenous concepts and vocabularies tied to the very past circumstances and social structures the State intended to transform, became, one by one, illegitimate from the point of view of the State and Party. It is only insofar as we can call these alienated and marginalized groups 'classes', though they were not distinguished economically from anyone else provided they kept silent, that one might possibly retain Voloshinov's idea that it is the class-struggle which determines the 'multi-accentuality' of the sign in political discourse.

In as much as any distincitvely Buryat political ideas (concepts expressed in the indigenously formulated terminology) had become illegitimate by the mid-1930s, we must consider the possibility that the entire Buryat people became a marginalized group in the above sense. This however was not the case. There is no doubt that the majority of Buryats participated in state politics as best they could. Nevertheless, this paper argues that minorities such as the Buryat perceived political activity differently from the Russians. The Buryats were the heirs of their own deeply-ingrained habits of thought, underlying political ideas. For example, the cyclical view of time, meant that the very notion of irreversible progress was, if not incomprehensible, not truly apprehended and internalized. Such 'possible ideas', latent for decades, might unexpectedly surface. Here is an illustration: by the Brezhnev era the consolidation of state power in a relatively defined social group had established something like a recognizably hierarchical social structure, and it was suggested by at least one Buryat linguist that the old honorific styles of address, earlier used for lords and Buddhist lamas and subsequently 'swept away by the Revolution' should be revived for address towards dignitaries of the Soviet state (Shagdarov 1972: 11).

This study will suggest that the most serious and brutal attempts to impose a single meaning in political rhetoric cannot succeed. Voloshinov was right, despite the reservations mentioned above, to point out the Janus-like, 'inner dialectical quality' of the sign, and it is this that we shall now explore.

The emergence of a Buryat political terminology

The Buryats live in south-east Siberia and speak a Mongolian language. Subjects since the seventeenth century of the Russian Empire, they nevertheless found themselves at the cross-roads of north Asia, a point where Russian, Mongolian, and Manchu/Chinese trade and communications met. The Buryats were not themselves ever politically unified. They were a collection of tribes, of varied origins in the north Mongolian world, each with its own dialect. The majority were converted to Buddhism by the early nineteenth century, but other groups remained believers in shamanism and in some areas were subject to rather cursory missionizing activity by the Orthodox church. Possibly because of these diverse influences on their development, the Buryats by the beginning of the twentieth century had a remarkable intelligentsia, multilingual, and adept in the manipulation of different cultures. It was from this class, remarkable for its energy and diversity, that there arose leaders determined to provide an indigenous political vocabulary to deal with the modern world.

The initial spur was the Tsarist land-reform of 1901–2, which threatened to transfer much Buryat territory into the hands of Russian settlers. By proposing peasant land norms for the whole population it threatened the entire Buryat way of life, which was based on extensive and often nomadic pastoralism. The 1905 'revolution' in Russia provided a new political discourse of democracy and revolt, and the overthrow of the Manchu dynasty in Mongolia in 1911, a regime which had seemed monolithic and eternal, suddenly showed that political change was possible. The Buryat intelligentsia was split: there were those nationalist traditionalists who clung to the hierarchical Mongolian ideal, there was a pro-Russian faction, and there were nationalist radicals who aimed for a modern transformation of Buryat-Mongolian society. It was this latter group which flung itself into activity: newspapers and brochures to raise Buryat consciousness, proposals for reform of the clan system and the Buddhist church, translations of European classics, reform of the cumbersome Mongolian writing system used by the Buryats, dictionaries and encyclopaedias. Out of all this, there emerged the new political vocabulary.

The new terms were not the simple translation of Russian or international words into Buryat. Potent nationalism made this course unacceptable. In some cases, words which were already present were given a new meaning. In others, new words were made up. Since words in the Mongolian languages are built up of meaningful roots and suffix morphemes it is possible for us to see the ideas behind the construction of the new vocabulary.

For example: *xubisxal* 'revolution'. In the nineteenth century this word had meant 'metamorphosis' or 'transformation'. It is formed from the root *xubi* 'fate' or 'destiny' and is one of a group of words built up on this base, including:

xubilaxu 'to be transformed', 'to deteriorate'
xubilgaxu 'to transform'
xubilgan 'a reincarnation', especially of lamas who are reincarnations of deities
xubiraxu 'to change', 'to fade,' 'to wilt'

xubiragulxu 'to make to change', 'to distort'
xubisgaxu 'to change' (transitive), 'to transform'

The word *xubisxal* is made up of the following elements: *xubi* 'fate', + *-s* (very forming suffix), + *-ga* (suffix making verb transitive), + *-l* (suffix forming abstract nouns). In this the -s suffix seems crucial, perhaps implying suddenness. Other abstract nouns formed from *xubi* have different meanings according to whether they employ the -l or the -r suffix, e.g.

xubilal 'evolution'
xubiral 'change (of a negative kind)'

We can see that the word *xubisxal* has a quite specific context in the Mongol languages. It was not used for the 1911 change of government in Mongolia, when the Manchus were thrown out and the autonomous regime initiated. Its use for 1917 was a quite deliberate extension of the reference of a word which previously had no political implications but rather religious ones. In the early period it was used for an abstract idea, the deliberate transformation of (one's) fate, but its reverberations in its linguistic context must have been given various connotations by different speakers.

There is no need to do a similarly extended analysis of other words created or re-deployed at this period. A glance at the following list will show the kinds of operation involved:

neyigem zirum 'socialism', derived from *neyigem* 'community', 'society', 'all'; *zirum* 'established order', 'code of laws'.

anggi 'class' (in political sense), derived from *ang* 'division' 'separation'.

eb-xamtu-yin nam 'Communist Party', derived from *eb* 'harmony', *xamtu* 'together', *-yin* (possessive suffix), *nam* 'people of a similar type, or belonging to a single group'.

zöblel 'soviet', derived from *zöb* 'truth', 'right', *zöblexü* 'to give advice', 'to consult'; *-l* (abstract noun suffix).

ed-ün zasag 'economics', derived from *ed* 'things', 'objects', 'property', *-ün* (possessive suffix), *zasag* 'rule', 'power'.

xamtu-yin azal 'collective farm', 'co-operative', derived from *xamtu* 'together', *-yin* (possessive suffix), *azal* 'task', 'work'.

tengri-ügei üzel 'atheism', derived from *tengri* 'sky', 'heaven', 'god', *-ügei* (negative), *üzel* 'view'

None of these words, nor others of the same kind, are now normally used by the Buryats, either in speech or writing. Although the 'new' vocabulary has not entirely disappeared from Mongolia, it has been replaced in Buryatiya by Buryatized forms of Russian or international words (*kommunis*, *parti*, *kolxoz*, etc.). Contemporary Soviet linguists explain this by saying that the lexicon of the 1920s was unwieldy and did not express the 'true meaning of the concepts', with the result that people were confused. It is certainly true that many of the new expressions were lengthy, e.g. for 'agronomist' (now *agronom*): *gazar taria-alang-iin uxaanda bolborson xün* ('a person educated in the science of tilling the land'). But such expressions are not unclear, and I shall argue that it is their over-determined character, their abstract intelligibility, which is one of the reasons for their demise.

Indeed, in the early period it was the borrowed foreign words which gave rise to misunderstandings. In the 1920s the Buryats used *xubisxal* interchangeably with the Russian *revolutsiya*. The latter was doubly alien, since ordinary people had little access to European history which might have enabled them to see what revolutions had occurred, or indeed that there might be different sorts of revolution at all. People told me of a folk-etymology at the period of the phrase '*oktyabrskaya revolutsia*', the adjective only adding an element of mystification, since it was not clear why the month should make any difference. People thought that there was a woman (perhaps because of the feminine ending *-skaya*, in itself a misunderstanding of Russian grammar) who was named after the month October, and that she led some kind of *revolutsiya* against the Tsar. This made sense to uneducated people because it was clear that one person's revolt – particularly one led by a woman! – should be different from another person's revolt, while the political difference between the February and October revolutions escaped them.

But during the 1920s a commutation took place: misunderstandings over Russian terms were short-lived and their referential meanings soon became crystal clear, and at the same time the meaning of the Buryat expressions clouded over as it became difficult to tell to what in the real world they applied. In order to understand this we must examine the general socio-linguistic context of the 1920s. The rapid political education of ordinary people was of course a priority of the revolutionary government. Commissions were sent out to record the dialects and vocabulary of the Buryats. One survey, conducted by the eminent Mongolist N. N. Poppe in various Buryat collective farms, is available to us and we may assume that it is a fairly exact record of rural speech at that time.

Then (late 1920s – early 1930s) the Buryat-Mongolian political vocabulary was still in use:

xubisxaliin erdem surgaal 'wise teachings of the revolution'
xagaan zasagai ülegdel 'survivals of the Tsarist (Khan's) regime'
bodolgo 'politics', etc.

But at the same time an extraordinary number of the words used in everyday speech were Russian, even where Buryat equivalents existed. Sometimes Buryat and Russian vocabulary was used interchangeably:

kolxooz and *xamtiin azal* 'kolkhoz'
xulaaguud and *bayad* 'rich farmers'
xot and *gorod* 'town'
nam and *parti* 'Party'

Very noticeable is the use of a purely Russian political vocabulary:

arganizaasa (Rus. *organizatsiya*) 'organization'
pirigib (Rus. *peregib*) 'deviation' (in political sense)
voyono kommunizami (Rus. *voyennyi kommunizm*) 'war communism'
splosnaa kiligtivizaasa (Rus. *sploshnaya kollektivizatsiya*) 'complete collectivization'
trudne momentuudta (Rus. *trudnyye momenty*) 'in difficult moments'

(Poppe 1934 and 1936).

What is clear, if we compare this with documents such as newspapers of the period, is that the ordinary speech of kolkhozniks was much more Russified than written texts. This has continued to be the case to the present day, although the two have come closer together, and we should look at the reasons.

In the late 1920s–early 1930s Buryat writing was still dominated by the arguments of the native intelligentsia. Buryat was written in the Mongolian script, an archaic form which differed markedly from any spoken dialect. This was thought to hold back educational development, because the script was difficult to learn, ambiguous, could not be used for reading aloud, etc. Opinions were hotly divided as to whether it should be retained in its present form (to preserve access to centuries of culture), reformed so as to remove ambiguities, or given up in favour of a Cyrillic or Latin transliteration of the spoken language. In the end the Party recommended the Latin option, which had long been in preparation by the Buryat scholar Baradiin and others. An orthography was finally agreed upon at the end of the 1920s, but it had a short and confused life. In 1933 the Central Committee of the Buryat Communist Party decreed that the language to be used as a base for writing was no longer to be Khalkh Mongolian but the Selenga dialect of Buryat. At the same time, 'archaisms' and 'Mongolisms' were to be abandoned, and international and Russian words to be introduced. Fear of pan-Mongolian nationalism and its links with Japanese expansion in north Asia were the background to these decisions. The disarray among writers of Buryat was only intensified when, in 1936, it was decreed that the dialect basis was to change again, from Selenga to Khori. In 1939, as part of an all-USSR policy, the Latin script was rejected and replaced with the Cyrillic. All of this constituted a devastating attack on the attempt by Baradin and others to retain a Mongolian culture in Buryatiya. It was now declared that Buryat was a separate language. The Party constantly urged writers to abandon 'Mongolisms', which were labelled 'bookish' and 'difficult for ordinary people to understand', and to bring their writing closer to the speech of the masses.

By the end of the 1930s, the early leaders of the Buryat intelligentsia, especially those associated with the Buddhist Church, had all been repressed. Those of their number surviving into the 1930s had been accused of 'bourgeois nationalism', and it is probable that for anyone to use their neo-Mongolian vocabulary of politics in writing would have been very dangerous. We can therefore see the disappearance of the Buryat terms in the written language as a matter of dire necessity – they were simply erased by decree.

But this does not explain why the spoken language was, even by the later 1920s, so markedly more Russified than Buryat writing. Even in Selenga, the district closest to the Mongolian border, the oral texts recorded by Poppe show that around 14 per cent of the vocabulary used in talking about political matters was Russian. The central organs of the Buryat Party were disingenuous in suggesting that the neo-Mongolian terminology was 'not known' among the people, or 'difficult to understand'. As the texts show, the terms were used and used correctly. I would suggest that the reason they were being abandoned in favour of Russian terms, even in advance of the Party's decrees, was that they were completely understandable as concepts, but what happened was that reality no longer corresponded to them. For the Buryat peasants and herdsmen, half-literate at best, and situated at the end of a complex administrative hierarchy of which the heights (in Moscow) were completely unknown to them, the socio-political reality of the 1920s and 1930s must have appeared bewilderingly arbitrary. Why War Communism, and then why the New Economic Policy, and then why De-Kulakization and Collectivization? Some of these expressions, such as 'the Ural-Siberian Method', floated briefly into vogue and then disappeared again. The drastic nature of the changes, and the fact that decisions about them were taken outside the known world, meant that no native Buryat concepts, even those specifically constructed for the revolution could accurately reflect the situation. Russians and Mongolians, faced with similar revolutionary upheavals, had only their own languages at their disposal and therefore tended to continue to use the old terms, however inappropriate they became. The Buryat solution was to turn to Russian terms which were used primarily as means of identification.

To take a very simple example: the Buryat word *bayad* (rich people) was the equivalent of the Russian *kulak* (rich peasant) in ordinary language. But as policy followed policy, it was soon apparent that kulaks were not *bayad*: the category 'kulak' was administratively defined, by criteria which changed from time to time for reasons which cannot have been clear to Buryat herdsmen. Initially these were essentially criteria from the Russian economy, such as area of land owned, number of cattle owned, or whether there were any employees on the farm. As the criteria widened many of the people defined as 'kulaks' could not have been rich in any Buryat understanding of the word. Buryats defined wealth by the number of cattle and horses owned, not by the area of sown land, nor the area of pasture, nor by the presence of employees. Furthermore, during collectivization the term 'kulak' came to be used for anyone who opposed the policy, i.e. it became a political category (Hirooka *et al.* 1988). In this situation, no-one in their senses would have used the word *bayad* to refer to kulaks; *bayad* meant rich people, and kulaks were *xulaaguud*, as the Buryats pronounced it. The sense of the term may have twisted out of sight, but the reference was entirely clear: 'kulaks' were found in every village.

The distinction between sense and reference is useful for understanding the fate of the Buryat-Mongolian vocabulary too. The terms had not only sense, but also their own implications of moral values which could not be forgotten. It would have been possible for the kolkhozniks to go on calling the Party '*eb xamtu-*

yin nam' ('the community of harmony and togetherness'), but to do so in view of the enormous changes which took place in the size, composition and socio-political role of the Party in this period, would have been to use this phrase as a clearly inappropriate even ludicrous label. No Buryat speaker could ignore a lingering sense, and an evaluation precisely linked with deeply felt aspirations of the specific social movement now long-since past, associated with these words. As a label 'Kommunis Parti' functioned much better.

Furthermore, with the Buryat terms it was not clear to what in the real world they should correctly be applied. In other words, while their sense was evident, their range of reference in many cases was not. The terms had first been defined by intellectuals in the capital and had, as we saw, reached the kolkhozniks during the 1920s. But the intellectuals became steadily less influential, and it is highly doubtful that as Soviet institutions changed, they could have established a more differentiated range of terms to deal with the situation in the countryside. Poppe's texts make clear that kolkhozniks used the term '*eb xamtu-yin azal*' ('work-group of harmony and togetherness') to refer without differentiating to communes, cooperatives, artels, and collective farms, but these were different kinds of organization, all but the last to be abolished in the collectivization drive. In discussing the present (1930s) the herdsmen simply used the Russian-derived *kolxooz*, since it was quite clear what a kolkhoz was. Who was to say that the reference of '*eb xamtu-yin azal*' was to be extended to include the kolkhoz?

If we return to *xubisxal* 'revolution', which today is definitely classed as an archaism, we find that contemporary Buryat dictionaries allow the word as a term for the February revolution, but not the October one, which in Buryat is *revolyutsi*.

Even in the period before the decrees outlawing 'Mongolisms', people must have sensed the official preference for Russian terms. At least with Russian terms, one could preserve the appearance of keeping up with the flow of policy which somehow or other had to be put into practice. Hold 'political discussions' and 'purge the leadership' of the 'class enemy'? – much the simplest was to say 'These are our discussions (Rus. *beseda*) and those are the class enemy (Rus. *klassovoi vrag*)', whatever the reality of the situation. The necessity of doing this was just as strong if no real attempt was made to carry out the instructions. All that was necessary was to report that a *beseda* had taken place and a *klassovoi vrag* had been unmasked. The fulfilling of instructions in a purely formal way (Rus. slang '*na galochki*' – 'for the record') was very common, indeed universal in the case of orders which had to be obeyed and which were difficult to check up on. In this situation having the appropriate label was most of what was required.

The function of Russian words as labels when they were used by Buryats becomes even clearer when we realize that many of them were used in current speech as abbreviations (this is true of native Russian speakers too), for example:

'*sotsialisticheskii*' becomes 'sots'
'*kommunisticheskaya partiya*' becomes 'kompartiya'
'*produktsiya*' becomes 'prod'
'*potrebitel'skii*' (consumption) becomes 'po'
'*snabzheniye*' (supply) becomes 'snab'

Unlike words in the Buryat language, which are made up of morphemes with meaning, no amount of working out from first principles will tell you what a foreign abbreviation stands for. The word *sel'po* (local branch of the consumers' co-operative) may not be understood, but the institution can be pointed out, 'There it is, right in the middle of the village'.

To use Russian is also a kind of protection of the Buryat language. Even if it is unconscious, people may wish to preserve their own values from the huge ideological pressure of the Soviet institutionalization – especially when those institutions, and even the ideological value attached to them is constantly changing. The corollary of this is that the Buryat language is increasingly kept for those situations in which an understood morality is shared – for example, in family life.

Written Tibetan and Mongolian and Buryat honorific speech have disappeared from the Buryat and Russian. Some idea of their use is gained from the following table constructed by Loseva on the basis of her field-work among kolkhozniks in the Aga Buryat National Okrug in the early 1970s (Loseva 1974: 123).

I would suggest, however, that the socially important difference now is between the formal or 'official' language, whether Buryat or Russian, on the one hand, and informal language on the other. The table shows that Buryat is ceasing to have much vitality as a written language. 'Informal language' is spoken Buryat, much interspersed with Russian colloquialisms.

The definition of linguistic codes of various kinds (known in Russian as 'styles') has been a matter of concern in the Soviet Union ever since the 1930s. In other words, the Soviet government

Use of language		*men*	*women*	*total*	*%*
Buryats stating native lang. to be:	Buryat	243	182	425	97.7
	Russian	4	6	10	2.3
Conversing at work in:	Buryat	90	60	150	35.7
	Russian	8	25	33	7.5
	Either B or R	149	98	247	56.8
Conversing at home in:	Buryat	170	136	306	70.3
	Russian	15	16	31	7.2
	Either B or R	62	36	98	22.5
Conducting correspondence in:	Buryat	13	24	37	8.7
	Russian	139	91	230	52.7
	Either B or R	95	73	168	38.6

has deliberately set out to create specific forms of linguistic expression for particular occasions. Numerous congresses and publications have debated the question of defining functional 'styles' and attempted to set out the number and type of 'styles' appropriate to given languages, the most important being Russian. The question of whether it was desirable to have such 'styles' hardly seems to have arisen. 'Style' itself was defined as a semantically closed, expressively limited and intentionally organized system of means of expression, corresponding to one or another genre of literature, writing, or social activity (Budayev, Dambayeva, and Shagdanov (eds) 1972: 13).

An influential All-Union Congress of 'stylistics' took place in Ashkhabad in 1966, attended by 360 linguists from all over the Soviet Union. It was decided that six functional 'styles' were to be differentiated: 1) artistic, 2) social-publicist, 3) official-business, 4) scientific, 5) production-technological, and 6) everyday communication. Academician Vingradov's objection to the notion of an 'artistic style' was swept aside. The Buryat delegates decided in favour of the Ashkhabad categories, with the qualification that in the relatively low state of development of the Buryat language it was not necessary to distinguish between the 'scientific' and the 'production-technological' styles (Budayev *et al.* (eds) 1972: 19).

The 'official' language

In fact, the social-publicist and official-business styles are indistinguishable. They constitute what I call 'official' language.

'Official' Buryat is so heavily influenced by 'official' Russian that it often gives the impression of being simply a Buryatized rendering of the latter. It is increasingly differentiated from any spoken form of Buryat, and although it is based on the Khori dialect, writers and speakers at meetings, etc. are discouraged from using any local-sounding words. Not only single terms, but also whole expressions are formulae ('exhaust all possibilities', 'liquidate deficiencies', 'make a categorical improvement' and so on) transferred directly from Russian officialese to Buryat. The sense, range of referents, and sometimes even grammatical characteristics, such as word order, are taken directly from Russian, e.g. Russian *denezhnyi oborot* ('financial turnover') – Buryat *müngenei er'ese*; Russian *obshchestvennyi stroi* ('social structure') – Buryat *olonshtyn baiguulalta*; Russian *imeni* ('named after' as in *Kilkhoz imeni Karla Marksa*) – Buryat *neremzhete*, etc. Even the strangely redundant Russian expression *rogatyi skot* ('horned cattle') appears in Buryat as *eberte mal*. Very common are terms consisting of paired Russian and Buryat words, e.g. *xütelberilxe shtab* ('leading staff'), *soyol kul'turyn emxi* ('organization of culture'). A large number of Buryat suffixes are now used in such a way as to correspond grammatically with Russian word endings, e.g. *-beri* corresponds with the Russian *-stvo*. Of course, literary Buryat contains a majority of words which have always existed in the language, but a large number of these have come to have specifically Soviet referents, and the 'old meanings' – which still obtain in ordinary spoken language – have been discarded.[2] An example is the word *bagsha*, which had the connotations of guru, mentor, or guiding spirit, but is now used in literary Buryat only with the meaning of 'teacher' in a school or other educational institution.

The guardians of the 'official' style are newspaper editors, broadcaster, journalists, Party officials, school-teachers. There is little distinction between written and oral modes, since speeches are written out and delivered to the letter. For important political meetings, the speeches are often written by specialists trained at the Higher Party Schools and distributed to the appropriate speakers. Frequently they are written in Russian and then translated into Buryat, as are the main (and perhaps all) regional newspapers. At less exalted levels, Party officials make a check on speeches before they are given.

Before *glasnost'* all over the Soviet Union articles and letters ostensibly written by members of the public were re-written by journalists in the appropriate style before publication. This was true even of the most humble newspapers. When Aleksei Losev was working on a local paper in a small town in north Sakhalin, it was his job to 'organize' the reactions (*otkliki*) of the public to current political events. He describes a morning in the newspaper office. A colleague says to him:

> 'I, Aleksei Vladimirovich, will take the working class – a workshop for making stools, and I'll do the scientific-technical intelligentsia, at Dal'tekhsnab. But you do a state farm, so we can have some representatives of the nationalities. And you, as a young man, can probably organise a woman.'
> 'But where am I to find her, Ivan Mikhailych?'
> 'Well, try ringing the hospital, or the library. Or you could try the post-office, Lyudmilla Vasil'yevna. She always gives us good reactions.'
>
> And we get down to it.
>
> 'Hullo, is that Dal'tekhsnab? Could you give me the Party Secretary please . . . Sergei Sergeyevich? Hullo, how are you? It's Ivan Mikhailych from the newspaper speaking. We have the idea of putting your reactions in the next number. To what? To the Plenum, to the Plenum, of course. Good. O.K. Shall I ring you and read them out when they are ready, or will you trust us? . . . Well fine. Thanks for your trust.'
>
> 'We got hold of the working class, the old Bolsheviks, women, the scientific-technical intelligentsia, the nationalities, and sometimes even pioneers and schoolchildren, and then got down to invention.
>
> 'I as a mother who has brought up four children . . . cannot help remembering the unforgettable days of October . . . and only with Soviet power has our little nation . . . I guarantee still more to . . . ..' (Losev 1978: 242–3)

In this style there is a limited range of adjectives and adverbs: success (*uspekh*) is creative (*tvorcheskii*), labour (*trud*) is also creative (*tvorcheskii*), help (*pomoshch'*) is brotherly (*bratskaya*), participation (*uchastiye*) is active (*aktivnoye*), and so on.

It is a truism to say that many political meetings carried out in this style were pure 'performance'. They achieved a change of state, for example the public 'decision' to take some action, but this was irrespective of the attitudes of those attending. In many cases such meetings consisted entirely of incantations. For example, from a meeting held in July 1973 to award the Buryat ASSR with the Order of the October Revolution, a speech made by N. F. Tatarchuk, chairman of the Krasnoyarsk Krai Soviet, selected at random from seventeen similar speeches, and of course in Russian:

> We, comrades, are heartily thankful and express our deep gratitude to the Leninist Central Committee of the Party and to our Soviet government for their continuous and attentive care for the development of the productive forces of the eastern regions of our country. Please, Mikhail Sergeyevich, convey to the Politburo of the Central Committee of the Party, to the Soviet of Ministers of the USSR, and to the Soviet of Ministers of the RSFSR our great gratitude for the great brotherly help which has been given, for the support in the strengthening of the economy and the development of the productive forces not only of the Krasnoyarsk Krai but also of all the eastern regions of our great multinational Homeland – the Union of Soviet Socialist Republics. (Applause)
> Long live the thrice decorated Buryat Autonomous Soviet Socialist Republic and her manly and work-loving people! (Applause)
> Long may the indestructible union and brotherly friendship of all the people of our international Homeland – the Union of Soviet Socialist Republics – live and flourish! (Applause)
> Glory to our Leninist Communist Party of the Soviet Union and her Central Committee headed by the General Secretary of the Central Committee of the Communist Party of the Soviet Union, Leonid Il'ich Brezhnev! (Applause) (Materialy . . ., 1973: 74–5)

The 'official' style has some further characteristics which stem from the Soviet ideological attitude to history. Both the sense and the reference of political terms are constantly in the process of being defined and re-defined. A stream of publications has this function: text-books, collections of speeches, directories for local Party workers, managers, chairmen of enterprises, etc., official records of current formulations of policy. Many such books are aimed explicitly at instruction and consist of chapters of explanation, with the significant words in heavy type, followed by a series of 'control questions'. To take a typical example, the first chapter of a book on economics in agricultural production sets out to explain the difference between 'socialism' and 'developed socialism' (Emel'yanov (ed.) 1977: 3–14). The 'control questions' at the end of the chapter begin:

> 1. What is the economic strategy of the Party and what are its basic elements?
> 2. What is the connection between the economic policy and the economic strategy of the Party? In what ways are they the same and in what ways different?
> 3. In what do the scientific bases of the economic strategy of the Party consist?
> 4. What are the characteristics of the contemporary stage of the development of the economy and how are they reflected in the Party's economic strategy?

Such questions do not bear too much thinking about in the abstract; it is clear that what the reader is expected to do is to answer the questions by referring back to the heavy type in the preceding chapter. What these 'guide' books are doing in effect is to provide a current definition of political terms. They sometimes give the sense of the terms ('Politics is the concentrated expression of economics') but they are mainly devoted to defining the reference, and usually not to some possible category, but to actually existing phenomena or processes which have occurred ('Socialism was built in our country already in the 1930 . . .'; or, 'One of the simplest forms of vertical integration is the sovkhoz-factory . . . .. Examples of such agro-industrial unions are the sovkhoz-factories 'Chuma' and 'Viktoriya' in the Moldavian SSR . . .').

Within the sphere of the 'official' rhetoric the 'struggles' over the evaluation of language have had a peculiar form. This is because, firstly, the definitions of the meanings of political words were established by high officials who did not take ordinary speech as a basis, and, secondly, while the current version of the reasoning behind these definitions was sometimes explained, in the text-books, the history of changes of opinion was assiduously erased.

It may seem incredible to Western readers that this really could be so. Surely old text-books and political speeches, visible evidence of different opinions, lie around undisturbed in provincial libraries? But a teacher in a small rural school in the Ukraine during the 1940s–1960s wrote:

> I did not observe any case of control by the organs of the state security over the school, but lists of publications due for confiscation were showered on us regularly and efficiently. The confiscated literature was destroyed in the presence of witnesses and with written confirmation. We were all amused when, after the 20th Party Congress, the new people in power hurriedly sent out circulars giving instructions for the confiscation of their own recent speeches and works. (Tiktina 1978: 80–1)[3]

People may notice, and be amused or appalled by changes in values, but discussion of such matters used to be dangerous and still is not without risk. The evidence is destroyed. As a recent article in *Izvestiya* on the teaching of history observes, 'The fact that Catherine II forbad the word "slave" did not mean that slavery disappeared' (21 July 1987: 3), but the existence of an effective 'social' evaluation (Voloshinov) depends on there being social means by which people can communicate on these matters – more or less absent for the Soviet rural population. Above all it depends on an understanding or *possession* of the concepts, which is difficult without a knowledge of their unfolding through time.

Essential to this process of re-definition of political concepts is the idea that the strategy of the Party is scientific. Processes in society develop according to laws which have the same objective character as the laws of nature. Consequently, the study of the laws of society becomes progressively deeper just as does the scientific study of nature. The laws of society and economics can be misunderstood. In the same way that past scientific theories were 'wrong', past political and economic theories were 'wrong' and are now superceded. The development of knowledge proceeds in parallel with the development of the economy.[4] Soviet ideology thus provides reasons for discarding past interpretations of economics, on which political policy is in theory based. Past values are at best useful indications of paths which should not be taken. At worst, they are dangerous misunderstandings. The orientation is away from the past and towards the future.

To the people responsible for defining the 'line' on some matter, a change from an earlier position need not seem blameworthy. On the contrary it is evidence of progress. This is true even if the matter under discussion is purely ideological, e.g. in literary criticism. In the Stalinist period, the Buryat 'Geser' epic was condemned, and the discussions separated out two incorrect views (that a bowdlerized version was acceptable, and that the epic merely suffered from an 'anti-people' character) which were contrasted with a correct 'scientific' view. (The term 'anti-people' is still used, but now applied to folk epics, which are widely published.) The critics in the 1950s felt aggrieved that they had not been given guidance from above, from the Scientific-Research Institute of Culture, thus allowing them to make incorrect judgements (Khadalov and Ulanov (eds) 1953: 196–7). But for the ordinary people, the recipients of the 'correct' line, all of the past is erased. They hear only that historians, philologists and philosophers have deeply studied the matter and arrived at a conclusion. In the case of economics and politics the 'line' is even more ineluctable, in that it is based on laws which are 'independent of the wishes of people' (Emel'yanov (ed.) 1977: 10).

Skinner has suggested that with historical change, words, if they are not dropped altogether, tend to accrete new meanings by specific types of social argument and re-evaluation (Skinner 1980: 562–78). Of course this does occur in large parts of the Soviet vocabulary, but the political lexicon has appeared until recently on the contrary to be subject to a narrowing process, both in sense and range of reference. I have suggested that there are two main reasons for this: firstly, the progressive cutting away of earlier evaluations of words, and secondly the definition of abstract concepts in terms of specific institutions, rather than in terms of principles. What remains is, essentially, a label.

Internalization of the 'official' language

The conceptual-linguistic resources of Buryat may impede the translation of certain crucial political ideas. To take one example, the concept of the 'bright future' (*svetloye budushchee* in Russian) cannot be adequately expressed in Buryat. The Mongolian languages seem to have no way of expressing a hopeful, definitively positive view of the future. This is consistent, of course, with the Central Asian cyclical view of time. In Mongolian and Buryat the 'future' is rendered by the following expressions:

xoito – 'after'; also, 'behind', 'northern side' (with connotations of coldness, uncleanness, peril)

ereedgüi sag – 'the time which has not come'
xozhom oixi sag – 'the afterwards time'

The expression 'bright future' is thus rendered in Buryat as:

ereedgüi sagai gereltei kommunisticheske baidal – 'the bright communist existence of the time which has not come', a phrase which is not as inspiring as its Russian original.

The concept may be understandable through this thicket of words nevertheless. How are we to know to what extent ordinary people think politically through the 'official' language? Almost no data exist on this subject for the Buryat, and we must make use of indirect evidence. A starting point is the same question applied to ordinary Russians of Siberia. Losev, the newspaperman mentioned above, has preserved some letters from his rural public. These, barely literate, and in their undoctored, unpublished form, he saw as important social documents, which should be read taking into account

> the special psychology of the author (it is not everyone who writes to newspapers), his inability to express his ideas (in itself this may be very expressive), and the influence of the stamp of official propaganda, undigested or misconceived, taken seriously or ironically, because written expression cannot be conceived outside this stamp (and this is also of social significance). (Losev 1978: 241)

Let us take the example of a letter from a schoolgirl of about 15 who wrote to take part in a discussion about the role of pioneer-leaders in schools.

> The vocation of man is the continuous, demanding realisation to help the masses, inactivity leads to stupidity, and then to idiotism. But man must work in contact with the mass and work graphically, according to the hourly graph and the plan!
> In the mass there is always the sputnik of biological fermentation and it is not recommended to get nervous and angry with the mass, since after work there is wear and tear of the organism, and man falls into a state of underdevelopment, it is particularly hard to work among children because they have so many 'Whys?' These 'whys?' monitor the personal character and therefore, according to the individual 'why?' it is possible to define whether this person is useful to society or not, and even the state of his health and the length of his fruitful work.

> All normal children engage in voluntary social work after school hours, but the underdeveloped are not in a fit state to engage in these questions – that is why there are pioneer-leaders: the leader is duty bound to set up the plan of work, so that the brain of man can begin to work according to his individual abilities, BUT the main thing is: 'The Regime of the Day!', 'The Plan of Work!', 'Why?' (Liz Sh)

One has the sense of someone who has learnt the labels and slogans (the 'mass', the 'sputnik', 'fruitful work', 'the regime of the day') and applies them mechanically. This is not simply childishness. Adults also make sense of the political ideology by incorporating parts of it into the practical world they know. Such attempts characteristically refrain from any individual interpretation and make almost desperate links between high policy and the people's wisdom. Losev received, for example, letters from an inventor – not a collector, an inventor – of proverbs (1978: 262):

> Livestock farming, as you know, depends on a sufficiency of fodder. The culture of legumes decisively raises the quantity of fodder. You know it was not by chance that the March Plenum of the Central Committee of the Communist Party of USSR devoted much attention to peas and legumes. And sufficient attention was given to the raising of productivity. Fertiliser, including organic fertiliser, plays in this matter a leading role. Do my proverbs not correspond to this?
> 'Take manure to the field and wheat will give you a great yield'
> *Vyvezennyi v pole navoz – eto i pshenitsy oboz*
> 'Sowing pea and bean will keep cows from getting lean'
> *Sei gorokh i boby i ne budet u korov khudoby*.

Such attempts directly to grasp the 'official' language are likely to occur in a bureaucratic society with centralized control of the means of communication. In Russia this is not new: peasants in Dostoevsky's *House of the Dead* familiarized the foreign '*kapital*' to '*kopital*' from the verb '*kopit*', to save or hoard. There are many such examples from the Buryats. A milkmaid in a newspaper interview says that it is the second year of our ninth five-year plan which has suggested to her the need to give some advice about massaging udders (*Buryaad Ünen*, 16 March 1972). Such examples are so common that we need not assume that they are invariably the result of journalists' re-writing.

This is unlike the cases of political participation in Africa studied by Bloch, Parkin and others in which a *range* of language codes, increasingly formalized, correspond to a range of increasingly ideologized political contexts (Bloch (ed.) 1975). In the Soviet Union any context (massaging udders) can be ideologized. People can make mistakes in the code, but they do not have a series of codes to choose from. The choice, in the public domain, is between Buryat 'official' language and Russian 'official' language.

It is interesting that 'official' Buryat often contains fewer Russian words than everyday Buryat speech of townspeople in particular. This is because, during the 1960s there was some concern in ruling circles at the extent to which the language was becoming impoverished. Attempts were made to create Buryat terms corresponding to Russian or international words. The central political lexicon remained untouched, but a number of words such as:

mergejelted – specialists
xüdelmergüidelge – unemployment
xütelberilegshed – leaders

were made up. The spelling of these new and complicated words was still not yet completely formalized in the 1960s (Shagdarov 1967: 90). Many of the suffixes used in their composition had only recently been taken up, and by linguists rather than ordinary people at that (Shagdarov 1967: 75). As pointed out earlier, some of these suffixes had themselves been created recently in order to correspond with Russian grammatical endings. A choice to use such words is thus *not* an expression of ethnicity, but of pomposity (in the Buryat mode).

Re-Buryatization of the 'official' language has created a situation which is in some ways the opposite of what one normally finds in situations of acculturation. In most cases, the familiar vernacular remains the more or less pure native language, while a range of public styles are acculturated. In the Buryat case, the vernacular is far more directly Russianized than the 'official' language. This arises from the different relation in neo-colonial and Soviet conditions between language and the state. The Soviet government has made an attempt to revitalize native languages, and it is also sensitive to the political need for them. But as earlier noted, most governmental documents, newspaper leaders, etc. are composed in Russian, and only subsequently translated into Buryat. This very political origin has created a gulf between the 'official' style, whether spoken or written, and ordinary talk. Important features of the Soviet case apply to both Buryat and Russian: the infusion of the 'official' style with ideology by means of 'suitable' combinations of words, and the consequent undertones of subversion in the vernacular which are possible through play with 'unsuitable' words and combinations of words.

Informal language

The Russianization of spoken Buryat started long before the Revolution. The economic and commercial vocabulary acquired in the nineteenth century was supplemented by the politico-administrative terminology of the revolutionary period and the vast array of technical words of the mid-twentieth century. However, there are several ways in which Russian makes deep in roads into spoken Buryat:

a) colloquialisms, e.g. Taahad tedeentei utarxai el soo *vozit'sya* bolono beshe gut? (Have you had to *bother* with them for a whole half year?)

b) word-order, e.g. *raekom parti*, instead of Buryat *partiin raiono komitet*

c) the take-over of whole social contexts by Russian, such as the sphere of organized work, where despite the existence of common and useable Buryat terms, Russian words are preferred, e.g. *oboroto* (work, from Russian *rabota*, instead of Buryat *ajal* or *xudelmeri*), *shaban* (shepherd, from the Russian *chaban*, instead of the Buryat *xon'shin*).

Interjections in vernacular Buryat, as in colloquial Russian, are still predominantly religious, taken from the traditional value system:

'*Ai, burxan*!' – 'Oh, God!'

'*Adxa shamai*! *Ene yamar haixan xubuun geesheb*!' – 'The devil! What a good-looking boy he is!' (an *adxa* is a small, evil spirit).

'*Noxoi*! *Morinhoo bu unysh*!' – 'Watch out!' (literally 'Dog!')! 'Don't fall off your horse!' (The dog is an unclean animal in the Mongol view.)

Interjections in the 'official' language, on the other hand, come from Russian: '*Ura*! *Exe oronigoo tülöö uragsha*!' – 'Hurrah! Long live the Mother-Country'.

There are many ways in which a bridging took place between the bureaucratic and the everyday styles. This was a general Soviet phenomenon, not merely Buryat. One of these was simply the ironic:

Ya malenkaya devochka,	I am a little girl,
Ya v shkolu ne khozhu,	I don't go to school,
Ya Lenina ne videla,	I have never seen Lenin,
No ya ego lyublyu.	But I love him.

Or:

Proshla zima, nastalo leto,	The winter has gone, the summer has come,
Spasibo Partii za eto,	Thank you, Party, for that,
Spasibo Partii za to,	Thank you, Party, for the fact that
Chto ya kupila sebe pal'to.	I bought myself an overcoat.

But what is remarkable is that it is frequently the very political labels and slogans, the armory of the Stalinist state, which were taken up and transformed. Let us look at the 'Sovet Narodnogo Khozyaistva', an organization set up by Khrushchev, ordinarily known as the Sovnarkhoz, or by its initials SNKh. Popular doggerel took up the initials and played with them, backwards and forwards:

Stalin Nash Khozyain,	Stalin is our leader,
Khozyain Nash Skonchalsya,	Our leader has died,
Strane Nuzhno Khozyain,	The country needs a leader,
Khozyain Nashelsya Sam,	The leader found himself,
Samyi Nakhalnyi Kohzyain,	The most bumptious leader,
Khrushchev Nikita Sergeich.	Nikita Sergeich Krushchev.

This kind of transformation recognizes the object-like quality of political terms. It is applied to ordinary labels, e.g. the registration letters on Soviet cars, which are given various idiotic meanings, but also to acronyms, to politicians' names, to standard expressions and definitions, to the official names for socialist countries (for example the People's Republic of Mongolia, which is officially called Bugd Nairamdax Mongol Ard Uls 'The Friendly-to-all Mongolian People's State', jokingly termed 'Bugderee Niilzh Manaid Arxi Uuya' – 'Let's all get together and have a drink at my place'). These are truly 'Janus-faced' signs. In the Buryat examples leaders are characteristically pulled-down, physicalized, and localized to their native origins. Often likened to animals (in the vast array of Buryat bestial terminology) the most dignified leaders are given nicknames which act like switches: one could be referring to politician X, or to the cow in the back yard.

Almost the converse as a style is the commandeering of ordinary language ('proletarian' language) in the service of bureaucratic ends. Characteristic of this is the one-sided use of the familiar *ty* (you) in Russian or *shi* in Buryat from the official to the addressee; or the bullying ('straightforward') manner: 'So you (familiar) think you can get away with . . .? The Party expects . . .. Got it?'

Colloquial Buryat is in effect one or other dialect, and only the official language is common to all districts. I was present at many meetings of people from different regions where the main topic of conversation was a dialect comparison. Sometimes the dialect differences are so great as to make mutual understanding difficult. This in itself may have contributed to the common use of Russian. It certainly creates an intimacy of expression, an intimacy based on the social experience of living in small, isolated communities. Such experience is not negated but fostered by the Soviet political structure, where vertical or hierarchical communication is emphasized at the expense of horizontal links.

Although officials 'speaking down' may occasionally use an odd dialect word, as it were in inverted commas, just as Russian bureaucrats may venture a phrase in Buryat, it is clear that dialect, like informal language, was not usable as a political resource in the public arena in the pre-glasnost' era. Not only Russian but also Buryat traditions insist on a heightened style in public discourse.

Ceremonial language

It would be a mistake to assume that there are no occasions on which ordinary Buryats spontaneously express in public and in their own language their sense of what it is to be a citizen of the Soviet Union. The Buryat culture is very rich in those social gatherings where people improvise in a traditional style on beloved themes. These include eulogies to the house and hearth, to local rivers and mountains, to the first mare's milk of spring, to the first hair-cutting of a child, to the birds arriving in spring, to horses, sheep, cattle, and goats, to winning horses in races, to champion wrestlers and archers, to ancestors and respected people. An elaborate cycle of such improvisations occurs at a wedding. They are significant in that the traditional form specifies the situating of the present event in the total cosmology and socio-political space of the celebrants.

The old framework of ancestors, clans, gods and princes has been replaced by the new Soviet cosmology. Let us take the example of the eulogy to a winning race-horse recorded in the Buryat collective farm in 1963:

May there be peace and tranquillity!
He who first ordained the reign of peace
On this earthly planet, and
Absorbed in himself learning accumulated
During hundreds of preceding epochs,
He who for the sake of all living beings
Established the clear and perspicuous revolution (xubisxal)
And was able to overcome the separation of classes (anggi)
His name is the great Lenin,
And the living creatures who listened (to him) were transformed
Into the nation of peaceful happy socialism (sotsializm).
Accomplished leaders of the workers,
Many thousands of people, all of you
Together, listen!
All of our numerous people in their places
Ordained by nature and the cosmos
Are made to grow by means of the grandiose seven-year (plan)
By our good Soviet (sovet) law
Towards the highest stage of socialism,
Widespread and flourishing,
And by further miraculous developments
And pure and good teachings
Our internal order is established.
I request your attention,
Glorious and powerful Chairman,
Custodian of the pure, sacred, fundamental order,
Clear as the golden sun,
Unadulterated as pure gold!
Under the rays of the Golden Kremlin,
The palaces of the sixteen republics (are)
Established as equal powers,
And the city of Ulan-Ude, capital of the Buryat people (is)
In a part of the earthly planet named south Baikal,
On the respected northern side of the river Ude

Which crosses the golden layered earth.
Right in the very centre
Of the fully rich white steppe,
Flourishing with a thousand blessings,
At the foot of the Xangil mountain,
By the decorative stream of Xan-Egetei,
Stands the growing settlement called 'Unen Azal' ('True Work').
It shines majestically, its red flag flying,
Its flowering trees decoratively spread,
And here is the joyful transparent festival,
And this is the day of the traditional great festivity!
Now is the time to sing to the glory of the
Accomplished pacer horse,
Which knows the Mongolian language,
Whose hooves are without dust,
Whose saddle-cloth is without sweat,
Whose gallop covers mountains in dust,
Who arrives from unknown places champing his bit . . . etc.
(Tsydendambayev 1972: 23–6)

Here we see transmuted elements of the earlier Buddhist world-view ('hundreds of preceding epochs', 'for the sake of all living beings', 'people in their places', 'pure and good teachings', etc.). And it is here that the Buryat political vocabulary, forbidden in real politics, re-surfaces (*xubisxal* – revolution, *anggi* – class). Turned into folklore – does this mean that these words have lost all vitality?

In Buryatiya, rural people differentiate between the public official culture and their own 'real' culture, but ceremonial verbal forms exist in a space somewhere between the two. Very little of ceremonial verse is ever openly expressed which has not been transformed into a Soviet civic version. Of course, there are some elements of 'folklore' which have never been Sovietized in this way (religious invocations, magical sayings, omens, etc.) and this very fact has changed their function in Buryat society and made them subversive even though they are not so in intent (Humphrey 1983). The continued existence of this fragmentary 'real' culture means that even now public folklore is not seen by officials as simply exotic – it continues to be in some sense dangerous, a possible repository of harmful, alien ideas, above all ideas with a history. Speeches like the one above are improvised, not tamely congealed in set phrases, and this makes them more active parts of culture than published literature which has been strictly censored. This is the situation the Buryats have had to play with. We can deduce that to include the early political terms in a safely optimistic eulogy was all right. To use them in a shamanist invocation or, far worse a real political speech, would have been quite another matter.

What is difficult to tell from all this is (a) how vital and creative are these public, ceremonial forms, and (b) whether this kind of discourse has been able to preserve the meaning (sense) of native political ideas.[5] Only an analysis of post-*glasnost*' debate, not yet available, would give some answers.

The history we have described here is that of a creative expansion of the language of politics in the revolutionary period, followed by a replacement of these terms by Russian vocabulary, and the crystallization of distinct linguistic 'styles'. In part this differentiation of language was imposed by the central government for the very purpose of limiting the ways in which politics could be discussed, but it also occurred because of the necessity for ordinary people of evolving modes of expression for functioning with Soviet society without attracting blame. Linguistic orthodoxy was a political necessity. As the Buryat terms, loaded with sense and history retreated into folkloric contexts, the official language of politics became increasingly 'label-like' and restricted, so that the merest hint of a double-meaning became suspect. It is in this vulnerability that the 'inner dialectical quality' of the sign lay. There is nothing really *wrong* about the doggerel of the little girl who never saw Lenin, it is just that there seems to be something not quite right about it – enough in its time to put someone in jail.

These developments are significantly different from historical change in the language of politics in the West. There is a different overall pattern of change in the political lexicon, related to the distinctive political relations which have existed in the Soviet Union. After the initial period of invention and transfer of new terms we are no longer dealing with disagreements (the 'struggle') over meaning, either as sense or reference. Both were fixed and enforced from above, by the State-Party complex. This removed the possibility countering orthodoxy with any kind of open heterodoxy.[6] But it left the official lexicon vulnerable to the slightest differences in evaluation. The necessity of upholding the correct evaluations of political terms may itself have contributed to the rigidity of the political system. As Skinner has suggested: because appraisive words have a function of legitimizing, as well as describing, people cannot in practice use them for any action, but only for plausible ones. In other words, people 'tailor their projects in order to make them answer to the pre-existing language of moral principles' (1980: 575–6). This may or may not have been the case in specific episodes in Western history, but it does seem a real possibility in the Soviet case, at least for the less educated and minority peoples deprived of the history of their concepts. One of the problems of *glasnost'* at this level may be the difficulty of dredging up a language for it.

But for the Buryats this paper would suggest that the difficulty is not insuperable. Their heritage of political concepts includes the timeless and hierarchical, in the Buddhist mode, but also the discourse of change and independence, resistance and cooperation, derived existentially from living as a minority through the revolution (in its widest sense). If such ideas have been preserved in the harmless talk of intellectuals and more publicly in the 'harmless' pond of folklore they may still be retrieved.

Notes

1 The author was able to visit collective farms in Buryatiya in 1967 and 1974–5 for short periods.

2 There have been disagreements, for example, about the conflict of grammatical and natural gender in sentences such as 'The doctor arrived', when the 'doctor' ('vrach') is grammatically masculine but the doctor who actually arrived is a woman, implying a feminine ending to the verb 'arrived'. Should one say in this case 'vrach prishel' or 'vrach prishla'? Asked this question, one worker replied that the masculine form should be used, because '*vrach est' vrach*' ('a doctor is a doctor'), while another responded that the feminine form should be used, because '*zhenshchina est' zhenshchina*' ('a woman is a woman') irrespective of her profession (Comrie and Stone 1978: 169).

3 A letter to Izvestiya from a teacher in Riga, V. Svirskii, complaining about the 'silence' of history as it has been taught in the USSR, cited the following: 'Not long ago there was a television programme in which the interviewer asked a school-leaver interested in history: "Who was the leader of the Soviet government after Lenin?" And how, after all, was he to know?! I am quite sure that tens of millions of viewers, sitting at their TVs, bit their lips: "And who was it?" One may query whether it was right to ask this question, but it did publicly demonstrate one of the numerous blank spots in our historical education' (*Izvestiya* 21 July 1987: 3).

4 The use of economic laws presupposes the calculation of the real conditions of development of the economy. But these conditions change, and this demands the perfecting of the mechanism of government of the economy, of the system of planning and economic stimulation. The rich experience of the development of our country demonstrates that, as conditions have changed, the Party has always found new, more perfect, methods of developing the economy.

And here, political policy does not simply passively follow the changes in the economy. The party, basing itself on profound scientific knowledge of the economy, forsees the tendencies of its development. And in accordance with this, it perfects the structure of the economy and methods of government in advance' (Emel'yanov (ed.) 1977: 11).

5 Austerliz discusses the vitality of the stock of inherited folklore (as opposed to new urban and industrial folklore) among a range of people of Siberia. He concludes, 'We therefore emerge with a final dilemma: in general twentieth century terms, all national cultures, the small ones included, are theoretically doomed to eventual extinction. However, in specific terms, the smaller and the more insignificant (culturally, economically) a group, the more likely it is to be pampered and its culture kept alive. That seems to me to be the circular dilemma of folklore, nationality, and the twentieth century in Siberia and the Soviet Far East' (Austerliz 1978: 145). I would agree with him on the importance of an extra-USSR 'anchorage', such as Mongolia for the Buryats, in maintaining culture, but I do not concur with the theory that all national cultures are doomed, nor that the pampering of tiny ethnic groups by the State will have much effect. Such pampering does not keep alive 'the culture' but superimposes an ersatz one.

6 There have been relatively few examples of terms imbued with the ideology of a previous era surviving, though with changed sense and/or reference into the Soviet period, i.e. of the mechanisms which have been the main forms of language change in the West (Skinner 1980: 572–3). Examples in the Buryat case would be: *namtar*, previously 'religious biography', now simply 'biography', or *surgaal*, previously 'Buddhist doctrine', now simply 'teachings'.

References

Austerlitz, Robert, (1978), 'Folklore, nationality, and the Twentieth Century in Siberia and the Soviet Far East', in F. J. Oinas, (ed.), *Folklore, Nationalism and Politics*, Columbus, Ohio: Slavica.

Bloch, Maurice (ed.), (1975), *Political Language and Oratory in Traditional Societies*, London: Academic Press.

Budayev, Ts. B., Dambayeva, D. Sh., and Shagdarov, L. D. (eds), (1972), *Stilistika i leksikologiya buryatskogo yazyka* (Stylistics and Lexicology of the Buryat Language), Ulan-Ude: BION.

Comrie, B. and Stone, G., (1978), *The Russian Language since the Revolution*, Oxford: Oxford University Press.

Dagurov, G. V., (1960), 'O mezhdumetiyakh buryatskogo yazyka' (On interjections in the Buryat language), Trudy BKNII, no 2, Ulan-Ude: Buryatskoe Knizhnoe Izdatel'stvo.

Emel'yanov, A. M. (ed.), (1977), *Osnovy ekonomiki i upravleniya sel'skokhozyaistvennym proizvodstvom* (The Foundations of Economics and Management of Agricultural Production), Moscow: Ekonomika.

Hirooka, Naoko, Hiroshi, Okuda and Uchida, Kenji, (1988), Review article on Yuzuru Taniuchi's *The Formation of the Stalin Political Regime*, *Acta Slavica Japonica*, Tomus VI, Sapporo.

Humphrey, Caroline, (1983), *Karl Marx Collective, Economy, Society and Religion in a Siberian Collective Farm*, Cambridge: Cambridge University Press.

Khadalov, P. I. and Ulanov, A. I. (eds), (1953), *O kharaktere buryatskogo eposa 'Geser'* (On the characteristics of the Buryat Epic, 'Geser'), Ulan-Ude: B-M NIIK.

Kuromiya, Hiroaki, (1988), 'The Stalin Years in the Light of Glasnost'', paper prepared for the SSRC Workshop on Soviet Domestic Politics and Society, June 1988, University of Toronto.

Losev, Aleksei, (1978), 'Pis'ma' ('letters'), *Kontinent* 16, Munich.

Loseva, E. G., (1974), 'K voprosu o dvuyazychii u buryat' ('On the question of bilingualism among the Buryat'), *Etnograficheskii Sbornik*, 6, Ulan-Ude: BION.

Materialy torzhestvennogo zsedaniya obkoma KPSS i verkhnogo soveta buryatskoi ASSR (50 let Buryatskoi ASSR), (Materials of the ceremonial meeting of the Obkom of the CPUSSR and the Supreme Soviet of the Buryat ASSR – 50 years of the Buryat ASSR), Buryatskoye Knizhnoye Izdatel'stvo, Ulan-Ude, (1973).

Parkin, David, (1975), 'The Rhetoric of Responsibility: Bureaucratic Communications in a Kenya Farming Area' in Bloch (ed.).

Poppe, N. N., (1934), *Yazyk i kolkhoznaya poeziya Buryat-Mongolov Selenginskogo Aimaka* (The Language and Collective Farm Poetry of the Buryat-Mongols of Selenga District), Leningrad: Izd An SSSR.

Poppe, N. N., (1936), *Buryat-Mongol'skii fol'klornyi i dialektologicheskii sbornik* (Buryat-Mongol Folklore and Lialect Collection), Moscow-Leningrad: Izd. AN SSSR.

Shagdarov, L. D., (1967), *Stanovleniye yedinikh norm buryatskogo literaturnogo yazyka v sovetskuyu epokhu* (The Establishment of Single Norms for the Buryat Literary Language in the Soviet Epoch), Ulan-Ude: BION.

Shagdarov, L. D., (1972), 'Sostoyaniye i zadachi issledovaniya stilei buryatskogo yazyka' ('The conditions and tasks of the study of styles in the Buryat language'), in Budayev *et al.* eds (1972).

Skinner, Quentin, (1980), 'Language and social change', in Leonard Michaels and Christopher Ricks (eds), *The State of the Language*, London: University of California Press.

Svirskii, B., (1987), 'Istoriya umalchivaet . . .' ('History is silent . . .'), *Izvestiya*, 23 July: 3.

Tiktina, Dora, (1978), 'A Rural Secondary School in the Ukraine' (in Russian), Soviet Institution Series no 2, Hebrew University, Jerusalem.

Tsydendambayev, Ts. B., (1972), 'O stilisticheskom pietete mongolizmov v buryaksom yazyka' ('On the stylistic piety of the Mongolisms in the Buryat language'), in Budayev *et al.* (eds) (1972).

Voloshinov, V. N. (Volosinov), (1973), *Marxism and the Philosophy of Language* (originally published as Markszism i filosophiya yazyka, Moscow, 1930), trs. Matejka and Titunik, New York and London: Seminar Press.

Some Italian Communists talking

Jeff Pratt

A rather impassioned Italian friend of mine once got up in a meeting of the local Communist Party to express his impatience at the apathy of his fellow comrades in the face of a current crisis. 'We sit around here and talk too much', he said, 'We should be more active, do more, we should have more meetings'. Although it was not the speaker's intention, his outburst is a suitable reminder that a large part of politics consists of talking, and we can perhaps add, following Steven Lukes's analysis of power, a large part of the rest is silence. Obviously there is more to politics than this, but in this paper I shall be concerned exclusively with the various kinds of language use found in the Italian Communist Party, and my primary focus will be how this relates to the distribution of power within the party. Many of my comments apply to other kinds of politics, and almost certainly to other Communist Parties, but I shall restrict the remarks to Italy, where the relationship between the rank and file and the leadership is a particularly sensitive issue.[1]

The examples come from Tuscany, where I did my fieldwork. As is well known, the Tuscan dialect became the official language of United Italy; the language of government, the law, education and the mass media. Within Tuscany it is true there are marked differences of accent and to some extent of vocabulary between the various provinces and towns, so that someone with a skilled ear can place a speaker to a particular province, and even to a particular village. But on the whole the language of a Tuscan farmer or textile worker is closer in this respect to that of his political leaders than is the case for a Communist from Sicily, Sardinia or the Romagna. Dialect is one variable, at least, that I do not have to deal with, though the question of class differences in language use is more complex and will be touched on below.

What follows is an account of the different ways in which rank and file and Communist leaders speak, both inside and outside formal political contexts, and my point is to examine how political dominance is related to language use. The illustrations and discussions of various styles of speech take up the bulk of the paper, while in the conclusion I examine more briefly the relevance of three more general analytical frameworks to the material presented: Tönnies, Bernstein and Bloch.

It is not my intention to illustrate all the various ways in which Communists speak, but I want to start by showing one kind of continuity between everyday conversation and the kind of contribution rank and file Communists make to a political discussion in a party section meeting. The first examples I give are all in a sense trivial, chat and backchat from bar-room conversation after work in the evening. The speakers are farmers, forestry workers, brick-layers and manual labourers employed by the local administration. They are all men, for the bar is still a male preserve in the small towns and villages where I studied, and in the Communist Party too, only about 10 per cent of the members are women, and these tend to be teachers, social workers or other professionals. In Tuscany working-class women do not on the whole join the party, even if they vote for it, although the situation is different in Emilia-Romagna and the large cities of the north. About half of those taking part in these evening conversations will be Communist party supporters, but in the first examples they are discussing matters and experiences which they share with their political opponents.

Here, then are three men drinking in a bar in the village of Montelaterone, all manual workers, but also part-time farmers and very much involved with the patches of land they own. The first remarks,

> 'I saw Moro (a nickname for a mutual acquaintance) walking home last evening. He was passing through the chestnut woods down by the mill'.
> 'Where?', asks the second.
> 'Down by poor Giovanni's place. [Poor means dead.] It seemed a long way round for him to walk home'.
> 'Perhaps he was looking for mushrooms', replies the second speaker.
> 'Ah yes, looking for mushrooms',

and the conversation, after a pause, moves on, as the third man present has remained significantly silent.

Two related aspects of this short conversation are worth comment. The first is that it deals with particular people, times and places which are part of the common knowledge of those talking. The second is what I shall call ellipsis.

In order to take part in, or understand, such conversations it is necessary to have a detailed knowledge of names of people and places, nicknames and relationships. Such a knowledge can only be acquired partially by a visiting anthropologist, it is the property of those who live at length in a given social environment (I shall return to this point), but all those who have such knowledge are free to talk, and in any order. Contributions tend to be rather short and pithy – indeed anyone who talks for too long is likely to be interrupted. It is a very egalitarian form of conversation. In this particular case the local knowledge which is common to the participants and the subject of the conversation includes much that is unspoken, for example that Moro has no land down by the mill and hence has no business there, that poor dead Giovanni was the father of the third and silent participant, and that mushrooms do not grow at that time of year. At this point we move into the area of ellipsis, the missing information or statements which complete an argument. The unstated information which is the subject of the conversation is the rumour that the silent participant is thinking of selling off the chestnut trees he inherited from his father, and hence the assumption that Moro had gone to look them over before making an offer. But the rumour is not common knowledge, and in any case selling off inherited land is a delicate matter, hence the elliptical form of the conversation – the speakers have not asked, the listener has not answered, and nobody else is any the wiser.

This may seem an unusually devious example, but in fact such conversational forms are extremely common and are used by women as well. Before going on to comment further I shall give a second slightly different example.

In another bar, a group of men has just ordered a last round of drinks. One of them, taking a gulp of wine, suddenly made a face and slammed the glass back on the table.

> 'Oh Onorio', he shouted, 'It may be 11 o'clock but we are not drunk yet.'
> The landlord stared back unabashed, raised his own glass to the light, and said, 'You can see Elba.'

He retired into his corner muttering blasphemies against his fussy customers. This is all part of a month long conversation, to the effect that the landlord substitutes cheap cloudy wine for his normal fare when he considers his customers sufficiently drunk or sleepy not to notice the difference. The comment about Elba refers to a proverb, the relevant part of which states that on a clear day, from the top of the mountain you can see Elba, hence the wine is clear and good. The landlord had in fact been conned into buying some bad wine and has to get rid of it somehow, but for obvious reasons refuses to acknowledge his problem. The customers for their part are stating that they are not fooled, but the substance of the matter is not made explicit to the landlord's face for fear of the long term consequences. Should the matter continue it is likely that a flaming row will develop and the customers move their trade elsewhere.

This use of banter, irony and veiled hints is the dominant tone in these public conversations, and even overflows and colours commercial transactions like hiring a labourer or buying a pig, contexts in which superficially it would seem that explicitness would be most prized. It reaches its most elaborate form when sexual matters are being referred to – the euphemism and allegory employed having something in common with the *sanza* talk of the Azande as described by Evans-Pritchard (1962), the skill in apparently talking about one thing while in fact talking about another. There is more to meaning than is covered by most accounts of semantics.

An important dimension of these conversations is contained in their form – they reveal a continuous probing and testing of the speaker's relationship to his listeners, the jokes at each others expense, the comments phrased with varying degrees of skill so that they will be understood by some of those present and not by others. In the course of an evening there is often a subtle shifting of boundaries within the group present created by these techniques of inclusion and exclusion. At another level the very force of irony ('Ah yes, he was looking for mushrooms') and the ability of the group to hold a conversation with a missing subject (ellipsis) depends on the shared knowledge of those present. A more detailed analysis of this material requires an excursion into the Italian concept of *amicizia* (friendship) in its various forms, a subject outside the topic under consideration, but I will give one last example of the principles underlying this kind of conversation.

The game of *briscola* is very popular throughout central Italy, and is perhaps a more subtle game than the naked power politics of Passatella, an 'economic game' analysed by John Davis (1964).

It is a card game played by two sets of partners, who are allowed to talk to each other, suggesting that high or low cards of particular suits be played,. or that they have picked up from the pack a card worth a high number of points. Success at the game requires a number of skills, the most crucial of which is the fine understanding with a partner so that you can talk to him without the opponents getting a clear idea of what you hold or what you want from your partner. Non-verbal communication, private sign languages of winks and scratches develop between regular partners, but these are usually banned at competition level, and they have to fall back on complicated systems of bluff and double-bluff, so that hopefully the speaker leaves everyone except his partner guessing. In a sense the game revolves around the axis of communication and concealment.

Up to now this paper has not referred to specific political issues of the kind that divide the contributors to these everyday conversations. Rather than go on to illustrate political discussion in public places, I shall give an example of contributions these same people, rank and file Communists, make at meetings of the Communist Party. The comparison to be made is that with the speeches of their leaders, but the material on Communist Party organization and the oratory of its leaders is held back for the next section.

The example comes from a meeting of the Party section in the same village, Montelaterone, as the conversation discussed above. It was a typical meeting for the area, though there are sections where a rather different kind of debate can be heard, and as will become clear, the character of debate does change the higher you move up the Communist Party hierarchy. It was held in 1978, prior to the PCI's 15th national congress, to discuss the overall strategy of the party, particularly in the light of the imminent elections. The main speaker was a young man of about 25, who was a member of the directing committee of the zone, and resident in a neighbouring town. There were only twelve men present out of the twenty-five party members and more than 200 Communist voters in the village. I shall be concerned with the comments of only two of them: the first, Angelo, is a manual labourer aged 40, one of the stalwarts of the local party but held in some suspicion by many of the older members, who remember that he was not always a Communist and suspect him of opportunism. The second, Elio, is also a manual labourer, in his mid 50s, and for a long time after the war a very influential figure in the party, but who has been quietly removed from all the offices he held in the section and in the *comune* administration, ostensibly in the interests of renewing the cadres, but probably also because of his opposition to the 1970s' policy of the *compromesso storico*.

After the visiting speaker had finished his long introduction, there is an awkward silence for some minutes, until after much prompting from the section secretary, Angelo is moved to speak.

'As everybody else is silent', he begins,

> 'I would like to give my personal point of view on this situation. Our comrade here has talked of the necessity of closer links with the Socialist Party, O.K., I don't like them. They want too much, they pretend too much. Now they've got the President of the Republic they want a Socialist Pope. We have seen here, we put Tongiani (a prominent local Socialist) in charge of the *Comunità Montana* (the zonal development agency), and he only brings water to his own mill. When there's a job going down at the slaughter house they insist on having a Socialist, otherwise they will resign.'

He then goes on to give a number of examples of Socialist favouritism and deviousness in the surrounding villages. He concludes,

> 'Where the Christian-Democrats are strong, they go with the D.C., where the Communists are strong they go with the Communists. They make me sick (*mi fanno schifo*). I think we should go our own way.'

Elio replies to these comments. 'Comrade Angelo here is wrong', he begins.

> 'When Togliatti returned from Russia he made it clear that we could not win the struggle on our own. I remember the coalition government after the war, when we were "inside" with the Christian-Democrats and the Socialists, and it was the Christian-Democrats who blocked us (obscenity), and expelled us from the government. And then we formed the Popular Front. And we must always work with the Socialist Party. They make many mistakes, but we must work with them, and coax them into seeing things our way.'

Angelo interrupts as this point.

> 'I was giving my point of view, and these things you are talking about happened a long time ago. I don't remember them, I was a little boy.'
>
> 'I remember them', rejoins Elio, and gives the coup de grâce: 'That's right, when these things happened you were a little boy running around with a basket of eggs.'

This quip needs explaining. At the Easter blessing of the house, the priest is assisted by small boys who carry a basket, in which, at least until recently, were placed the eggs the priest received as a return gift for the blessing. Angelo had been such a priest's helper, and the public reminder silenced him for the rest of the evening, though I am not sure the young visiting speaker understood the extremely barbed allusion.

The characteristics of this kind of political discussion can be summarized very briefly. When the rank and file do speak there is a tendency for bar-room habits to persist, and for a hubbub to break out and speakers be interrupted, especially if they go on too long. This is in conflict, however, with what the participants consider should be correct procedure on such occasions, and they usually give the chairman their support if he calls the meeting to order and insists on precedence between speakers. When we turn to content, we find that Angelo's comments contain no words or concepts which are not found in everyday conversation. The condemnation of the Socialist Party is in terms of the concrete and the particular, what that man in that place did, drawing on the common knowledge of a particular locality. The phrasing is personal (I think, I dislike) and the judgements are on the moral characteristics of persons. For example the owners of a local hotel will be described as a bunch of thieves, not the system as exploitative. Even when referring to the Socialist Party as a whole, it is as they, a generalization of particular individuals, and the comment is not that *the party* forms an *alliance* with the DC, but that *they go with* the DC, a conscious reference to prostitution.

Elio's comments, which I have had to abbreviate considerably, have a different style.There is far less use of the first person singular, and a far greater range of reference in terms of national politics and the history of Communist Party strategy. There is also a greater tendency to present an argument in abstract terms – a historical struggle, social classes – but the movement is still in a sense from the particular to the general. This is a difficult matter to illustrate by quotation, but I would suggest that for men such as Elio, such abstractions are generalizations from particular political experiences and perceptions, rather than as for another kind of oratory and another kind of Communist, the particular being simply an illustration of a general principle. Whatever, the differences in style between Angelo and Elio, and these in turn reflect differences of political experience, they both share, in comparison with the oratory I shall be considering below, a simplicity of syntax and a low level of abstraction, as well as the characteristics I have discussed in connection with bar-room conversations, including ellipsis and profanity. Even Elio cannot resist combining his attack on the historical compromise, for such it became, with an ad-hominem attack on the priest's little helper. (There were two major interpretations of the 'historical compromise' then current policy in the party, but the important point to note in this context is that both involved closer ties with the Catholic world. Opponents of the policy within the party, such as Elio, stressed instead the fundamental importance of alliance with the Socialist Party, with the aim of forming a left-wing government. Although, as we shall see, party leaders did not deny the importance of links with the Socialists, it received a very different emphasis in the overall strategy.)

The leadership

Before moving on to the second kind of oratory, it is necessary to say a little about Communist party organization, however libellous this becomes because of abbreviation. The party has a classic hierarchical structure, with a number of organs at the national level, including the central committee, and below that a series of regional and provincial committees, the latter being known as the federation. Below the federation we often find a zonal organization, and then each individual *comune*, finally reaching the section, the smallest effective unit, based on a village or town quarter. The cell, based on the place of work, has been virtually abandoned. In theory, according to the statutes, each level elects the membership of the congress and committee at the next level up, a rule which ensures for example, that the delegates to the national congress do not come from the rank and file, but are already militants at the federation level. However, in practice, the form of democratic centralism which obtains in the PCI concentrates power at the top. Not only can any committee suspend and reorganize the party structures at the next level below (e.g. the federation suspend and reconstruct the *comune*), and discipline individual party members (now rare), but the membership of a particular committee is in practice often recruited through co-option. That is, the choice of who becomes a member of the federation congress and hence of the directing committee tends to be made, in a variety of ways, by the pre-existing members of federation, rather than by the party at zone or *comune* level. Similarly the choice of section secretary or town mayor tends to be made on high. A young activist who makes his mark as a *comune* secretary or mayor at the local level can rise very fast, be pulled out by the federation and given a permanent post in the apparatus or be elected to parliament.

The party leaders at the local level in Tuscany tend to be young, mostly in their thirties. The majority are the children of working-class or peasant families, who having done well at school, go on to higher education. They are teachers, lawyers or accountants, though many have been selected by the party for office before finishing their training. They will all have been to at least one session at the national schools run by the PCI. These sessions, which last a few days or a few weeks, provide a very intensive education in party history and strategy, and in problems of public administration, during which the participants live a life of seclusion. The Party attaches considerable importance to these training sessions, and detaches some of its most prestigious scholars and leaders from other duties to teach at them. In addition a local leader will read the party daily, *L'Unità*, a newspaper which was known for its heavy prose even by the standards of Italian journalism, and also probably *Rinascità*, a weekly devoted to wider theoretical problems. This curriculum vitae, although typical of the present generation of local leaders, is not applicable to the previous generation which came to prominence in the resistance and the Cold War, but it is beyond the scope of this paper to deal with the changes which have taken place in the last forty years.

The kind of oratory I shall be discussing deals with very general issues, so it is worth mentioning again that I am not attempting to deal with all the kinds of language use found within the Communist Party. The party has the most efficient political machine in the country, and the same leaders who can talk for hours about strategy can attend to detail and get things done – instruct x to canvass one side of the street, y the other and to report at 8 o'clock in headquarters. And just as at the rank and file level Elio can silence Angelo by referring to a basket of eggs, so, it is rumoured, Togliatti the post-war national secretary used to embarrass his hot-headed rival Pajetta by asking in the middle of a central committee meeting whether the machine guns had arrived yet.

The average party meeting lasts about three hours. The main speaker will talk for an hour or an hour and a half, comments from the floor, which may be slow in coming, take up the next hour, and then the speaker will wrap up the meeting, responding to the points made. The speaker will always come from the next level up the hierarchy. In my experience it is extremely rare for a section to meet without the presence of a leader from the *comune*, if the zone then an activist from the federation, often an MP or Senator, will be sent. Votes are rarely taken, at least at this level, even if what is at stake is the party line to be agreed at the next national congress. Generally what happens, as in the meeting referred to above, is that the visiting speaker expounds the line, and at the end responds to any criticisms made. This is known as consultation, or ample discussions.

The two essential qualities of such a speaker are that he should be prepared (*preparato*) and should speak at length. The cumulative effect is to create considerable inhibitions amongst the base, as is widely acknowledged within the party. Thus a member of the rank and file who wishes to comment after such a speech invariably begins with some kind of apology. 'I am not prepared' (*Io non sono preparato*) or 'I am only giving a personal opinion', as with Angelo. In Italian, the leaders make a *discorso*, or present an argument, the others just talk (*parlare*) or chat (*chiacherare*). The style of a *discorso* is very close to that of a *comizio*, an election address or rally, where by a long Italian tradition one speaker holds forth from a platform, with no heckling or reply from those present.

The length of a speech has already been mentioned. The general secretary of the party, on a grand occasion, may speak for up to five hours – this is known as a *discorso fiume* (river). A number of elements go into making a 'prepared' speaker, and I shall deal with them rather arbitrarily under the headings of content and style.

Content

The first necessity is that the speaker should be able to place the issue under discussion in the widest possible context. It is obviously appropriate that the general secretary addressing the national congress should devote a great deal of time to the international context in which the PCI operates, but even at the local level speeches tend to begin, rather like certain anthropology articles, with a short history of the world. For example, a meeting I attended which was devoted to the financial difficulties of the *comune* administration began with an outline of the crisis of late capitalism, the fall of the dollar and the price of crude oil. This is known as setting the context, or framing (*inquadrare*) the situation. If there is another speaker on the floor of the meeting, who wishes to *inquadrare* the situation in a different way (and this is more likely the higher you go up the party hierarchy), the meeting may last for five hours. The movement of the speech is always from general to particular, from international, to national, to local. At this point the speaker usually draws breath and starts again with an examination of the role of the PCI in Italian society, sketching the past strategy of the party and emphasizing the contribution of its leaders in such a way that at the end the present day policy of the party (for example the necessity of certain alliances) is shown to be part of an unbroken tradition, to have a pedigree. This is in every respect a contrast with the personal and parochial interests of a speaker such as Angelo.

Style

Speeches by party leaders tend to avoid the first person singular – they make not personal but collective statements, and if 'I' is used, it is conspicuous, and for a particular effect. The syntax is complex and close to written prose – indeed many speeches are to a greater or lesser extent written out beforehand, and if not may contain the mannerisms of prose. For example a speaker who wishes to widen the framework (*inquadramento*) of his argument will say 'and here I open a parenthesis', and then eventually will close it. There are certain usages in phrasing an argument – 'in the degree to which', 'not only because', etc., and a much greater use of subjunctive and conditional tenses than is found in everyday conversation. Finally there are elements which belong to both style and content, conceptualizations of the world which are specific to this kind of speech. They include the famous stock phrases to be found in all the oratory: the intervention of the popular masses, democratic and anti-fascist tradition, cultural patrimony, the centrality of the party in the democratic life of the country, political directives, and so on.

It is not my intention to give a lengthy example of this kind of oratory. Before moving on to a summary, I will give one short extract from the closing speech of Berlinguer at the national congress of 1978, an extract which deals with the Socialist Party, like Angelo at the section meeting. It is a relatively simple part of his speech, chosen only because I have a written copy.

> 'Let us appeal to our Socialist comrades, so that, abandoning every equidistance, leaving on one side their rather ambiguous directive of a fight against both the largest parties, they commit themselves as well to a clear and decisive battle. The force of a more united left, we repeat it, is an indispensable condition for the development, on its basis, of that fuller popular and democratic unity which our country needs. In any case, the flag of unity, the unity of the left-wing parties, of the working classes, and the unity of all the democratic forces will be our flag.'

Summary

I have outlined two kinds of language use found in the Italian Communist Party, the first of which is that of the rank and file, though a modified form is used on certain occasions by the leadership, the second of which is exclusive to the leadership. What can we say about the differences between the two?

In part this difference relates to the classic sociological difference between *gemeinschaft* and *gesellschaft*, and I have stressed this aspect at a number of points. The rank and file when they contribute to political discussions tend to do so in terms of the particular and the local, of known events, people and their moral qualities. A similar theme emerged in the comments on techniques of inclusion, exclusion and ellipsis in everyday conversation. The leadership on the other hand deal with the more universal, or at least with historical processes on a national scale, an aspect which was dealt with under the heading of *inquadramento* or framing.

I will say no more about an analysis in these terms, except that it does not exhaust the differences between these two types of language use, and though it can help us understand different kinds of speech, it does not help us understand how the different kinds of speaker are related within the party. In this I am simply echoing Pitt-Rivers's comments on Redfield's version of *gemeinschaft* and *gesellschaft*: that he has not examined how the peasant society is *sociologically* related to the literate culture of its civilization (Pitt-Rivers 1963: 10).

Bernstein's distinction between restricted and elaborated codes, although originally developed as part of an investigation into working-class and middle-class speech, is in many ways 'the old polarity of gemeinschaft and gesellschaft in another guise' as the author himself acknowledges (1971: 54). Applying this framework to the material illustrated above presents, however, a number of serious difficulties, not least because the key distinction has been gradually modified by Bernstein and his colleagues, and different emphases given in the process of defining and re-defining the contrast. Some discussions of the distinction between restricted and elaborated codes are much more relevant to the speech types discussed here than others. In brief, the speech of party rank and file quoted shares many of the characteristics of Bernstein's restricted code (meaning is context dependent, implicit), though I have not stressed its function in creating social solidarity (cf. Bernstein 1971: 147). However, the speech of party leaders is more complex. Although it shares some of the characteristics of an elaborated code (abstraction, syntactical complexity, is more universalistic), it is not a form of speech particularly well adapted to the exploration of individual experience or differentiation. Although this possibility is itself covered by Bernstein's later distinction between positional and personal modes of the elaborated code (cf. Bernstein 1971: 150) this raises difficulties which cannot be dealt with here. Instead I want to make the tentative suggestion that the subordination of the 'I' to the 'we' in the speech of Communist Party leaders (cf. Bernstein 1971: 157) is a characteristic which would emerge more clearly if a comparison were made with speeches of leaders in other parties, and that this in turn is a reflection of the different place of the individual in the party, and has to be related to other features of Communist Party practice.

This leads to a further consideration. In discussing the speech of Communist leaders, I drew attention to factors such as length, preparation, and syntactical complexity, but we can only fully understand how it constitutes a 'dominant language' if it is put back in its context (including decision making practices within the party), if it is 'grounded in institutional practices'. In other words the dominance achieved through and reflected in this particular language use (to which I return) also has to be placed in the context of the organization of the Communist Party, its de facto rules and practices, and the role of leaders within it. In turn this needs to be related to the party's own ideology, and what it attempts to achieve. In other words, and this would constitute another paper, there is considerable, though not complete, consistency between the party's ideology, formal organization and mode of doing business, in which I would include the avoidance of factionalism and the ritualism of much party life.

I have said that in part the leaders achieve their dominance through the use of language, so is it possible to use Bloch's concept of formalization (Bloch 1975) to reveal how this is achieved? Certainly there are many aspects of the leaders' oratory which correspond to Bloch's formalized speech: the operation of stylistic rules, the illustrations only from a limited range of sources, some fixity in the sequencing of speech acts and the use of composite phrases, all of which contribute to the 'arthritic' character of these speeches. Certainly also, the net effect of this oratory is close in some respects to the traditional authority expressed in formalized speech; the leader is not offering personal opinions but speaking for a collectivity which values above all its unity, and the rank and file member who disagrees with specific propositions is inhibited by the fact that he is thereby forced to disagree with a whole weight of historical analysis of the nation and of the political role of the PCI. The structure of a '*discorso*' means that specific disagreements appear as a challenge to the whole party line and the authority of the person who has presented it.

Yet does the concept of formalization account for all the differences between these two types of speech? Perhaps if I had compared the Communist leaders' oratory with let us say a group of university students discussing the latest political scandal, the formalization aspect would be revealed more clearly. However, strictly speaking this is irrelevant. Angelo of the rank and file, and Berlinguer the (then) party secretary were both talking about the alliance with the Socialists, but are doing so with a different syntax, and above all with different frames of reference and different conceptualizations of the world. It does not seem to me that we can simply say that one is a formalized or impoverished version of the other (Bloch p. 13: many of the different language uses described by contributors to that book are not susceptible to this reduction, particularly those which are least concerned with traditional authority in the Weberian sense).

My final comment returns to the question of form and content. Bloch's analysis is designed to reveal the form of speech, and his point is that the greater the formalization of language use, the less capacity it has to make propositions about the world. The most formalized end of his continuum is speech which is meaningless in the normal sense of the word, or rather has illocutionary rather than propositional force. 'Not to report facts but to influence people'. To this unconvincing opposition of Austin's, Bloch adds immediately '– and here we are back to politics'. But it is the politics of mumbo-jumbo. In other words the politics that Bloch is analysing involves traditional authority, the kind where a person claims authority because he is the lord's annointed, or is in communication with the ancestors and through him all blessings flow. Such claims are in an important sense false, and the politics are the politics of mystification.[2] Clearly such an analytical framework will be less useful in the handling of authority which is based on a different kind of legitimacy. Perhaps the usefulness of the framework in this kind of political analysis is increased if we turn the equations around, and say that where we find the development of formalization in political discourse, this is evidence of 'mystification' and the intrusion of some measure of traditional authority into a system which is basically of another type.

Certainly not all Communist discourse is mystification, but Bloch's analysis is not designed to reveal the fact that before the last instance when 'maximum formalization' is reached, the speech continues to contain propositions about the world, ideology, and that the politics is here too. Despite what some of its critics say, the oratory of the Communist leaders continues to contain a good deal of ideology, and there are subtleties of choice available even amongst the most abstract composite phrases with which the leaders fill their speeches. Thus when a leader talks about the *blocco nuovo* rather than the *compromesso storico*, the middle classes rather than the *borghesi*, the centrality of the party rather than its hegemony, these indicate shifts in party strategy which are understood by the *conoscenti*, and are reflected in changes at other levels too.

I have not attempted to discuss the inter-connection between the three theoretical approaches contained in the writings of Tönnies, Bernstein and Bloch, instead I have applied them briefly to some material collected on a hierarchy of forms of language use found within the Italian Community Party. In each case important aspects of party life were brought into focus and further questions generated (for example the place of the individual in the party, the basis of a leader's authority, or the important question of the way in which leaders 'translate' local issues into national issues and back again). No one approach could cover all the connections between language and politics, but from the discussion above three inter-related analytical comments can be made. Firstly there is not one, universal form taken by dominant languages (for the British educational system it was Bernstein's elaborated code, for the Merina it was formalized speech, and these are fundamentally different). Secondly the dominance of a language is not revealed by the analysis of its formal linguistic properties alone. Rather dominance can be understood only by analysing the formal properties of the language and the wider context, including differential access to certain linguistic codes, and institutional practices surrounding the language's use. Thirdly, one of the most influential recent accounts of the relationship between language and politics, that by Bloch, concentrates on language *form*, because he found that all content was missing in the political events he was studying. Consistent with that, he claims that his formalized speech lacks all propositional force, thus excluding any possibility of analysing its content. Whatever the merits of such a position when dealing with traditional authority, it is clear that in many contexts the content, including the ideological component, will be an important dimension of the politics of language, and even 'reporting facts' may 'influence people'. The ideological component may itself take a number of dimensions. The dominant language may be embodying a dominant ideology, against which other accounts and constructions struggle to acquire authority. Or, we may be dealing with different levels at which ideology is manifested and articulated, corresponding to what Gramsci termed systematic ideology and common-sense. Both kinds of ideological difference were to be found in the Communist Party discussions reported above. The hierarchy which emerges in those discussions involves form, content and practice.

Notes

1 This is a slightly revised version of a paper given at an SSRC conference on European anthropology in 1979. The ethnographic material relates to a particular historical moment of the Italian Communist Party: the shifting debates on strategic alliances under the leadership of Enrico Berlinguer. The material was collected in a particular social environment, specified in the text, and does not pretend to cover the way issues are discussed and decisions reached in all Italian party sections.

2 Bloch in a later article (1977) would call this one of the systems by which we hide the world, though by this point, he had abandoned the category of traditional authority for a much more all-embracing and less useful concept of 'instituted hierarchy'.

References

Bernstein, B., (1971), *Classes, Codes and Control*, London: Routledge & Kegan Paul.
Bloch, M. (ed.), (1975), *Political Language and Oratory in Traditional Society*, London: Academic Press.
Bloch, M., (1977), 'Th Past and the Present in the Present', *Man*, 12 (2): 278–92.
Davis, J., (1964), 'Passatella: an economic game', *The British Journal of Sociology*, 15: 191–206.
Evans-Pritchard, E., (1962), 'Sanza, a characteristic feature of Zande language and thought', in *Essays in Social Anthropology*, London: Faber & Faber.
Pitt-Rivers, J., (1963), Introduction to *Mediterranean Countrymen*, Paris: Mouton.

Word of honour

Michael Gilsenan

Introduction

A turn to rhetorics, to the analysis of modes of persuasion and the force of statements, the powers and contests over representing reality as one sees it and wishes it to be seen, has begun to take more of our anthropological attention. Words such as story, performative, style and appearance take on rather greater resonance than they have previously had. In concentrating on the poetics of ethnography and the poetics of power we may blithely ignore 'the politics of power and, of course, power politics' as Scholte has trenchantly remarked.[1] It is easy to finesse the question 'who speaks?' with an over-elaborated treatment of that siren word 'meaning'. There is no inherent reason why a focus on performative aspects of language, performance and practice, the intentionality of the act and of responses to the act, should allow the study of politics and language to drift into aestheticizing self-indulgence.

This short paper has its roots in my difficulty with a naggingly persistent sense of the centre of inquiry being 'data', notes about events and information referring to an everyday sense of 'what really happened'. The limits of my naivety in this regard were rarely reached with enough of a concussive force to shock me into any awareness of their existence. I suspect that the whole discourse of evidence as distinct from mere anecdote, that powerful rhetorical tool of the scientist against the non-professional in the defence of boundaries and practices, also made me nervous. For a long time I thus did not wish to take cognizance of the fact that one crucial element in my fieldwork was that I was being told stories; that I was hearing about and attending to reenactments of acts, moments, situations, conflicts between persons on the field of honour; that the manner of the stories created and recreated the manner of what was performed, and that in both cases manner and matter were indistinguishable, the what and the how were one question.

The vividness of the tellings and retellings successfully performed one of their critical functions – to blind the listener, or at least this listener, to the fact that it was these accounts and reports and reminiscences that constituted 'the event' of which they were apparently just the vehicle. The stories appeared to be transparent. I could see through them too well as it were. Transparency became invisibility. I have had to recuperate an awareness of the forms and language of dramatic enactments as constitutive of the actualities of honour in practice rather than my simply recounting in my notes or some articles a set of encounters to illustrate honour events in all their supposed typicality. It is not what you do but the way that you tell it, and hear it. This turning from the notion of seeing to that of hearing, stressed by James Clifford and Johannes Fabian, is more difficult to accomplish than I realized.[2] Perhaps I should have been more attentive to the old procedures for validating the *hadith* (Muslim Prophetic traditions) with their insistence on 'I heard it from X who heard it from Y' right back to the first source. The politics of narratives, the way they convince people (or fail to) of the force of this version of events, that reality was thus and no other, the beauty and excellence of the honorable man manifestly demonstrated upon the other, these kinds of issues took a long time to impinge on my consciousness.

Two recent books have explored some of these issues. Michael Herzfeld's *The Poetics of Manhood* examines the construction of male identity in a Cretan mountain village through the analysis of poetics as praxis in a context predominantly characterized for him by a fundamental concern for *simasia* (glossed as 'meaning'). Men must steal sheep to show that they are, as Herzfeld puts it, good at being men. They must tell the story and be told of in performances the criteria for the success of which he writes very tellingly. Lila Abu Lughod's *Veiled Sentiments* highlights the relation of a specific poetic form characteristic in the main of women among the Awlad Ali tribe of the western desert of Egypt to politics and gender. Her discussion of emotion, vulnerability and visibility in that society suggested whole areas of which I had never really thought (and from which in a key regard, the lives of women, I was virtually excluded throughout my fieldwork in north Lebanon in 1971–2).[3] Both works concern themselves with how 'poetic' discourse is related to that of ordinary social life, a relation which may of course include violation (see Abu Lughod, p. 32 and Herzfeld, pp. 10 and 18, drawing on the writings of Kenneth Burke).

Extended treatment of their ideas is not my purpose here, but these books and a rereading of Pierre Bourdieu on honour and Kabyle society inform what follows.[4] I want to elaborate on a classical theme in the study of honour, that of 'the word' as 'the person' by metonymic substitution.

I also want to suggest that if we are to understand the words of honour we need to follow out and interpret a whole discursive formation. This entails not only analysis of speaking, rhetoric, performance, action and so forth but also deciding just what constitutes the formation of honour as a discourse understood as a range of social practices. In my view this would mean giving equally serious attention to a set of themes which are not generally treated as an integral part of the subject either by natives or by outsiders: comedy, joking, the full nature of insult and injury, the meaning of winning and losing, obscenity, pollution of the self and other threads that go to make up the material of honour in a historically changing world. I have argued elsewhere, for example, that it is essential to look at the topic of lies and the creation of social artifice and appearance to understand the realities of status, integrity and significance or insignificance in the north Lebanese society in which I worked. Life there at times seemed to be a constant testing of one's own and others' actions: what was true, what false? What could be made to seem true and what false, and how?

Behind the figure of every 'heroic man of honour' was the shadow figure of the buffoon. I say shadow but in fact its substance was no less than that of its counterpart in social practice. Moreover, the same initiative might win admiring exclamation from one audience but mocking laughter from another. The drama might be turned into at least melodrama and at worst pantomime. So I have come to see that comedy and comic narratives of failure, shame and the reversal of all one's schemes are quite as central to the question of the meaning of the telling of stories about honour as those which present the triumph of the 'real man'. In interpretation and analysis they must be considered as integral to the understanding of the relation of words to honour, for they are aspects of the same discourse and reality.

Honour and narrative re-enactment

The man of honour, and it is always with men that we have to do in this context, is literally 'as good as his word'. That is what he is worth, morally and socially in other men's eyes. That word given, the individual is bound by its reified active and public force which is taken to express both his autonomous will and his irreversible commitment to a course of action which will involve him and others in a stream of events which he may well not in practice be able to determine in two major respects. For on the one hand there are all the objective uncertainties of what may happen to whom over indeterminate intervals of time in cases of feud and vendetta for example. And on the other he will become subject to words, be made into a subject by words in the discourse of honour, control over which is always to be secured and cannot be taken for granted.

The man of honour is also only as good as other peoples' words. For an event to become 'an event' it must be told, selected by collective processes of recognition of appropriateness. It has to be made into a sequence. It will be fashioned by others into a story, or, in the double sense of the term as report and assessment, an *account* in which the good of the word is held to be demonstrated. It has to fit the repertoire of the honourable and people have to show that that is indeed the case. So to become a hero a man has to become a character in the story and subject to the demands of the discourse of tales of honour, though we must never lose sight of the fact that the tale will be retold, remembered and reenacted as if it flowed from his single autonomous will and character. He appears unambiguously as the author and agent.

How all this becoming-a-story happens is no less part of agonistic competition than any specific challenge to his honour. Not all claims to have fulfilled the demands of the code are recognized. The claim has to have force, to compel or seem to compel its telling (just as is true for example of miracles). Not to be talked of, for a story not to become established as worth telling over a period of time, and the longer the period the more significant it is of course, is social insignificance. The wider balance of forces in the socio-political field is always in play. There are those about whom one does not tell such stories, those disprivileged defined by the dominant groups as outside the charmed circle of honour altogether. It is the interest of the powerful that stories should tend to be told about those of whom one tells stories, the old familiar circle of power.

Each retelling is part of the public rhetoric of honour, always imposing or seeking to impose a sense of the inevitable form of what was done and how it fitted to the ideal, how it incarnated what a man should be. Such performances structure as well as being structured by relations of power. They are part of the field of honour, contextualize action and interpretation, take on a life of their own in the talk and memory of social groups whose being as individuals and groups they help to reproduce.[5]

Such narrations take many forms which I can only indicate briefly here. One of the most important is the dramatic representation of an event in which the central figure, as he and others present him, reenacts his part to an audience of peers, if he acknowledges any, and inferiors. He tells in word, gesture, movement and theatrical reconstruction, and with the proud self-aggrandizement that is exactly what is demanded of such a figure, of the time when he did the extraordinary things he did. People who act as minor *dramatis personae*, kin in a subordinate position but sharing in some reflected glory, attendants who were there when it happened, may set the situation up for him to embark on his performance. They begin by evoking that story-everyone-has-heard of what Abu Ahmad did that day in that place. They perform their socially conventional role. The hero sits quiet, unspeaking in the silence of the truly fearful, leaving mere words to the subalterns as heroes do. But he is urged on. Expectation grows. The tellers cannot do it justice, they have not the style, they cannot act the form that is integral to what was done, only one person can do that. Abu Ahmad begins to speak in a dark, harsh voice: abrupt cadences, piercing looks suddenly switched from one hearer to another, cutting and precise gestures, everything apparently pared down to its absolute, iconic rightness. As the tension rises he rises to his feet, draws on to the denouement in which twenty-seven fully armed men were turned back by him alone. He repeats key phrases in an emphatic voice, pacing and suddenly halting or swinging round as the audience, utterly attentive and showing it in their eyes, ways of sitting and murmured exclamation that act as a kind of choral accompaniment, are borne along to the moment of triumph. It is the force of his being – for what could his single rifle do? – that triumphs and that animates the rhetorics of the performance in which we are privileged to participate.

Such is the display of *marajul*, of manly performance. It is difficult in the sober columns of learned journals to convey the impact. To this outsider it was oppressive, grotesque, horrifying, impressive, riveting, frightening and yet unwillingly admired. In the gloom of a dimly lit and cold room at half past one in the morning, squatting on thin rugs and already half numbed by chill and what had seemed until then interminable and none too consequential talk the context of which I had not fully grasped, this eruption brought a flood of cliches to my mind – flashing eyes, imperious presences, majestic glances and so forth. Perhaps the fact that these stock responses of a Victorian travel writing kind arose, was a kind of witness exactly to the degree to which the sheikh was indeed acting a stock character, a hero who was both only and entirely himself while also being almost impersonally a stereotype of a transcendental figure.

This example was produced in a wider political frame. The leading sheikh in question, an outlaw wanted for killings that were well into official double figures and a leader of a major clan in the most powerful large village at the top of the mountain, was making a formal visit under cover of darkness to our village, the most powerful of the settlements in the foothills overlooking the plain that leads to the sea. A skilled local negotiator of years of experience was trying to patch up relations threatened by a case (not untypical) in which a member of one of the poor village families had taken off and married a distant relative to the sheikh without the parents' permission. The drama was therefore in appearance totally spontaneous and yet it might be read as a calculated intervention for effect. It established in an absolutely classical mode the honour and immense capacities of the hero, carried implicit sanctions, focused minds wonderfully, and was no doubt exactly what was expected as well as immensely enjoyed as a performance. So although such an enactment needs no justification for its intrinsic quality justifies itself, none the less it was strategically employed in the sense delineated above as well as being set apart and framed as a separate, intensely dramatic event as if for its own sake and for no other reason.

There is an enormous number of such displays. This one was especially striking but very much of a type in style and formed part of a chain of stories about the sheikh in question. He was spoken of, not least by himself. Senior men of known families will commonly tell of their exploits, or allow others to repeat versions in their presence. The audiences vary – kin, dependants, visitors and strangers, potential opponents of similar stature, all those who may repeat it in appropriate settings. A man shows his current allegiances in factional and wider politics by speaking for such a leading figure (who may or may not be present but will be told by others later if he is not) at a gathering in someone's house, or at a funeral ritual, or a feast celebration, a wedding or a *mulid* ritual honouring the Prophet Muhammed. He tells an appropriate story, possibly refers to several great confrontations of his champion. Others notice who is telling what about whom in what mode. There may be barely veiled competition on such public occasions liable to bring various groups and families together. Subordinates must sit silent and unattended to while talk is dominated, I use the word deliberately, by those having or claiming predominance. It is the role of the subalterns to serve, efface themselves and mark their loyalty by deferential witness to the speech and presence of the great. Hierarchies within and between families are marked in this way. Those who are 'inaudible' may at the limit tell stories of others. They may use words, but only of others. This censorship is constitutive of the relations and practices of difference and power. Lowly witnesses are integral to the occasion. They are the contrast turn to the hero.

Such narrative occasions go to create what I shall call the aura essential to power and honour. Crudely put, the greater the figure the greater the number of tellings, though it swiftly becomes a chicken and egg question about which only an anthropologist would be concerned. I could not possibly record the number of times I was told (and not in response to inquiries) of incidents in the life of the type case of the powerful lord who had been killed fourteen years before my fieldwork began (his only son had been assassinated five years before that).[6] They were often one-line evocations which triggered in memory other like moments: they say he shot a young peasant who was building a wall, like that, just for fun, to test a new rifle; he threw a man out of a window of his palace in a rage, or for the hell of it in another version; he defied the labourers in one of his many villages single-handed and then had them all beaten up and chased out; he knew every sheep and goat in his wide domains and no one dared steal from him (highly significant where theft is one of the constant themes in peasant-lord relations and is linked to the idea of power as nothing but force which can be mitigated only by the stealth of those who have nothing).

This aura, of a man who came to own many villages and to run huge estates and became a major capitalist entrepreneur and farmer in the process, is clearly part of what power is felt to be. It creates the dispositions to believe – in his capacity to go beyond mere mortal capacities, to do, say, see, know, hear whatever he liked of whomsoever he chose.

It makes him feared. The stories create fear and depend on fearful anticipation. They create the vulnerability which Lila Abu Lughod has identified in another setting as a thread in the whole discourse of honour and hierarchy, in her case in a bedouin society, but I think it holds with some modifications for my rather different material. Men of 'place' and 'station in life' must not show vulnerability, whether emotional, psychological or physical. Their language excludes emotion or reference to 'private' feeling. Patterns of dependency are highly visible, in contrast to Abu Lughod's material, and marked by a strong public emphasis on rank and honour. These stories invest a man and a whole system of rule with a kind of transcendental force. They do that in part by highlighting the vulnerability that admired and feared force exposes in others. That vulnerability is marked by gesture, tone of voice, patterns of silence and deference behaviour in general, a whole rhetorics of subordination. It is, in short, a very public matter.

As well as having their own narrative time stories are themselves of course within historical processes. They change in major or minor ways in the telling and in the significance they bear for other generations. This is difficult for an anthropologist to map out but I can give one example. Consider the account always given for the reason for a grove of olive trees being called 'the grove of the orange' (*karm al leimun*). The local mayor used to say how his grandfather on his father's side was riding with one of the lords on the plain during the years of severe famine at the end of World War I. The lord was eating an orange and the *agha*, his regular companion, said: 'I would give anything for that orange.' The lord asked: 'Would you give your olive grove over there?' to which the reply was 'Yes I would'. Later, in the lord's reception room where many were present for he was a man of power he calls out to the *agha* 'What, Abu Ali, aren't you a man of your word!' His companion, puzzled since he has long forgotten the brief incident on the plain, replies: 'Of course I am.' Then comes the challenge. 'Well didn't you say that you would give me that grove in exchange for an orange?' The answer, inevitably, is: 'Take it.'

Here the word of the man of honour is summoned up by a man of power who challenges him to make it good. The story shows that it was not at the time thought of as 'giving his word' in the conversation of the two men, members of the superior status honour estates riding together (the use of horses being restricted at that time to true 'horsemen', that is beys or *aghas*). The bey makes it so later, in front of an audience, perhaps relying on the agha not deigning to make even the tiniest concession to any reality save that of the word which becomes the grand gesture. To the lord's challenge he gives the superb response. For the most precious thing in the world he gives up the key indicator of landed wealth at the time, the olive grove, land in all its symbolic and material importance and the olive trees which endow that land with the greatest crop value (told about a wheat field how different the story would be). He is outwitted by the lord, forced into a literal reading of an utterance and his only way out is to cover the way in which the lord has played with him by a splendid disregard of all save his honour. He wins his story by surrendering his land.

His grandson ruefully said to me that that was how they (the *aghas*) had lost their land over the years; by being unthinkingly prodigal, vulnerable through the very code of honour itself to the strategems of the unscrupulous who play on the code to oblige them to disadvantage themselves in the act of being honourable. Symbolic capital destroys material capital would be my way of expressing his reading. We preferred the glory to the material substance, he said, generosity to calculation. A history perceived as one of decline is registered in the honour mode now transformed into a collective agent of self-sabotage, aided and abetted by the tension with the dominant lords always scheming to limit the independence of the aghas in terms of property and wealth. But 'that's how we are'. To the grandson the story witnesses to a fatal weakness for stories of honour and the splendid moment. Others would cite it in contexts where 'our' current feebleness and backwardness became the theme. It showed a kind of loyalty to practice that subverted honour in the long term because it forsook all for formal aesthetics and sacrificed the property so essential to status and autonomy. The lords have exploited the word, our word, to our historical detriment in a process of both alliance and competition. For a later generation pride in true genealogy of honour is haunted by the implications in a world of transformed economic and political relations where dispersal of the patrimony more than ever weakens the solidarity of the patrilineal group. The account now illustrates an uneasy, double consciousness of honour as reason for being and as a cause of historical decline.[7]

Property becomes insidiously more visible, and the line between the noble and obligatory honouring of 'word' (a classical virtue) and fecklessness (a classical vice) looks to the descendants not so much fine as non-existent. Yet the tale can be told and has certainly remained in the repertoire to demonstrate that we knew how to be real men at that time; those were the days, which no longer exist, not least because of the way we followed the code. We no longer have the measure of the moment. We have failed the ancestors, whose fault it none the less is if we cannot measure up to them.

It is in the active memory, to call it that, a memory which is constantly activating as much as being activated, that the notion of community is generated and given sense. The 'community of shared memory' in Weber's phrase, is in such story performances represented in its most transfiguring form.[8] This transfiguration is a key ideological function. The 'beauty and excellence' of groups claiming social honour is incarnated in these tellings. Acts come to seem as if they were done in order to be told and recalled. They are given an emblematic quality. They are directed, not only to their timeless present of honour-in-its-essence (which is also simple present again in the moments of performance), but to a future in which they will be memorialized in words as constituents of a shared past. The question hinted at above in the orange grove story as to what happens if they come to be figures of only a time past, of how it was then or how it could be then as distinct from how it is or can be now is something we shall consider later.

Remembering means being told collectively. It is where we might say that Marx's famous phrase 'the tradition of all the dead generations weighs like a nightmare on the brain of the living' is actualized. There is a burden on those following, a charge upon the next generation, though it is imagined as part of being and a glorious living out rather than a bad dream. For the stories, amongst their many dimensions, constitute benchmarks of significance for 'us', the beys and *aghas*. In any case they appeal to the wider society's standards of truth and necessity in morality and social action. They represent the only way to be. In this sense they are represented as having as much an ontological as a political relevance.

No less than the act of challenge or response the story is agonistic. Not only is it 'about' challenge; its telling reproduces the sociologics of honour and makes every performance part of the process of struggle. Each telling is new and renews, however apparently repetitive of what has been told many times before with very similar though never quite the same gestures, postures, intonations, phrases. It draws boundaries between a 'we' and a 'they', of people like us symbolized in our champion who recognize and act on the imperatives of honour versus people like them who do not, or cannot, or fail. Consensus cannot be assumed, and such narrative events may be ways of testing reaction or the degree of persons' assent to inclusion in or alliance with a group on a relatively short or much longer term basis. A story may be related in public as a direct challenge to others. If the audience is entirely ourselves on a given occasion there is undiminished pleasure in the re-experiencing of our social truth and distinctiveness as against theirs. There is always some political dimension.

Repetition is of the essence. The pleasure given is as inexhaustible as the group's sense of itself. It is integral to the form of life it helps to perpetuate or about whose perpetuation it is reassuring in worlds of whose precariousness people are only too conscious. The re-enactment is an assertion of worth and continuity, a kind of renewing of the guarantee of significance. All are sensible of the fact that others have other versions of events told in very different registers, or that they see 'nothing worth talking about'. Rhetorics depend so much on one's group interest in the event, and on one's own social perspective. People are acutely aware that the line dividing the great hero from the posturing buffoon may be, or may be represented as being, uncomfortably thin. 'The same' events may thus be recounted in opposing ways by opposing groups. Others, however, have to dare to ridicule by making farce out of our high drama. Their joking or demeaning renditions of our great events are politically delegitimizing only if they can make them good in public arenas too. They had better get it right. The balance of forces, that potentially unstable and delicate set of processes, is at issue as always.

Comedy and the world reversed

This is the sense in which the often ignored dimension of comedy becomes relevant. What is fine speech for one may be taken to be bombast by another, or rather performed as bombast by another; what you represent as the noble gesture of the true man of honour I may pantomime as the ludicrous melodrama of the cheap actor.[9]

When told within a group comic narratives are frequently performed by those whose lower social status is marked in part by a joker role they have acquired over time (a role quite inappropriate for a man of social standing). The audience is often predominantly made up of young men, whose position precisely because they are not socially mature and in the fullness of the position of married men with sons, their own independence and biographies as men to be reckoned with, makes them suitable respondents. They too are vulnerable, unheard, silenced on most occasions. The leading men who are present smile quietly, shake their heads deprecatingly while laughing in a restrained manner, murmur ironically that only God knows when it comes to dealing with the joker or some such phrase, and generally hold themselves on the edge of the performance.

The teller and his immediate audience have the licence that goes with the social constraints on their positions. It is expected that they should laugh a lot rather than displaying the gravitas and *maîtrise de soi* of the seniors. They are 'light', not yet weighty. Not knowing how to restrain their passions by reason and judgement formed by experience they show a playful excess of words, just as in some situations they may show a dangerous excess in action. Their places are thus ambiguous: that of the joker because he has come to be socially marginalized through poverty, lack of social discrimination and reliability, failure to secure his family's material wellbeing for whatever reasons, or dependence of an uneuphemized kind, for example as a lord's servant for cash rather than as a companion for honour to whom money is a 'gift' indicating 'respect' rather than a wage; that of the *shebab* (young men) because they are crucial in the mobilization of the group for violence and in the reckoning of forces, yet not fully socialized and liable to disrupt delicate social and tacit negotiations with unreasonable action in the name of an honour whose practices they do not master.

The comic performances may centre on the joker (or one of the young men who assumes the role), or on the member of another group, or on someone who has come to be seen as a fit object of such narratives. The comedies are frequently a major phase in *saharat* (evening talk among a group of friends), between the furious mock insulting and obscenity of card games, loud political dispute, news gathering, evocation of times past and so forth. Repetition is again a principle. The hilarity at the umpteenth re-enactment with formulaic parodying and frequently marvellous timing and imitation is no less genuine each time than the admiration for the nth version of the great challenge or riposte. The ambush that went disastrously wrong, the catastrophically ill-judged expedition to sort out some crisis which instead blew the whole thing up to impossible proportions, the duping of the innocent and the not-so-innocent in positively Chaucerian elaborations of cunning and deceit, the tables turned on the speaker who begins as full of sound and fury and ends in the nothing of ignominious discomfiture, there are many such in the repertoire. Everyone knows them, demands another telling, another acting out, anticipates with delighted relish the exact moment of come-uppance, collapses helplessly at the hugely caricatured outrage of a victim.[10] Honour is reversed, its greatest fears made a subject of group laughter contained within specific frames of reference. Play enters the high seriousness of honour, elaborates on what is silenced, exposes no less fatally than a challenge, and creates the complementary and contradictory aesthetics of the hero and joker.

I must emphasize the importance of ambush and duplicity in these narrative performances. Here is no head-on, one-to-one or indeed one-to-many, direct, uncomplicated, single-minded honour of the stories. Rather we have tales of indirectness, duping, coming at things from an angle. Calculation, which as Bourdieu has rightly argued is seen as alien to honour (*tout se passe comme si* again) is central. Where economic and personal interest are almost invisible in honour enactments they are frequently overtly motivating in the comic routines. The one is represented as something in itself, the other as always *for* something else. That crassness of purpose is often illustrated in the accounts of thieving, stooping to the low-life reverse of the honorable land seizure by the true *qabadi*. In the former a mere something is dishonestly taken, in the latter an essence is demonstrated (from the man of honour's perspective of course . . .).

In joking about a theft which was successfully accomplished the laughter springs from the fact that the victim's switch from say bravado and the high rhetorics of response (present in shadow form behind the comedy) to grovelling sycophancy after a cuff to the head is a sly revelation of the reality lying behind language, giving the lie to language and mere appearance. Ruse, so aptly figured in the ambush trope, and sharp nose for who is and who is not a possible target (i.e. fraud) are the qualities comically exalted. The joker/thief is an agent of unmasking those who affect valour. He is paradoxically also an agent of truth achieved through challenge and a humiliation that is as much self-inflicted as anything. For the victim shows himself to be one who can be made a victim, who 'gives himself away' in our revealing phrase. The thief reveals, as does the gifted liar with his insight into the secret motives of others so vital for the true *mal'un* (close to the antiquated phrase a man of devilish cunning, literally 'cursed', someone with dangerous and devious capacities not least to see those same capacities in others and outsmart them, use them without their even knowing it etc. It is a useful word in the context.). He can play on appearances, his own and others, and in this way triumph in act and performance.

And if the ambush was a failure? If the joke is that everything went wrong for the teller? Risk is always present and the comedy may lie in the mis-calculation, the fact that the presumed victim's show of resistance turned out to be a reality. He was what he said he was. Then it is the would-be master of the ruse who is hoist with his own petard and who in the telling mimics his own unwilled self-exposure, turning it into a triumph of comic narrating.

In both cases the joker is an agent of uncovering and revealing, one of the dominant metaphors in the discourses of power. His tales are commentaries with their moral within the immoral context of dishonourable robbery. The latter itself is recognized as the way of the world and made representative of that universe of lie, appearance and interest opposed to yet always hidden in honour, always threatening and always present. The universe of power in all its operations is served by the ruse and the manipulative, calculating strategy quite as much as by the man of honour who is so often imaged as its true emblem. After all, the great bey uses his *qabadi* in the most interested of ways and for the most ruthlessly calculated ends, however euphemized the relations may be.

Vulgar theft implicitly comments on high-born, not to say high-flown seizure of property. The rhetorics of honour are parodically assaulted, but always safe-guarding the central notion that 'true' honour has been served by the exposure of pretence. Hence the moral and political significance. Theft remains of course a term of the deepest disapprobation in general for the aghas and beys. *Yisruq*, he steals, marks a man out as low, *wati*. It marks dependence and is something to which he has been reduced, as well as demonstrating a character flaw. And it is what peasants do. Those excluded from status honour act that way, it is expected that they will, it is their style. If one of us, the *aghas*, does it that blurs the key distinction. Yet the reality is that times are hard, some men have nothing and in material terms are no better than many fellahin, a man has to eat, what can you do? This other deep social ambiguity is contained in the joking tale.

Much of the joking turns on fear. This powerful and feared emotion is represented grotesquely in pantomime of rolling eyes, snivelling tones, shaking hands and the roars of the victim beneath the blows, which come complete with their own masterly sound effects. Virtuoso gestures mimic the collapse of form and the supposed master of form, the ruin of the aesthetics of honour in often wonderfully contrived comedy. The nightmare of fear and the revealing of fear within the core of honour and respect becomes a performance generating explosive laughter and unrestrained amusement at the seemingly unambiguous world of the joker. It is not 'serious'. The individual, so much a fetish of the honour tales with their celestializing of the all-powerful will, is shown in comic realism as all too human, which perhaps eases the burden on the brains of the living. In playing with the stern, exhilarating demands of honour things can be shown of which we are all aware in one way or another but which we must all suppress.

The great comic theme of reversal, of both roles and expectations, is carried through other kinds of events-become-stories in which authority is parodied and subverted. Certain of the *shebab* become known for the quickness of their eye and tongue in exploiting a social possibility others may not have seen to their own and maybe their group's greater glory unless the whole point is to distinguish themselves from the rest of the collectivity. Two simple accounts will indicate something of this kind of capacity to fashion reality against the odds into a triumph for the teller.

On my arrival there was a certain competition to be associated with a stranger who by that position, mode of introduction and what was understood of his background might constitute some kind of social asset as well as whatever more personal interest might develop out of his curious and ill-defined role. It was appropriate for the sons of men of the *aghas* to act as quasi-attendants on me, subordinate and respectful but of course knowing the way things were in ways far beyond my ken. Since you do not often meet social innocence of that degree in north Lebanon the pleasure was spiced with this even rarer experience.

Some days after my entry into the village one of the sons of the old bey, whose family lived mostly in Beirut and Tripoli but would spend time in the *dai'a* in the spring and summer or during elections, invited me on a *kazzura* (an outing, an enjoyable trip purely for the pleasure of it). He proposed a drive to Bsherri, place of the few remaining cedars of Lebanon high in the mountain due east of Tripoli. As a tourist resort this was completely outside the social range of the *shebab* who could never afford such visits and did not conceive them as part of their possible life chances. They were totally out of place there except as drivers or waiting on one of the *bekawat*. The young bey fancied the trip; I had a car while he did not, and he could use me and the occasion to show off (*fannas*) in front of the village lads and emphasize a privileged relation between the privileged. Or so he thought.

As we drove past the mosque and the great tree over the spring at the entrance to the social space of Berqayl we were spotted by those sitting around the little shop at the roadshop where there was always a group of the *agha* young men idling away time and watching the world go by, something my passenger had counted on. He had not counted on one of them swiftly leaping into the road and stopping us: 'Where are you off to *in sha' allah*?' Had I been there longer I might have lied and evaded the question in any of the standard ways which would have been conventionally used by anyone to fob off such an inquiry. The bey tried to do so, but my naive truth-telling gave the real answer that we were off to the mountain. In a flash the young man was in the back seat of my battered VW beetle, grinning all over his face and announcing his undying enthusiasm for our company, the honour it would be, and his duty to accompany me. My host said, and it was an acknowledgement of defeat had I but realized it at the time: '*Hatigi ma'na ya Abdo*? (Are you coming with us then Abdo?) The answer was that he would go anywhere with the ustaz Mikhail and Mustapha Bey, follow us wherever he might at our service. These replies came with vast sanctimonious enthusiasm as he lauded the bey to the skies in all the fitting '*awatif*' of subordination, but in what to me was such an overblown way that even I felt nervous at the transparent play of it all. Compliments flowed as the grin grew wider and he kept up a stream of talk all the way.

At the restaurant visited by wealthy Lebanese to which we went my unfortunate host did the social equivalent of exposing his Queen at chess. As I looked at the menu and admired the dramatic view over the scenery of the mountains, he advised me to take half a chicken and a dish of aubergine (*nusf farrug wa sahn bitinjan*). Abdo fell on this opening with ruthless speed. 'What!? This was a lord's invitation?? Of course I should eat this and that and the other. The table should be covered in dishes. Did not Arab, and especially the lords' invitations know no bounds?' Classical virtues were invoked, imagery of the table and the sacred link of guest and host swamped the bey who almost visibly drowned in the rhetorical tide. The table was duly covered with food, demolished with particular enthusiasm by Abdo, and the bill was obviously many times more than half a chicken and a dish of aubergine would have cost. I enjoyed this all the more as some inkling of what might be going on dawned on me.

All the way back the defeated bey was subjected to recitals of the glories of his house, his own qualities as *sheikh ash-shebab* and Hatim Tayy, a legendary figure of generosity. I was given the most outrageously complicitous smile in the driving mirror. Game, set and match to the village boys.

In the days that followed Abdo told the story in *sahras* and wherever he could and '*nusf farrug wa sahn bitinjan*' became an instant catch phrase for miserliness. The delights were many. First, he had hijacked the whole trip in front of the very audience (myself) before whom the bey thought that he would be the one to parade his rank. The latter was thus hoist on his own petard. Abdo *finessed* the *fannas* (show off) and did so as a member of a group whose champion he made himself. Second, his use of language and social manipulation were infinitely superior to that of his supposed superior. Sitting 'in the back seat' he actually conducted the whole trip. Every compliment was hollow, yet just so calculated as to be unchallengeable, at least by the unskilled victim who had so disastrously misread the possibilities of the situation. Abdo employed the '*awatif*' and rhetoric of hierarchy as his instrument in the control of the bey, making it very difficult for the latter to operate and yet giving him no obvious means of calling the miscreant to account as he was on the surface saying all the right things. That included complimenting me, which further restricted the lord's freedom to respond since everything was taking place before the stranger. Third, he could play on the codes of generosity and the invitation with virtuoso ease. He was entitled to join us, as it would be incorrect to refuse him once we had said where we were going and that it was an '*azima* (invitation) to me. Abdo would be there as my attendant and companion. More, he acted as the very mouthpiece of the great Arab tradition of generosity and feasting, specifically discomfiting the host with his evocations of transcendental virtues of Hatim Tayy and days of glory. None of this could be denied. The bey was compelled to fulfil the conditions of Abdo's verbal performance that followed on the uttering of the fatal phrase *nust farrug* . . . The *bakhil* (miser) was forced to act as if he were prodigally open handed, having condemned himself out of his own mouth. Abdo, out of his own social setting among the Lebanese bourgeoisie and tourists but not out of his social depth, had the wit to play also on the code of the 'Western' invitation: the menu from which a few dishes are carefully chosen, the privacy of host and guest. This was exhuberantly subverted in the name of the imperatives of Arab ways and a true invitation.

In every department therefore he was the winner. He had picked his victim unerringly, because there were a couple of the lord's sons with whom he would probably never have tried it on so blatantly. I was a perfect stooge and witness all in one, and of course was integral to the whole operation anyhow. (I could not be a narrator myself back in the village, as I had no identity with the collective and had neither the skills nor the role fitting to such a joking and bravado performance. I can tell it here, released by different circumstances to the relative one-dimensionality of academic writing.) So Abdo appeared as in a special relation to me, as guardian and educator of the Englishman who was to be especially linked to his descent group and prised from the clutches of the *bekawat* who felt that he naturally belonged with and to them. My innocence was the ideal foil, as my vindication of his account was the perfect guarantee. Had I been displeased and willing to show it there would have been difficulties but I clearly gave enough behavioural clues on the drive to show that I really had no objections at all.

This same young man had accompanied me to Tripoli in my VW a week or two previously. Not knowing the city I headed off in the wrong direction on one of the boulevards and executed a quick U-turn on Abdo's instructions. There was an immediate and imperious sound of a police whistle. A young constable came over in full uniform and utterly in control of the situation. He began to note the infraction and assert his function as agent of the law. Abdo jumped from the car and gave him a lecture on the importance of tourism, the Prime Minister's own orders that visitors were to be welcomed and treated with the maximum helpfulness since they did so much for the Lebanese economy. Here was an Englishman, a university person to boot, being treated in a way that defied the rules of hospitality and the state (I do not remember if God was invoked but I do not think so). Moreover, *ihna min Berqayl*, we are from Berqayl, a large and important village, so the 'tourist' was suddenly revealed as part of a local universe of relations in some unimaginable way. The constable by now looking battered and uneasy tried to insist, threatened with loss of face in public and taken by surprise by the torrent of words, adjurations and rhetorical questions from a younger man with no official standing whatsoever. He would continue. At that point Abdo said peremptorily, as if fully in command of the situation: '*Ar-raqm ma'ruf. Wein az-zabit*?': 'We know your number. Where is the officer?'

His dismissive look at the number on the policeman's epaulettes and obvious willingness to continue this outraged performance to an officer who might well find the spectacle of a foreign visitor with who knows what position or links was sufficient to crush resistance. We drove off, I bemused and Abdo exultant.

The incident immediately became a story in which one of us (of Berqayl, of the family) turned the tables on one of them (the city, the state). The man in uniform was challenged on his own ground in response to his challenge based on his official functions, and he was routed. Speed of reaction, an instant assessment of the disposition of resources was used to surprise the other in his own over-confident deployment of authority by someone apparently in an inferior position (a parallel with the previous story). We were in the town, the *balad*, and yet could invoke the weight of the village, the *dai'a*, against the representative of the central power, and win. The name of Berqayl could be introduced to show the man he had completely misconceived the context and implications of what he was doing. The revelation that I was English and at an English university was a further blow, as he must have assumed the driver in the car with Lebanese number plates was local, my moustache and short hair enabling me often to pass as Akkari. He had misread both actors and situation. Abdo's employment of his own police number and the threat against him of his own higher authority was the final coup. Narratively speaking it played the epigrammatic, clinching role of *nusf farrug* and was often used later to invoke the entire scene.

The fact that the constable was acting quite correctly and on his turf made the victory one even more to be relished. The encounter was essentially between two persons who did not know anything about each other outside the frame of the face-off. One of them was able to introduce elements which moderated the apparent frame of the action in ways quite unanticipated by the other. The third figure turned out to be English and not what he had seemed to be Akkari, as well as being classified as representing a category of privileged stranger (foreign tourist). Abdo played with the rules and overthrew the one who thought he was the master of the moment. The challenge was thrown back on the challenger; the initiative and advantage seemingly with the policeman was snatched from him by rhetorical adroitness.

Both incidents, and the narratives which they became, depended for their effect on improvization, a capacity to seize any opening and for spontaneous play on language and setting. Both pivot on the capture of a situation from the actor who presumes himself to have the power to define its nature and appropriate course (in which case it would never become a 'story'), very much as in honour stories. The hero of the stories, also usually their narrator to audiences from his own *agha* group, plays with the language of the other who knows or fancies that he knows himself to be in the superordinate position. Abdo is not like the great sheikh *qabadi* in his *murajil* performances, with a reputation and a large force behind him. He is at this time one of a small set of brothers, the fourth of them and therefore very junior, living on his wits as much as anything for he has left school but has no training and only very intermittant work. What he does have is a devastating sense of timing and rhetoric, sharpened in the day-to-day encounters of which, after all, these stories were just two. He made one situation, the invitation, into a test of wit and nerve; the other was thrust upon him and he converted potential embarrassment, for if I had had trouble he would certainly have been described as being at fault back home by his *shebab* rivals happy to discredit him, into a different kind of reversal of authority.

In both events there were other possible outcomes. Abdo had summed up the young lord correctly and I have suggested that he probably would have been shrewd enough to avoid those of the old bey's sons who were quite sufficiently *mal'un* to put him in his place. The policeman might have been more flexible, or well-connected, or simply brutal. Many of the other young men of the village would have neither been capable of the first response nor of the dexterity and temerity required had they blundered into a confrontation.

What was at stake had nothing to do in formal terms with *sharaf* (honour bound up in controlling the sexual purity of group and individual) or *karama* (more specifically a man's personal honour and integrity) of course. But it had a great deal to do with winning or losing in playing on the potentialities of social situations and refusing to accept the apparently dominant classification. Things do not work out at all as the young bey or constable imagine they will and they lack the social imagination to visualize the other stories that could be made out of the material. Taking the encounter too much for granted they are both shown their miscalculation, and that miscalculation becomes a story to be recounted with delight at the expense of representatives of both the local power elite and the forces of the state.

So I would want to argue that such comic performances and usage of language are also part of what I have called above 'benchmarks of significance' and constants of social morality and action. They too are part of an ontology as much as of a 'game of honour', political oppositions, and of a social ethos in general.

It will be obvious that suppressions and silences play a basic structuring role in the words of honour. I am speaking now of the level at which everyone recognizes, just knows, what must not be told, what must be kept secret or euphemistically glossed. Certain things have to be forgotten, as they do in the imagination of all communities. This forgetting may be no less precarious than the remembering in stories. People err in judgement, something is blurted out by someone whose social acuity is limited (an anthropologist's knack too), someone who lacks the *savoir faire*, *savoir dire* and the sheer mastery of timing so admired by Bourdieu.

Stories in the shadows

One thing is certain. Others will speak of what we suppress, given the right circumstances and occasion. If we guard a secret, well and good. If not, then we must be strong enough to ensure that it is worth more than anyone's life, metaphorically or literally, to repeat it. Some events cannot simply be passed over in complicity, the murder of a paternal first cousin for instance. That is a guilty secret that cannot be kept. However immediate the peacemaking, however quickly the descent group notables close ranks, the crime is right there at the centre of the patrilineal world, on the edge of fratricide, striking at the heart of the political unit of males bound by kinship and violence, and at a privileged relation of authority between father's brother and brother's son as well as of marriage preference ideals for father's brother's daughter. It contradicts the logic of family, patriarchy, endogamy, and the solidarity of a violence group sharing a name. It is a paradigmatic self-violation. Accounting for it or giving an account of it presents huge difficulties.

Rhetorical persuasiveness in the case of which I am thinking depended on imaging the victim as responsible for his own death through his irresponsibility; he was beyond the pale, asocial, capable of anything and therefore dangerous to anyone, including his own kin. This is close, terribly close, to the highest figures of power who are represented as transcending all the limits of others, moral, social, and familial in an excess that bursts the banks of any coding of honour (though that is of course a classification itself). The ambiguity is fundamental. Violent, ready for anything, brave, fearless, unpredictable, this could be the very type of what the Lebanese call an *qabadi*. Or it could be the picture of one who, exactly because he refuses to acknowledge limits or implications for others, poses as much of a threat to his own as to outsiders. For he may drag them into conflicts where far too much is at risk, the field is not of our choosing, and thus imperil relations constructed out of political or other interest.

Significantly in this case the murdered man had intruded disruptively into relations between the beys and the descent group of those linked to them in next position in the hierarchy of status honour, the aghas. Extortion, threats and blackmail against certain of the lords, actions admired by some for the embodying of individual nerve (and perhaps for putting the lords under pressure too), to others within the group were a destabilization of key links. The real *qabadi* was becoming, as real *qabadis* may do, embarrassing and dangerous.

When I was being told of his career and death, on the quiet and by someone who had no status within the agha group of which he was a member as he had squandered his patrimony when a young man and was basically no more than a minor outlaw and servant for one of the lords, the murdered man was described as *makhlu'*, beyond the pale. This seemed to be the accepted term for labelling his entire life and character.

And yet . . . It was a killing, and by his paternal first cousin. The victim had been a 'real man' whose exploits were exactly what would in other circumstances be recounted, not whispered or held close in the secret heart. Young men too young to have known him personally might look regretful or mutter *'aib* (shame) if a conversation among them somehow led to his name briefly surfacing. Killed by an outsider he would no doubt have been spoken of as a hero, dying the right death for heroes (often very nasty and the result of treachery or sordid entanglement) and to be avenged, even if people in fact were desperately hoping not to be embroiled and were looking for every possible rhetorical way out. Killed by an insider his name was off everyone's lips though known to all. And, in the version I was given, there was the image of the dogs licking his blood as he lay dead in the street in the heart of 'our' quarter. That was drama, but a drama of shame and impiety however you read it. The horror and dramatic aptness of that image of the unclean scavenging the human waste is part of the aesthetic of honour stories no less than representations of the grand gesture.

Peace had been accomplished by, at least in part, the rhetorical device of the *makhlu'*; he was one for whom vengeance was doubly inappropriate, not only because of the close kinship proximity where vengeance is taken to be a nonsense since it destroys what it is supposed to defend, but because you do not avenge one who has passed beyond all codes and ceased to be in the full sense social.

Both murderer and victim had brothers. They 'avoided' each other and all conspired in the descent group to maintain invisibility and its necessary accompaniment of silence. But what if one day they were to become visible or audible to one another because of arbitrary and unanticipated circumstance?

The story is always thus hovering in the shadows. It is known but not heard, or heard only in a kind of whisper in the dark. But it is known to many others. Groups of the *fellahin* in the village ('peasant' stratum in the status honour idiom) say nothing of it in public either. They, however, are mutes rather than mute. They dare not name names or tell the story save in complaints among themselves about how 'they', the aghas, *really* are. The story then becomes testimony to the nature of the dominant stratum and part of the catalogue of oppression by those who very consciously see themselves as the oppressed, those who cannot and dare not speak. Speech, public and challenging, would bring violent retribution by these superior forces whose violence is often seen as part of their very nature as much as of the nature of the hierarchical order in practice. Speaking it only amongst themselves the *fellahin* acknowledge their own sense of being controlled. The story is part of the tissue of their lives also and their experience of language and domination, though with a quite different significance.

In the discourse of power they have neither the right nor the capacity to 'speak'. They have no 'word', and no words can properly be spoken by or of them (in that sense my writing here would seem unthinkable to someone local in the village – how do you write about peasants?). In the extreme form this may be lived as an internalized sense of mutedness and a constituent part of personal and collective identity. A man cannot speak, not only because he is fully aware of sanctions if he does, but because he is in himself unable to speak. It is not of his nature. In this limiting case the subject appears unable to conceive of 'speaking' save in the language of the subordinated.

Less extremely, exclusion from language and signifying power of status honour may be spoken among the peasants somewhat ambiguously in terms of a devalorization of status honour as a code and ideology as a whole, *and* of the dominant groups' practices described as not in fact even true to the code which legitimizes hierarchy. Their acts are not honourable, merely tyrannically oppressive, beyond measure unjust (*zulm*, a term with considerable religious weighting and closely linked with the idea of arbitrary and absolute powers). Their word is not good, but falsehood (*kizb*). The beys and aghas are represented as both deceiving, telling and using *kizb*, and self-deceived, for they do not realize that their show of honour is a lie. This is what characterizes them in general, whatever judgements about particular individuals' qualities may be. The only trouble is that they can make their lie good in the social world, something we cannot do with our truth.

There are exceptions to all rules. One of the *fellahin* achieved through a capacity for violence the status of one of whom stories were told. He was feared (*biyfazza'*, he frightens) and respected (*muhtaram*). At a period when the lords wanted to subvert the position of the aghas they identified a couple of the peasant young men as likely lads, good strong-arm men and bodyguards. This endangered the previous monopoly on force and status honour shared with the lords that sometimes enabled the aghas to threaten a lord's place. It was thus an attempt to shift the balance. One of the young peasants became a well-known figure in the familiar career of challenge, elimination of rivals, taking on those of whom others were afraid, defying agencies of the state such as the police or army, and so forth and so on. He was eventually killed, and for various reasons the overall strategy ran into the sand. His exploits were spoken of by the aghas and the beys as a case of idiosyncratic importance but never possessing a more generalized status, nor as far as I know, on social occasions such as the *saharat*, formal visits and so on. He was figured as one of a kind, on his own in the literal as well as the figurative senses, frightening but not a threat to a system within which he had played a disturbing and a confirming role. His function in the beys' scheme of things was quite clear to the aghas, but he became his own man, his acts did earn their 'respect', were taken to speak for themselves, and his name did weigh with them. The man of violence is remembered. Some years after his death when I was in the region his name was evoked without question as a man who 'needed no one', went beyond the ordinary, lived out the tropes (not least in his death). This *qabadi* never politicized relations between the peasants and the other strata, though he was part of that wider frame. Rather he acted according to the social and symbolic logic of violence in which his individuality alone was his glory.

Conclusion

Pierre Bourdieu begins his article on the sentiment of honour in Kabyle society with three cases in which the observance of proper form in language and action breaks down. He goes on to use these episodes to distinguish 'the rules of the game of challenge and ripost' (p. 197). It seems to me that almost inadvertently he raises a somewhat different but no less crucial set of questions about rhetoric and social form which he never really addresses.

The breakdowns arise where one party to a dispute cannot, or possibly will not follow the rules and the dialectic. In each instance this is the offended party who is in some significant way an *outsider*: one is described as 'having forgotten the technique and spirit of what he called "Kabyle rhetoric"'; the second is a city-dwelling landlord 'ignorant of the nuances' of that rhetoric; and the third has 'lived abroad and had little knowledge of local custom', and therefore of the appropriate rituals of peace-making. The three have become 'strangers', and though Bourdieu uses the words 'ignorant' and 'forget' it seems at least as possible that they *refuse* the 'rhetoric' (used in a pejorative way and meaning something like empty and meaningless form), in one example by rejecting the mediation of a delegation of venerable persons, an unprecedented action. Their rules are different. Their perceptions of the *enjeux* have altered (they are referred to as educated and well-to-do as a result of their move away from Kabylia, and we should remember that the region was marked from relatively early in the French colonial period by its high rate of emigration to France). Their socio-logics and ways of making accounts are not merely different but are seen by them to be opposed to the time-honoured ways of acting and accounting for social action. Such new rationalities displace the old, they do not complement them. The challenge is thus to 'the game' as a whole, not from within it.

This is surely crucial. When, therefore, Bourdieu goes on to say that from these stories, and a 'host of similar episodes could be related' (p. 197), 'one can distinguish the rules of the game' it seems to me that he is treating those rules as if they were part of a homogeneous world of meaning and practice rather than being subject to radical change in form and habitus.

My feeling in rereading the material is that the focus on habitus is in fact associated with an underlying nineteenth-century division of a *gemeinschaft-gesellschaft* kind in which Kabylia is made to stand for the former in an unequivocal way. This may not be entirely without benefit if it enables Bourdieu to unravel the complexities of habitus, doxa and the like. But it does mean that the language battle over the language of honour and social distinction itself is lost. This is of course a consistent failing in the standard anthropological mode when historical transformations and developments are elided or suppressed altogether, not because of a complicity with colonialism but rather because of discursive traditions within our subject to which even innovators like Bourdieu are subject. Like the rest of us he too has his *méconnaissance* built into his system.

Much is involved in these episodes, and sometimes the outsider protagonist who causes the unforeseen problem is counselled to the greater wisdom of accommodation to local practice. If he is going to live and maintain strategic interests there it would at the very least make good 'modern, rational' sense to do so. In the last case, however, he refuses any kind of tempering of his claim and, intentionally or otherwise it is difficult to say, insults the assembly of notables by virtually accusing them of taking money to intercede as they have done. In other words he suggests the single value of cash, as if they were merely shopkeepers rather than guardians of the social integrity of the collectivity whose acts are utterly without interest or the very notion of exchange and recompense. 'The worst curses were predicted for the offender.' One can quite see why. One wonders also whether they had any effect . . ..

This is a different kind of nightmare on the brain of the living. What if the worth of the tradition of the ancestors, who in my fieldwork experience were no dead generations but stalked the streets in person and in narratives, were called into question?

What if more recent hegemonic discourses of power are established in which the tradition comes to be an image of what is merely and emptily 'past', irrelevant, mere 'Kabyle rhetoric'? What are our words then? There arises a double fracture of language and experience: first that we are unable to replicate and fulfil the demands of the tales (save comically), for we no longer command the symbolic and material means to do so; and second, that those tales themselves no longer compel attention in our social universe in the same ways because that universe as a whole has become subordinated to others through changes in political, cultural and economic relations which we neither control nor can even self-deceivingly imagine we control.

Language becomes doubly ironical. There is always and increasingly a gap between word and reality of honour, a gap which indeed structures the discourse of honour. Vulnerability and fear are given new dimensions. It can begin to seem as if there is nothing but mere show and mere appearance; that even 'the truth' will be taken to be just *kizb*, or empty words, rhetoric; that all tales are turned into bombast or buffoonery by the times. The mayor's story of his prodigal grandfather and the orange grove has elements of this, and it gives the comedies a particular edge. Perhaps the repetition is in part an attempt by the collective unconscious of the aghas and those like them to attempt magically to reproduce what is felt to be cruelly threatened, namely the honour on which they have built all their claims to value and precedence? For members of the peasant stratum, on the other hand, the nightmare is diminished when the burden of the rhetoric is weakened. And for the younger lords, accustomed to flats in Tripoli or Beirut and boutique culture the whole local scene can be just a kind of joke, still with its serious side if their fathers depend on the olive crop so they had better not be too offensive on a visit back to the country seat, but a joke none the less.

Other values and schemes of precedence intrude, as they do in the persons of the Kabylian outsiders. As in Herzfeld's study I was struck by what he calls an 'introverted' aspect to the discourse of the person (a subject I have not been able to deal with here at all). Younger men of the aghas felt vulnerable, not because of a lack of personal courage or manliness, but because they had partly at least absorbed a realization of the inadequacy and 'backwardness' of their peripheral region and ways of life in the perspective of the 'centre'. There were many ways in which they were compelled to see how poor was their education; just where in the job market they entered and the realities of that new phenomenon 'being without a job'; how 'rural' was their speech; how cheap their clothes, how crude their manners were taken to be by the Beirutis amongst whom many of them worked, schoolteachers, job givers, city slickers, business men coming to trade olives, those few who had 'made it' to any degree at all and preferred to live in Tripoli.

They spoke of themselves as lacking, without, deprived of real power or real capacity to live up to themselves and the dead generations in the images of honour. 'Call us a people? (*sha'ab*). Are we real men? This bunch of useless bastards? There's nothing to us.' There was a pessimism not least about the performative powers of language. It was as if words no longer were or did and could not possibly be and do what they were supposed to have done. Ambiguity had become central, irony sometimes appeared omnipresent. The question was what new words and ways of imagining the community were there, or was there really, as so many of the *shebab* said, 'no future?'

Notes

1 Scholte, (1986), p. 9.
2 Clifford, (1986), p. 12.
3 As a single male I was virtually confined to the company of other males in the village. After many months I was occasionally able to participate in more informal family gatherings where women were present and contributing in word and action, but these were rare. I have written in various places about my place of fieldwork in Akkar, north Lebanon and for my purposes here will offer only the briefest sketch. It was described as 'feudal' by most writers and many educated Lebanese, when they had a view of it at all. By that was meant that the region, straddling the Syrian border north of the port of Tripoli, was dominated by a landed aristocracy with the help of others also associated with the ideology of status honour and the title of agha (often self-awarded) whose military force was crucial in the lords' rule. The peasants (*fellahin*) had for a long time been held in a virtually serf-like position, and in some areas still were, even in the early 1970s. I am now finishing a book on the subject of politics, violence and culture in the region.
4 I am not sure that Bourdieu does not sometimes overdo the 'game' metaphor, but acknowledge a great debt to his writing.
5 There are major methodological problems in this whole analysis which will have to be clarified in later work. Richard Bauman's research on stories is most helpful, but does not really treat of the dimensions of power. It does indicate, however, just how much I have to do on performance and 'internal' properties of the narratives. Unfortunately I have no tape recordings of the tellings as it was not my practice to do so because of what I saw as local difficulties it would pose. And as the whole point was that the tellings were inextricably woven into social life and the setting was always crucial I am making do for the moment with very general analysis of rhetorics.
6 It might be noted that I very rarely heard stories about the son, who lived rather

the life of the sophisticated 'outsider', who became a minister while his father continued his local and regional political career with a greater attention to affairs directly in and around the village.

7 Some version of this theme is found in many analyses of societies in which, for example, the maintenance of social honour necessitates the sale of land and goods and a decline into genteel penury, with only the name on which to live.

8 I have cited this phrase in Gilsenan, 1986, p. 27.

9 Young men in their late adolescence used to rehearse little 'plays' of comic comeuppance which they put on more or less spontaneously for their elders. To be a *mumaththil*, an actor, was a term often used to characterise particular individuals, and social life was informed by the keenest sense of the dramatic that I have ever known.

10 In my *Recognising Islam* I deal with an episode in which a religious man was, entirely without his knowledge, socially destroyed in this way.

References

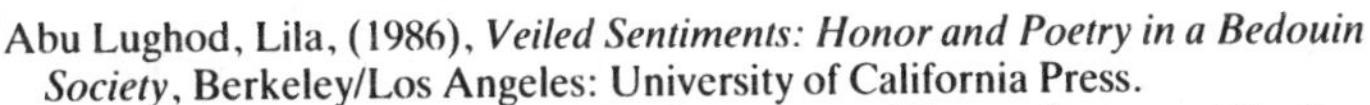

Abu Lughod, Lila, (1986), *Veiled Sentiments: Honor and Poetry in a Bedouin Society*, Berkeley/Los Angeles: University of California Press.

Bauman, Richard, (1986), *Story, Performance and Event: Contextual Studies of Oral Narrative*, Cambridge: Cambridge University Press.

Bourdieu, Pierre, (1965), 'The Sentiment of Honour in Kabyle Society' in Peristiany (ed.) 1965.

Clifford, James and Marcus, George E. (eds), (1986), *Writing Culture: The Poetics and Politics of Ethnography*, Berkeley/Los Angeles: University of California Press.

Gilsenan, Michael, (1976), 'Lying, Honor and Contradiction' in Kapferer, B. (ed.), 1976, pp. 191–219,

Gilsenan, Michael, (1982), *Recognizing Islam*, London, Croom Helm.

Gilsenan, Michael, (1986), 'Domination as Social Practice', *Critique of Anthropology*, vol. VI, nr. 1 (Spring), pp. 17–37.

Herzfeld, Michael, (1985), *The Poetics of Manhood: Contest and Identity in a Cretan Mountain Village*, Princeton: Princeton University Press.

Kapferer, Bruce, (1976), *Transaction and Meaning: Directions in the Anthropology of Exchange and Symbolic Behavior*, Philadelphia: ISHI Press.

Peristiany, John, (1965), *Honour and Shame: The Values of Mediterranean Society*, London: Weidenfeld and Nicolson.

Scholte, Bob, (1986), 'The Charmed Circle of Geertz's Hermeneutics: A Neo-Marxist Critique', Critique of Anthropology, vol. VI, nr. I (Spring), pp. 5–15.

'We condemn apartheid, BUT . . .': a discursive analysis of the European Parliamentary debate on sanctions (July 1986)[1]

Gill Seidel

Introduction: the discourse on sanctions

In Western Europe sanctions are debated in a number of contexts, formal and informal, using a variety of modes: spoken, written, iconic, kinesic, musical; and, in popular culture, through a combination of these modes. In terms of formal talk, debates take place in parliament and are relayed by the media. At the same time, the issue of sanctions is fought over in the extra-parliamentary arena: in local and national campaigns and boycotts which receive scant media attention, in international bodies, as well as in trade and financial circles.

The sum total of these discussions, confrontations and campaigns may be seen to constitute 'the sanctions debate' or 'sanctions discourse' in a broad sense. The different ways in which sanctions are 'seen' and articulated by the pro- and anti-sanctions lobbies, that is, the meanings and images which are put into circulation and fought over contribute to the destruction or maintenance of apartheid respectively, and, at a more general level, to the anti-racist and racist discourses at large.

Language, politics, ideology and discourse: a brief note on the analytical framework

In terms of European Parliamentary (EP) debates, given the plural linguistic status of the Community institutions in which all official communications are interpreted/translated into the recognized Community languages, any purely formal linguistic investigation into interaction (which would normally assume a shared language) would be difficult to sustain; and, arguably, would be skewed from the start.

From my own perspective, however, as a discourse analyst, this consideration is not so crucial. I would maintain that the meanings of words and phrases have very little to do with purely formal linguistic properties; and that there can be no universal semantics. Meanings are primarily socially constructed; and this fundamental insight, obvious to even the most naïve observer, has been ignored in the formal work on semantics. The prevailing view is articulated in John Lyons's account of semantics (1981). He recognizes three main levels of analysis: word-meaning, sentence-meaning and utterance meaning. From an anthropological perspective, the most significant fact is that the first two levels are distinguished from the third on the basis of the relevance or otherwise of the social context to the determination of the meaning. In a critique of this position, Grillo, Pratt and Street (Coates *et al.* 1988) provide a very clear synthesis of anthropological studies of semantics, focusing on the limited and therefore problematic meaning of the *social* in much linguistic work, where it is reserved for interpersonal relationships. This is comparable to the body of work on racism, centring on 'prejudice' as interpersonal relations, thereby ignoring the force of institutional racism and discourse and their material effects. Both in linguistics and in 'ethnic studies', this interpretation, influenced in part by an older paradigm in social psychology and by a certain euro-centric and a-historical pragmatism, has served to depoliticize much of the work in these areas, including pragmatics, the main focus of inquiry into 'social meaning'. My own position is closer to that of the anthropologists, and I would reiterate that the social context is crucial, and that all levels of analysis of meaning are constructed in conflicting discourses. Language may be seen as a shared resource, but with differential access. It is also a social practice intersected with different discursive histories and struggles.

Discourse, then, of any kind – text as a suprasentential unit of meaning – is a site of struggle in which social meanings are produced (not reflected), sustained and challenged. This is most clearly the case with political discourse, since the theory and practice of politics and political talk is seen to be primarily concerned with power. Ideology is part of discourse, and does not exist outside of it. This statement assumes a conflict, not a consensus model of society, and a model of language-use seen as part of social action and concerned with the relation between action and structure (Seidel 1985).

Ambiguity and the reproduction of racist discourse

I propose to explore the hypothesis that the opponents of sanctions, who may be termed collaborators, articulate an ambiguous discourse on apartheid; and that they reproduce a set of meanings which sustain racist discourse.

All EP political groupings condemn apartheid. In a number of cases, however, this rejection of apartheid is combined with a rejection of sanctions, despite the list of demands they put to the Botha régime. This makes for an *ambiguous discourse on apartheid* which is operating in a larger context. The formulation of some of the demands would seem to suggest that apartheid can be 'reformed'; and that 'dialogue' followed by negotiation can or should ensue, as if between equal partners. Interestingly, this is the position of the liberal Progressive Federal Party of South Africa, as exemplified in Helen Suzman's stance, and is using an argument already rehearsed by liberal capitalists in South Africa. It suggests that not only is the system evolving in a positive direction, but that sanctions would hamper this development. This liberal discourse bears little relation to the definition of African realities and arguments for sanctions as articulated notably by representatives of mass political organizations in South and Southern Africa (including ANC, PAC, SWAPO, trade union federations such as CUSA-AZACTU, as well as the Front Line States and the signatories to the Lomé Convention) (see Appendix B).

The kind of ambiguity that exercises us here is not primarily of a formal kind. I refer to the shared basic presupposition of the anti-sanctions lobby which runs through the debate, and is contested, and would seem to be that apartheid can be reformed. The presuppositions entailed and other encoding of realities (including lexical choice, collocation and agency) will be fought over as a stake in the reality-making mechanism. We are referring here to a presupposition that is rooted not in the linguistic meaning of a sentence (Lyons 1977: 601–5; 1981), but which is dependent on the particular reading of an ideological and political text which also has material effects. The relevance of context dependency for interpreting presuppositions and ambiguities in language must also take account of discursive strategies and ideological struggles within discourse. That reading, that articulation, may itself be considered as a form of praxis.

In the debate on South Africa it is abundantly clear that 'dialogue' and 'negotiation' are part of the code of those in power. They are also part of a consensus-making mechanism. Also at work in the debate, and outside of it, are relativist arguments about violations of human rights in other parts of the world which trivialize racism and fascism. This particular strategy is discussed elsewhere (Seidel 1988). This paper identifies a particular set of ambiguity markers present in the speeches of those opposed to sanctions which may symbolize a particular view of South African reality. These are the lexicalization of 'dialogue' and 'negotiation'.

I would further suggest that apologists of sanctions are reproducing an established, patronizing discourse in relation to Africans, which may be seen as a component of racist discourse.

Data: criteria for selection – why the 1986 European Parliamentary debate?

In the introduction I referred to the different terrains in which the debate on sanctions is being promoted, including initiatives at a local level. Politically, extra-parliamentary initiatives are of the greatest importance. Parliament will not, indeed, cannot lead the struggle for sanctions. The pressure, therefore, must come from outside. Yet in terms of official discourse, parliamentary debates in general call for particular attention since they articulate the arguments of the legislature. And, specifically, the parliamentary debates in Western Europe, in the European Parliament in Strasbourg, and in Britain may be seen to be politically significant in view of the important trading and financial relationships pertaining between South Africa, the EEC and Britain.

It must be stressed that the EEC is South Africa's largest trading bloc, while Britain has a considerable economic involvement, and hence heavy responsibility. Britain is South Africa's third largest *trading* partner, but is by far the largest foreign *investor* in South Africa. Precise estimates vary. According to figures given by the British Industry Committee on South Africa to the House of Commons Foreign Affairs Committee in July 1986, Britain's investments in South Africa total £6,000 million, and represent 40 to 45 per cent of all foreign investment in South Africa. This amounts to 70 per cent of British overseas investment. This is also the figure given by the UK South African Trade Association (UKSATA). The Anti-Apartheid Movement, however, estimates the UK's share of total overseas investments in South Africa at 38 per cent (Labour Research Department 1986). South Africa's investments in Britain are worth £700 million, representing 1.9 per cent of all foreign investment in the UK. Visible British exports to South Africa amount to £1,010 million a year, while visible South African exports to Britain total about £990 million a year.

These figures would suggest, therefore, that any debates and resolutions taken by the EEC and the British government in relation to sanctions necessarily have implications for the anti-apartheid struggle, with repercussions on the whole of Southern Africa and the SADCC states. In the particular case of the EEC, in the context of the Lomé Convention (which an independent Namibia would be expected to join), and the ACP-EEC Convention,[2] they have implications for a number of other African, Caribbean and Pacific States (see Appendix A). So the potential, over-all impact is enormous.

There is another reason for focusing on the EEC and British parliamentary debates – although my analysis of the British debate is not included in this paper. In structural terms, these two Assemblies (the European Parliament and the British Commons) currently entertain a particular and close, almost symbiotic, relationship. I refer to the dual status pertaining at the time of the debate of the new British President of the European Council of Ministers, Sir Geoffrey Howe, who at that point is simultaneously the Secretary for Foreign and Commonwealth Affairs in the second Thatcher administration which has made no secret of its opposition to sanctions.

Because of the structural arrangements of the European Community, legislative power lies with the Council of Ministers, not with the European Parliament itself, which is purely a consultative body. Sir Geoffrey Howe was currently, therefore, the most powerful figure in the EEC. Although in his capacity of President he spoke officially for the Twelve and not in his national capacity as spokesman for the Thatcher government, clearly there is tension between the two positions. Arguably, the reason he was shunned by a number of African leaders during his tour of Southern Africa in July 1986, as delegated by the Council of Ministers, was precisely because he was perceived not as the representative of the EEC, a number of whose constituent member states have adopted restricted sanctions, but of the Thatcher government.

Debates on South and Southern Africa, including the sanctions issue, have taken place in the European and British Parliaments prior to 1986, and subsequently (in the case of the European Parliament). However, it is generally agreed that the July 1986 debates were the most significant to date given the context of

1. The South African régime's re-imposition of the nation-wide state of emergency on 12 June 1986, with an unprecedented wave of repression and arrests, and unlimited powers to suppress all opposition;
2. South Africa's war against its neighbours fought by surrogate armies ('destabilization') as an extention of apartheid's second front (Hanlon 1986 a and b);
3. the dissension within the Commonwealth at the Nassau Summit of October 1985 in which Britain refused to accept the Commonwealth sanctions package (which led to the August 1986 Boycott by 32 countries of the Thirteenth Commonwealth Games in Edinburgh);
4. the determined moves taken by the US Senate to implement sanctions in the face of presidential opposition;
5. the determination of the Botha régime to go ahead with new elections (6 May 1987) which totally excluded South Africa's black majority.

These, then, are my reasons for choosing these debates as illustrating the official discourse on sanctions in Western Europe today.

Contextualizing the debate: the European Parliament – structural parameters and constraints

The debate of 8 and 10 July 1986 was ostensibly an historic occasion: it was the first EP vote in favour of sanctions. The voting was 228 for the motion, 114 against, and 29 abstentions. (An official summary of the debate as published in European Parliament's *The Week* constitutes Appendix A.)[3] But before euphoria takes over, it is important to remember that the EP has no executive power: EP votes and decisions have the status of expressions of opinion. In other words, the EP is simply a talking shop.

Debates on South and Southern Africa in the EP and British Parliament have tended to be a complete charade. They have been characterized by delays, emasculating amendments, ambiguities, hollow relativist arguments, and other stone walling tactics. For the most part, the debate of 8 and 10 July was no exception – and the contributions often stilted and artificial. This wooden impression may partly be accounted for by the rigid EP rules: each of the nine political groupings is given a fixed time allowance. If a speaker exceeds this entitlement, the excess time is deducted from the over-all allocation in a subsequent debate. Time is even more at a premium since Spain and Portugal acceded to membership. In practice this ruling also has the effect of virtually dispensing with interruptions and extempore exchanges. Hence the over-all impression is of a formal debating chamber with delegates reading from prepared texts. The only brief moment of excitement that led to short, unscheduled exchanges was caused by a noisy demonstration on 10 July protesting against French nuclear tests in the Pacific which some right-wing MEPs[4] tried to use an excuse for interrupting the debate.

In the EP, the anti-sanctions lobby comprised all the political groupings, with the exception of the Socialists (S), Communists (C), Rainbow Group (ARC), and individual members of the Independents (NI). The debate in question was the outcome of a report drawn up by the Political Affairs Committee (Doc A2-58/56) in May 1986 on the political situation in Southern Africa and future prospects.[5]

The report included two statements of minority opinion by the Socialists and the Communist and Allied Groups respectively. The report was tabled by the Committee Chairman, Mr Formigioni, a Vice-President of the EP (PPE) (Italy), since the *rapporteur* (COM) (Greece) had officially disassociated himself from the original report amended in Committee beyond all recognition. This had entailed a dispute about Rules of Procedure which was briefly involved by the debate by CAMPINOS (SOC) (PT).

A month earlier Mr Formigioni had introduced the joint declaration against racism and xenophobia (86/C 155/01) which was adopted by the Presidents of all three Community institutions (the Commission, the Parliament and the Council) on 25 June 1986. It placed racism as a priority problem for the Community. This declaration was the outcome of a special Committee of Inquiry of the EP into the Rise of Fascism and Racism in western Europe, chaired by Mr Ford (SOC) (UK). The original report (Doc A2-160/85) was drawn up by the late Mr Evrigenis (PPE) (GR) in December 1985 and debated on 16 January 1986. The Committee was set up following the European elections of July

1984 which returned 16 fascist MEPs (10 FN, 5 MSI and 1 EPEN).[6] This led to the creation of the new European-Right group (DR) chaired by Le Pen[7] of the *Front National*, whose party won almost 11 per cent of the French EP vote in the first PR ballot. The irony is that the EP structures entitle all parliamentary groupings, including the DR, to financial support and representation rights on all committees. Le Pen attempted to prevent the enquiry being set up by appealing to the Court of Justice at Luxembourg. He failed, and subsequently boycotted the proceedings. But the DR is not the only marauding group in the EP. A number of crypto-fascists and racists in other right-wing groupings such as the PPE (Christian Democrats) sat as members of the Committee, and later drafted volley after volley of amendments.

This same kind of political absurdity and argumentation strategies that characterized the Committee of Inquiry into the Rise of Fascism and Racism were also present in the debate of 8 and 10 July 1986 on Southern Africa and in earlier and subsequent deliberations. This Committee actually succeeded in jettisoning the concept of fascism en route: it no longer figures in the title of the official declaration. During the sanctions debate, Sir James Scott-Hopkins of the ED group actually accused the left-wing in the European and national Parliaments of stirring up racial hatred. So when at the outset of the Southern African debate Mr Formigioni chose to refer to the relation between the two debates, thereby emphasizing the shared anti-racist dynamic, it was doubly ironic. The same political patterns emerge: the racist and anti-racist discourses present in the reports and deliberations of both Committees. All speakers condemn racism and apartheid. On the Right, the condemnation is no more than en empty ritual gesture towards a form of consensus politics. The Left on the other hand, (Socialists, Communists, the Rainbow group and some Independents) call for a less ambiguous resolution, immediate and effective sanctions, support for the ANC and SWAPO and an end to the illegal occupation of Namibia; and they include a very clear statement about the position of women in South Africa. In the rest of the debate, the links between racism, apartheid, the structural oppression of women, and sanctions are not clearly articulated. The Right refuses to take any account of the clear expression of the majority of the black population in South and Southern Africa who have called for sanctions; or of South Africa's undeclared war against the surrounding black majority states. And, as K. Focke

(S) (G), E. Glinne (S) (B), Miranda da Silva (COM) (PT) and others point out, the question of Namibia is entirely absent from the original resolution. Nor does the Right make any distinction between oppressors and oppressed. We are dealing with the political semantics of Bitburg transposed from the European arena (Hartman (ed.) 1986; Seidel 1986, chapter 1).

The Right's opposition to sanctions: the struggle between racist and anti-racist discourses

It is abundantly clear, despite a number of dubious opinion polls thought to be conducted on behalf of Western interests, that the majority of black political groups in South Africa are in favour of sanctions against apartheid. As early as 1959, the ANC, then a legal organization, welcomed moves to boycott South African goods. In the 1980s that call became louder, despite the fact that it is illegal in South Africa to advocate disinvestment, boycotts and sanctions – as they are equated with 'economic sabotage'; and for some white supremacists in the National Party like the Minister of Manpower, Piet du Plessis, the advocation of sanctions verges on high treason (Hanlon and Omond 1986: 18).

I wish to argue that the Right's opposition, and the sanctions debate as a whole, should not be seen as a discrete issue. The discourse on sanctions is part of a broader struggle between racist and anti-racist discourses which engages the politics of culture in the west. The *politics of culture* (which may also be construed as the *politics of meaning*, as it is a terrain in which meanings are fought over) engages an ideological struggle that is carried on through discourse. It is a symbolic battle ground where these meanings are constructed. At times, this struggle to affirm a particular set of meanings may appear to be issue-orientated, with single specific targets (e.g. education or the 'nuclear deterrent', very much in evidence around election-time). But these issues, or targets, do not stand on their own. They derive from a particular way of 'seeing' the world, from 'positional politics', that is, they are informed by a particular view of history and culture, dominant, or otherwise, which has particular social representations (nationalist/internationalist, north/south, class, gender, minority status, etc.); and these representations may contain contradictions and tensions. The political theories from which they derive tend to be underwritten by a particular view of 'human nature' (Rose

1985). I would argue, therefore, that the discourse on sanctions needs to be understood and analysed in this broader ideological perspective. And that the opposition to sanctions, frequently presented as a single issue, in common with the discourse of the pro-sanctions lobby, is clearly one which is shaped by a particular ideological and discursive baggage. It is a discourse in which the defence of vested western economic interests are couched in liberal or anti-communist arguments and phraseology and translated into an array of verbal strategies. While, at the same time, the scale of South Africa's undeclared war and destabilization of the neighbouring black majority states[8] is not widely reported and little understood in the western media.

This discourse of the anti-sanctions lobby articulates and symbolizes the defence of western economic interests. In so doing, it bolsters up the system of apartheid, and hence justifies the South African incursions into neighbouring black states, destabilizing the region. It follows, then, that although these verbal exchanges are *symbolic*, they, nevertheless, have a *material effect* which is translated into institutions and practices. They have a *material effect* (the material counterpart of discourse in general) on the quality of the lives of the black population of South and Southern Africa.

I suggested earlier that particular sets of representations (for example, a vision of European civilization) which structure discourse representing ideological choices may also contain contradictions. To develop this same example, political groupings to the right of centre will argue that although colonialism was responsible for destruction of all kinds – of human lives, communities, economies and cultures – it, nevertheless, had a number of 'positive features'. Similar arguments are circulating in Western Germany, and not simply on the far right, seeking to revise the history of the Third Reich (ICA 1987; Pulzer 1987). These ambivalences are very disturbing. In both cases, they would suggest that colonialism, or fascism, have 'good' and 'bad' features and therefore, are capable of reform and positive or constructive developments. In the US, the idea that sanctions will halt 'reform' has been lexicalized in the anti-sanctions lobby as a recommendation for a policy of '*constructive engagement*', a phrase of Dr Chester Crocker, US Secretary of State for Africa. It has also been taken up by South African radio and Gavin Relly of the Anglo-American Corporation (Hanlon 1968: 68–9). The politico-lexical response to this semantic representation (semantic guerrilla warfare), and to the very real aggression to which the victim states have been subjected, is the use of the collocation 'destructive engagement'. This phrase also appears in the title of a book by P. Johnson and D. Martin with a Foreword by Julius Nyerere published in 1986. I would submit that this same racist ambivalence is present primarily on the right, but to a limited extent on the left, too, in relation to the apartheid régime. And that this political and discursive hypothesis may in part be demonstrated empirically.

I have already mentioned that all speakers condemn apartheid. This posture, or posturing, cannot therefore be read as a measure of their political attitude to the Pretoria government and white majority rule. We are accustomed to living with political hypocrisy. There are two linked parameters, however, whose presence and, particularly, perhaps, co-occurrence translate this ambivalence to the Pretoria government as one with which it is possible to treat. These two terms are 'dialogue' and 'negotiation'. The contexts in which these items occur, or co-occur, in the same speech, are reproduced below (Table 1).

Table 1 *Dialogue negotiation: Parameters of political ambiguity in the European Parliamentary debate on sanctions* (*8 and 10 July 1986*)

8 July 1986

Formigioni (PPE) (IT)

(. . .) In this blind alley, in this spiral of violence, there is only one means of finding the way out, and that is by resorting to reason, to NEGOTIATIONS between the opposing sides (. . .) In the same way I think it is appropriate that we call on the opposition groups for a clear official acceptance of DIALOGUE and NEGOTIATION, and a rejection of the methods of violence (. . .) so that there can be a justice and solidarity for all; so that a DIALOGUE can be reopened and sure and certain guarantees offered that cannot be postponed . . .

Focke (S) (D)

It (the Committee on Development and Cooperation whose basic positions are shaped by its terms of reference and responsibilities to the front-line and SADCC states party to the Lomé Convention) calls for political NEGOTIATION with the real representatives of the population as a whole, and for that reason –

though not only for that reason – for the immediate release of all political detainees, because only if they can take part in such NEGOTIATIONS will these hold out any prospect of success.

Vergeer (PPE) (NL)

(. . .) Is a peaceful solution still possible? The state of emergency, under which the freedom of the press is restricted, people have been arrested, houses searched and so on, does not make the situation look very hopeful and must be seen as a fresh obstacle on the road to DIALOGUE (. . .)

We again refer to the need for a national DIALOGUE with the real representatives of South Africa, who are excluded from the present government structure. We endorse the view of the Heads of Government, again expressed in The Hague, that this DIALOGUE cannot be conducted as long as recognized leaders of the black community are held in detention and their organizations are banned (. . .)

(During our visit to Southern Africa and discussions with Church leaders.) To be honest, one question that was asked was this: 'If the Churches no longer speak to each other – and that is the case – how can one expect there to be the national DIALOGUE which the partners are under so much pressure to conduct from all kinds of groups at grass-roots level and from the media?' (. . .)

Following on from this, I wonder whether Europe might not achieve more by trying in the immediate future to *encourage talks* outside the glare of the media in and outside South Africa at any level, in any environment, with a view to creating the right atmosphere for DIALOGUE (. . .)

(Debate interrupted for question time; resumed on 10 July 1986)

10 July 1986

Prag (ED) (UK)

(. . .) Our first objective must surely be to bring the South African Government and the representatives of the black majority together (. . .) If people do not talk *intelligibly to each other*, how can they *even begin to reach agreement* (. . .)

If we wish to end apartheid and bring democracy to South Africa not in bloodshed and destruction, but in peace and prosperity and freedom, we must try, try and try again to bring blacks and whites to the NEGOTIATIONS table (. . .)

Ephremidis (COM) (GR)

(Criticises contradictory resolution in that it avoids asking Parliament to vote for effective sanctions and speaks to amendments to this resolution from the Communist and other groups)

(. . .) amendments which can steer Parliament's decisions towards a commencement of sanctions against the regime because this is the only thing that can bring about DIALOGUE and peaceful solution (. . .)

Piryl (PPE) (D)

(Adopts relativist approach: political oppression and infringement of human rights also exists elsewhere; and against the 'destabilization' of South Africa which he sees as the inevitable result of any application of sanctions, which would have devastating consequences on the rest of Africa and on 'our' economies. Finally he offers some suggestions for a coherent policy on South Africa which condemn violence and acknowledge positive internal developments). (. . .) Second, we must do all we can to ensure that DIALOGUE takes place with South Africa.

Bethell (ED) (UK)

(Refers to violence and injustice of South African government, the hypocrisy of the left, and black on black violence, and encourage *power sharing* among blacks and whites in South Africa.)

Scott-Hopkins (ED) (UK)

(Argues that sanctions are a negative approach, and that the left in some national parliaments is stirring up racial hatred; and that much of the violence has been black on black.) (. . .) We want to take a positive attitude and give help to South Africa. While condemning apartheid, we also want to make certain at the same time, that something is done to encourage and to help the whites come to the NEGOTIATING table.

de Clercq, Member of the Commission (NL)

(. . .) This debate is taking place at a time when the administration in Pretoria faces a once-and-for-all choice: either it enters into a political DIALOGUE with all genuine representatives of the black population or it runs the risk of civil war. The situation in South Africa is now deteriorating day by day. Despite this, the government has still not opened the door to NEGOTIATIONS on the future of the country (. . .)

Ambiguity markers: 'dialogue' and 'negotiation'; and the evidence of ambiguity

In terms of the occurrences (Tables 2 and 3), on the basis of the *maximum totals* (including paraphrases), 75 per cent of ambiguity marker D is to be found in the PPE (Christian Democrat) group,

Table 2 *DIALOGUE and NEGOTIATION: occurrences and co-occurrences*

i *Occurrences*

D	: 10 (+ 2)
N	: 7 (+ 2)

ii *Co-occurrences*

D + N : 3

Note: These totals include 2 occurrences of *negotiating table*: and N in singular and plural case are not shown here separately: (+ 2) indicates a paraphrase.

Table 3 *Occurrences and co-occurrences of DIALOGUE and NEGOTIATION on the basis of EP political groupings*

Occurrences in descending order

Political groupings	D	N
PPE	8 (+ 1)	2
SOC	–	2
ED	– (+ 1)	2 (+ 2)
COM	1	–
DR	–	–
LDR	–	–
NI	–	–
ARC	–	–
RDE	–	–
Commission	1	1

ii *Co-occurrences*

	D + N
PPE	2
ED	(1)
Commission	1

Note 1: See Table 2, Note 1 above
Note 2: PPE: D (+ 1) = 'to encourage talks'
ED: N (+ 1) = 'power-sharing'
(D + N) = 'If people do not talk, how can they ever begin to reach agreement?'

These are shown below in tabular percentage form (Table 4).

Table 4 *Synthesis of findings in relation to D and N*

maximum D	75%	PPE
maximum N	44.4%	ED
maximum co-occurrences	50%	PPE
	25%	ED
	25%	SOC
minimum D	80%	PPE
(including Commission)	10%	COM
	10%	COMMISSION
minimum D	89.9%	PPE
(excluding Commission)	10.1%	COM
minimum N	29.3%	PPE
(including Commission)	29.3%	SOC
	29.3%	ED
	12.1%	COMMISSION
minimum N	33.3%	PPE
(excluding Commission)	33.3%	SOC
	33.3%	ED

44.4 per cent of N in the ED (Conservative); and in terms of co-occurrences, interestingly enough, in these two groups alone, 50 per cent (including a paraphrase) is to be found in the PPE, 25 per cent in ED and in the representative from the Commission respectively. On the basis of the *minimum total* occurrences of D, 80 per cent is present in PPE; and as regards the *minimum* total occurrences of N, it is equally present in PPE, SOC and ED, that is, 28.3 per cent; and 12.1 per cent in the Commission representative. Discounting the Commission, in terms of *minimum N* (which, in theory, at least, on the basis of the statutes, is independent of party affiliation), 33.3 per cent is equally distributed among PPE, SOC and ED; and in terms of *minimum D*, 89.9 per cent is present in PPE and 10.1 per cent in COM.

These statistics and their distribution (albeit on the basis of a limited number of occurrences) confirm the higher preponderance of ambivalence in those groups opposed to sanctions. 75 per cent of *maximum occurrences* of N (excluding the Commission) are present in political groupings opposing sanctions; and 90.9 per cent of *maximum* occurrences of D (excluding the Commission). This is quite an interesting result, and confirms the initial hypothesis. It should be remembered, and is worth stressing here, that PPE introduce the Report and, therefore, arguably, set the discourse framework; and the speakers for ED are all British Conservatives: Mr Prag, Lord Bethell and Sir James Scott-Hopkins. It was Scott-Hopkins who drew up the earlier report on behalf of the Political Affairs Committee in 1982, and while condemning apartheid, he declared that 'sanctions are a folly'. We are dealing here with a continuity of discourses, both internal (to the EP) and external. I shall return later to the pragmatics of the pro-sanctions group.

Afrikaner coded language: an example of a dominant discourse frame

With Vergeer (PPE) (NL), we find the collocation 'national dialogue'. This is not explicit in the other speakers in which 'dialogue' is not immediately qualified, yet this frame is clearly implied. Scott-Hopkins (ED) (UK) goes even further: he calls for something to be done 'to encourage and to help the whites to come to the negotiating table'. This statement may only be read as an invitation to appeasement. At this point, it is illuminating to introduce a quotation from a speech by P. W. Botha given in 1986 to the federal congress of the National Party in Durban, a year after his 'Rubicon' speech about reforms dashed any hopes of significant changes. Botha's heady rhetoric about proposed constitutional changes proved to be totally vacuous. Botha and other Afrikaner Nationalist leaders had already used the terms '*dialogue*' and '*negotiation*' – as part of the Afrikaner nationalist code. Botha spells out the Afrikaner nationalist meanings and the precise racist parameters, which are given material reality in terms of the Constitution. Hence both *NEGOTIATION* and *DIALOGUE* are entirely on the terms of the white minority.

To this analogy and decoding, we may add more recent speeches from P. W. Botha during his visits to the townships of Sharpeville and Sebokeng on 4 June 1987. The emphasis is on 'negotiations' with 'moderate', that is to say, traditional black leaders. His speeches were reported in the *Independent* of 6 June 1987, by Tony Allen-Mills in Johannesburg in a piece appropriately entitled: 'Botha presses blacks to negotiate':

> Undeterred by the point-blank rejection by blacks of his power-sharing proposals, President P. W. Botha is pressing on with

> plans to begin negotiations with moderate black leaders (. . .) Not one reputable black leader has yet come forward in support of Mr Botha's plans.
>
> But Mr Botha appears confident his political supremacy will persuade moderate blacks to do business. In Sebokeng he warned the black community: 'The time for excuses is over. There is no justification for hiding behind demands for "models", "blue prints", and declarations of intent as excuses for not negotiating'.

This would suggest that Botha is still 'on course', determined to 'negotiate', in a clearly polarized and irredeemable situation, when even traditional leaders, totally dependent on the white racist government for their resources (and seen as suspect increasingly by their hitherto unpoliticized followers within their ranks) are re-assessing that situation. And this would again confirm the relevance of the first set of ambiguity markers.

Ambiguity on the Left

How can we explain the presence of these ambivalence parameters, part of the dominant discourse framed by Botha and shaped by the western media, in the speeches of the pro-sanctions lobby? Let us look at the Table 1 concordances and Table 3. We need to look closely at the context of the two occurrences of N in the Socialist group (Focke, G) in the early party of the debate, and the single occurrence of D in the Communist and Allied Group (Ephremidis, GR).

Focke's intervention is politically significant in that she speaks on behalf of the EP Committee on Development and Cooperation. This Committee's position is shaped by its terms of reference and responsibilities to the front-line and SADCC states party to the Lomé Convention. The Lomé Convention, sporadically the forum for pressure by the ACP countries on the EEC, was singled out by the journal *West Africa* in its issue of 11 August 1986 as the forgotten factor in the current debate.

Whereas the Chair of the Committee, Formigioni (PPI), opening the debate explicitly called on the opposition groups, to accept *dialogue* and *negotiation*, Focke speaking on behalf of her Committee, and indirectly for the SADCC members and the Front Line states (Signatories to the Lomé Convention), appears to be calling for *negotiation* with authentic representatives of the black majority. But this is puzzling – as it assumes a non-named co-negotiator. For the Left, this cannot be Pretoria. Nor can it be the EEC which has no power in this situation. There is no way either in which the EEC could take over from London, as it were, in a re-run of the Lancaster House negotiations for Zimbabwe independence, substituting that analogy and arrangement for South Africa. The two situations are not identical. So the identity of the potential co-negotiator needs to be constructed and possibly determined through struggle; and for the moment cannot be known.

The second occurrence of *negotiation* in the same speech is similarly vague and ambiguous. '*Negotiations*' is not articulated by Focke in the context of 'reform': rather, it is predicated on the basis of the immediate release of all political detainees as a basic precondition. Nevertheless, given these pre-conditions, *negotiations* (with the Pretoria government?) is articulated as an imminent possibility, or reality. In linguistic terms using a simplified Hallidayan model, 'they' is a participant in a process. That process here is restricted to one of 'negotiation':

THEY	TAKE PART IN (modalization: CAN)	NEGOTIATIONS

'They' here refers to the 'real representatives of the population as a whole', which includes political detainees.

The problem with this construction is that 'they' ('the real representatives of the population as a whole') are not speaking here as autonomous historical subjects – but they are *spoken for*; and the limited, politically unacceptable framework in which they are *spoken for* is clearly set out complete with modalization. I am aware that the kind of ambivalence we are considering here is congruent with an older patronizing colonial discourse about black Africans. Attempts to deconstruct N in this way are part of the *process* of oppositional discourse. The political culture of the European left is not/cannot be entirely free from such representations and linguistic habits. It is primarily a structural phenomenon sustained by dominant discursive practices.

Let us now look at the single occurrence of '*dialogue*' in the Communist Group. Ephremidis's use is no less ambiguous than Focke's '*negotiation*'. However, it is emphatically not constructed in the same way as Formigioni in the opening of the debate discussed above. Ephremidis is not calling upon opposition groups to accept *dialogue*. The political pragmatics is quite diffent.

It is *sanctions* which activate a process resulting in *dialogue* – and a '*peaceful solution*'. Ephremedis seems to be using the same discursive frame as Focke. Although an active supporter of effective sanctions, and commenting, ironically as it turns out, on the contradictory nature of the resolution, Ephremidis's formulation adds an additional dimension to the contradictory messages.

ONE THING	BRING ABOUT	DIALOGUE
(Sanctions)	(modalization: CAN)	
ONE THING	BRING ABOUT	PEACEFUL
	(modalization: CAN)	COEXISTENCE

From the perspective of the majority of black political groups, neither *dialogue*, nor a *peaceful solution* can now be on the agenda. It is an example of reformist discourse. Ephremidis (like Focke) sees himself promoting the black majority cause in the European arena – whereas, in fact, this ambiguous collocation both supports and rubbishes it. Like Focke, Ephremidis would seem to be imposing his perception, or that of his political grouping, on the black struggle for liberation. For the black majority organizations, particularly following the state of emergency, there can now be no such perspective in view. This, then, would seem to be another example not only of vague but of reformist, patronizing discourse, of speaking *for* an oppressed group, however, well-intentioned.

Conclusions

The ambiguity markers that were identified in relation to apartheid and the presence of the relativist, trivializing argument, give some measure of the ambivalence of the Right in relation not only to sanctions, which, as I argued earlier, is not to be seen as a discrete issue, but to *apartheid as a crime against humanity*. This UN definition is not taken up by the right; and qualifications such as 'racist state' are largely the property of the left. And I have indicated, the refusal of this debate, by its very relativization has resonances with European debates confronting Nazi crimes. They set in motion the most important moral values of our time and challenge the foundation of our civilization, engaging the politics of meaning.

On the Right, sanctions are not only talked out, but, using another kind of relativist strategy, it is argued that it is the blacks in South Africa, and the neighbouring majority States, that would suffer the most. (For a summary, see Hanlon 1986.) This is another example of political hypocrisy. The representative mass organizations, SADCC and the Front-Line states have made their position clear. This is the focus of Buchan's passionate intervention. But the west knows best. We are dealing with another dimension of the dominant, patronizing discourse, which seems to be largely self-generating in relation to western interests; and has its counterpart in the dominant images of Africans presented in charity organizations (though these are changing) and in media stereotypes (Palmer 1986: 1987). Deconstructing and contextualizing the images of black alterity is important for the development of anti-racism. This involves a number of related strands: it means challenging the long-term processes which have articulated blacks into European society, bringing blacks into history outside the categories of problem and victim, and establishing the historical character of racism in opposition to the idea that it is an eternal or natural phenomenon. This needs to be done not in terms of a jarring anti-racist populism, but part of the mode of understanding the interpretive community (Cohen 1985) of the black diaspora and dimensions of affirmative black oppositional practice which are not reducible to the narrow ideas of anti-racism (Gilroy 1987). These images have frequently been constructed as dependents without a history, incapable of speaking for themselves,and rarely as autonomous, historical subjects. There are overlaps with sexist discourse (Thalmann in Seidel (ed.) 1988). B. Heinrich's (ARC) (G) contribution to the debate, representing the Committee of Women's Rights, articulates this relation very clearly with reference to women's legal status in South Africa as 'perpetual minors' (Capitan in Seidel (ed.) 1988). These patterns of meaning further reinforce and extend the related discourses of racism and colonialism which are operating today within a larger context (Third World First 1987).

I shall end with a quotation from J-P. Sartre. In France Sartre was the conscience of the intellectual left. However, it is not generally known that Sartre was one of the founders of the French Anti-Apartheid Committee. The text was written in 1968 and quoted in a recent essay by Olivier Desouches, General Secretary of the Anti-Apartheid Movement in France (*Les Temps Modernes* 1986). As early as 1968 Sartre was arguing that in the absence of any mass struggle against apartheid not only in France but world-wide, the virulent neo-fascism of Pretoria would re-enter Europe. And to remain passive would make us accomplices.

> Si nous ne pouvions pas réussir, non seulement ici en France, mais partout ailleurs, si nous ne réussissions pas à amener à la lutte la majorité, et dans un état d'esprit profond, serieux, nous serions responsables et complices, par passivité, d'un néo-nazisme intolérable et virulent qui viendra d'Afrique du Sud et qui infectera jusqu'à l'Europe. Si ces pratiques sont tolérées, si nous continuons à les tolérer, alors cette plaque tournante du fascisme qu'est l'Afrique du Sud nous renverra les fascistes qui nous apprendront notre douleur.
> Jean-Paul Sartre, Paris, le 9 novembre 1968

What Sartre failed to see was the reburgeoning of neo-fascist movements in Western Europe. In the anti-imperialist discourse today, the necessary relation between North and South is articulated primarily in terms of economies and finances, like the call to cancel 'Third World' debts. Nearly twenty years ago Sartre was stressing a different dimension: the linked struggle in the North and South against neo-fascism and racism on a global scale. It is a very crucial insight.

Notes

1 This is a shortened version of an invited paper presented to the African Regional Conference of UN Associations on the Eradication of Apartheid and the Liberation of Namibia:
Intensifying the World Campaign, 15–30 June 1987, Accra, Ghana.
I am indebted to Bradford University Research Committee for making it possible for me to participate in this Conference. Librarians at Bradford, Information Officers at the European Parliament and the European Commission offices in London, and the Assistants to Alf Lomas (Chairperson of the Socialist Group. EP) and Richard Caborn MP helped me enormously with documentation. I am also indebted to former MEP Bob Cryer for a most useful discussion.

2 At the ACP-EEC Joint Assembly held in Vouliagmeni, Greece, in September 1986, the general *rapporteur*, Christopher Jackson, presented the 1986 General Report, 'Towards the Year 2000 – people-centred development', which was denounced as 'Thatcherite' by its political opponents; and a 'soft' resolution was adopted on South Africa (*Courier*, November–December 1986: 15–19).

3 ANC members were present at the debate. However, Sir Henry Plumb, a British Conservative (ED) and EP President, did not exercise his initiative and invite the ANC to address the Assembly separately.

4 Two right-wing French representatives from the RDE and DE, one Dutch (LDR), and one British Conservative, D. Prag (ED) (UK). D. Prag was the Vice-Chairman of the Committee of Enquiry into the Rise of Fascism and Racism.

5 An earlier report on Southern Africa drawn up on behalf of the same Committee in October 1982 was eventually debated, after an extraordinary delay, on 8 February 1983. The *rapporteur*, Sir James Scott-Hopkins (ED) (UK), emphasized the view that 'sanctions are folly'. In the subsequent voting, trade embargoes were rejected by 130 votes to 96 with 7 abstentions.

6 A list of abbreviations for EP political groupings is included in Appendix B.

7 Le Pen was a contender for the 1988 French presidential elections. He was invited to address a fringe meeting of the 1987 Meeting of the Conservative Conference, with the support of Sir Alfred Sherman, former adviser to Prime Minister Thatcher. After some controversy in the press, Le Pen later declined the invitation.

8 Hanlon states that more that 10,000 people have been killed, many of whom have starved to death in Mozambique as a result of South-African rebel activity which prevented drought relief. Ormond suggests that 3½ million have been forcibly removed, while another 1.8 million are under threat of removal, and that this figure is likely to rise to two million. According to the SADCC Conference, over the five-year period 1980–1986, the South African offensive cost the region $10,000 million (Hanlon 1986; Omond 1986: 131; SADCC Newsletter, September 1985).

References

Africa Confidential, (26 November 1986), 'South Africa: A Total Strategy', 27 (24).

Africa Confidential, (10 December 1986), 'South Africa: the ANC', 27 (25).

Allison, C., (1986), *'It's Like Holding the Key to Your Own Jail': Women in Namibia*, Geneva: World Council of Churches.

Amin, M. and Lindsay-Smith, I., (1987), 'Death on camera: the role and responsibility of the media in third world disasters', paper presented to a meeting of the Royal African Society (London), 27 February.

Association of West European Parliamentarians for Action Against Apartheid (AWEPPA), (September 1985), 'Government action in Western Countries, Amsterdam: AWEPPA International Conference.

Association of West European Parliamentarians for Action against Apartheid (AWEPPA), (September 1985), 'The continuing illegal occupation of Namibia: the failure to act', Amsterdam: AWEPPA International Conference.

Bernal, M., (1987), *Black Athena: The Afro-Asiatic Roots of Classical Civilization*, vol. 1, Free Association Books, London.

'Black and White Media Show', (1986), BBC Television.

Bloch, M. (ed.), (1975), *Political Language and Oratory in Traditional Society*, London: Academic Press.

Brewer, J. D., (1987), *After Soweto*, Oxford: Oxford University Press.

Capitan, C., (1987), ' "Status of women" in French revolutionary/liberal ideology', in G. Seidel (ed.), *The Nature of the Right: A Feminist Analysis of Order Patterns*, Amsterdam: Benjamins.

Coates, R., *et al.* (eds), (1988, 2nd edn), *Horizons in linguistics*, London: Penguin.

Cobley, A., (1983), '*We all die together*': *crisis and consciousness in the urban black community of South Africa, 1948–1960*, unpublished MA thesis, University of York, Centre of Southern African Studies.

Cohen, A. P., (1985), *The Symbolic Construction of Community*, London: Tavistock.

Davies, R., O'Meara, D. and Dlamini, S., (1984), *The Struggle for South Africa. A Reference Guide to Movements, Organizations and Institutions*, vols 1 and 2, London: Zed Books.

Desouches, O., (juin-juillet-août 1986), 'La Politique Sud-Africaine de la France: Quelques Réflexions', *Les Temps Modernes*: 506–16.

Van Dijk, T. (ed.), (1985), *Handbook of Discourse Analysis*, vol. 4, New York: Academic Press.

Van Dijk, T., (1987), *Communicating racism. Ethnic prejudice in thought and talk*, Beverly Hill, California: Sage.

Ebel, M. and Fiala, P., (1983), *Sous le consensus la xénophobie*, Lausanne: Institut de Science Politique.

Eco, U., (1984), *Semiotics and the Philosophy of Language*, London: Macmillan.

Fowler, R. *et al.* (1979), *Language and Control*, London: Routledge & Kegan Paul.

George, S., (1985), *Famine and Power*, London: Writers and Readers.

Gilroy, P., (1987), *There Ain't No Black in the Union Jack*, London: Hutchinson.

Grice, H. P., (19785), '*Logic and Conversation*', in P. Cole and J. Morgan (eds), *Syntax and Semantics 3: Speech Acts*, New York: Academic Press.

Grillo, R. D., Pratt, J. and Street, B. V., 'Anthropology, Linguistics and Language', in R. Coates *et al.* (eds).

Gumperz, W., (1982), *Discourse Strategies*, Cambridge: Cambridge University Press.

Hanlon, J., (1986), *Apartheid's Second Front: South Africa's War against its Neighbours*, Harmondsworth, Middx.: Penguin Books.

Hanlon, J., (1986), *Beggar your Neighbours: Apartheid Power in Southern Africa*, London: Catholic Institute for International Relations in collaboration with Indiana University Press.

Hanlon, J. and Omond, R., (1986), *The Sanctions Handbook*, Harmondsworth, Middx.: Penguin Books.

Hartman, G. H. (ed.), (1986), *Bitburg in Political and Moral Perspective*, Bloomington: Indiana University Press.

Hunter, J., (1987, revised edn), *Undercutting Sanctions. Israel, the US and South Africa*, Washington: Washington Middle East Associates.

Institute of Contemporary Arts, Symposium on Modern German History, London, 30 May 1987.

Johnson, P. and Martin, D., (1986), (Foreword by J. K. Nyerere), *Destructive Engagement: Southern Africa at War*, Harare: Zimbabwe Publishing House.

Kramarae, C., Schulz, M. and O'Barr, W. M., (eds), (1984), *Language and Power*, Beverly Hills, California: Sage.

Kress, G. and Hodge, B., (1979), *Language and Ideology*, Routledge & Kegan Paul, London.

Labour Research, (August 1986), *Tory MPs stake in Apartheid*, vol., 75.

Labour Research, (May 1987), *South Africa: UK pays for poverty*, vol. 76.

Labour Research, (1986), *Profiting from Apartheid – Britain's links with South Africa*, London.

Labour Research Department, (1986), *Profiting from Apartheid – Britain's Links with South Africa*, London: LRD Publications.

Les Temps Modernes, (Juin-juillet-aôut 1986), 'Afrique du Sud: Demain le feu'.

Links 22, (1985), *Dying for Profit: The Real Cause of Famine in Africa*.

Lyons, J., (1977), *Semantics*, vols 1 and 2, Cambridge: Cambridge University Press.

Lyons, J., (1981), *Language*, Meaning and Context, London: Fontana.

Makhosikazi, V., (1985), *South African Women Speak*, London: Catholic Institute for International Relations.

Minsky, M., (1975), 'A Framework for Representing Knowledge', in P. Winston (ed.), *The Psychology of Computer Vision*, New York: McGraw Hill.

Mommsen, J. H., and Townsend, J. (eds), (1987). *Geography of Gender in the Third World*. London: Hutchinson.
Munslow, B. and O'Keefe, P., (November 1985), 'South Africa: Sanctions and Counter-Sanctions',*African Events*.
Nolte, E., (6 June 1986), *Frankfurter Allgemeine Zeitung*.
Omond, R., (1986, 2nd edn), *The Apartheid Handbook. A Guide to South Africa's Everyday Racial Politics*, Harmondsworth, Middx.: Penguin Books.
Orkin, M., (1986), *Disinvestment, the Struggle and the Future: What Black Africans Really Think*, Johannesburg: Raven Press.
Palmer, R., (December 1986), 'Out of Africa, out of focus', *Times Higher Educational Supplement*.
Palmer, R., (April 1987), 'Africa in the Media', *African Affairs* 86 (343): 241–7.
Pêcheux, M., (1982), *Language, Semantics and Ideology*, London: Methuen.
Political Social Economic Review, (July 1986), 'NOP on sanctions and South Africa', 60: 7–14.
Pulzer, P., (1987), 'Erasing the Past: German historians debate the Holocaust', *Patterns of Prejudice*, 21 (3): 3–14.
Quine, W., (1953), 'Two Dogmas of Empiricism', in W. Quine (ed.), *From a Logical Point of View*, New York: Harper Torchbooks.
Rich, P., (1983), 'Landscape, Social Darwinism, and the Cultural Roots of South African Racial Ideology', *Patterns of Prejudice* 17 (3): 9–13.
Rich, P. B., (1986), *Race and Empire in British Politics*, Cambridge: Cambridge University Press.
Rose, S., (1985), Invited oral Testimony to the European Parliamentary Committee of Enquiry into the Rise of Fascism and Racism in Europe.
Schank, R. C. and Abelson, R. P., (1977), 'Scripts, Plans and Knowledge', in P. N. Johnson-Laird and P. C. Wason (eds), *Thinking: Readings in Cognitive Science*, Cambridge: Cambridge University Press.
Seidel, G., (Octobre 1981), 'Le fascisme dans les textes de la Nouvelle Droite', MOTS (Paris): 49–59.
Seidel, G., (1985), 'Political Discourse Analysis', in T. van Dijk (ed.), *Handbook of Discourse Analysis* vol. 4, New York: Academic Press, pp. 45–60.
Seidel, G., (1986), 'Representations of culture, "race" and nation in the British and French New Right', in R. Levitas (ed.), *The Ideology of the New Right*, Cambridge: Polity Press, pp. 107–35.
Seidel, G., (1986), *The Holocaust Denial: Antisemitism, Racism and the New Right*, Leeds: Beyond the Pale.
Seidel, G. (ed.), (1988), *The Nature of the Right: A Feminist Analysis of Order Patterns*, Amsterdam: Benjamins.
Seidel, G., (1988), 'The white discursive order: the New Right's enemy within: "the anti-racists" ', in G. Smitherman-Donaldson and T. van Dijk (eds), *Discourse and Discrimination*, Detroit: Wayne State University.
Seidel, G., (1988), 'Verbal strategies of the collaborators: a discursive analysis of the July 1986 European Parliamentary debate on South African sanctions', *Text* 8 (1): 111–17.
Smitherman-Donaldson, G. and van Dijk, T. (eds), (1988), *Discourse and Discrimination*, Detroit: Wayne State University Press.
Stone, J., (July 1986), 'When Botha goes: South African society beyond the era of apartheid', *Ethnic and Racial Studies*: 412–25.
Sullivan, S., (20 April 1987), 'Ghosts of the Nazis', *Newsweek*: 20–8.
Sykes, M., (1985), 'Discrimination in discourse', in T. van Dijk (ed.), *Handbook of Discourse Analysis*, London: Academic Press.
Tambo, O., (29 May 1987), 'The white world's moment of truth', *Guardian*.
Thalmann, R., (1988), 'Sexism and Racism', in G. Seidel (ed.), *The Nature of the Right: A Feminist Analysis of Order Patterns*, Amsterdam: Benjamins.

The Arusha Conference, (1985), *Conference on Southern Africa of the Socialist International and the Socialist Group of the European Parliament with the Front-Line States ANC and SWAPO*, 4–5 September 1984 (Co-Chairman: J. den Uyl and J. Nyerere), London: Socialist International.
The Commonwealth Group of Eminent Persons (1986), (Foreword by S. Ramphal) *Mission to South Africa: The Commonwealth Report. The Findings of the Commonwealth Eminent Persons Group on Southern Africa*, Harmondsworth, Middx.: Penguin Books.
Third World First, (1987), 'Altered Images: Media Myths and Misunderstanding', *Links* 28, Oxford: Third World First.
Trade Union Congress, (1986), *Beating Apartheid: The Current Crisis in South Africa – and the TUC's programme of action*, London: TUC.
Tutu, D., (1986, 3rd edn), *Hope and Suffering*, Glasgow: Collins.
Tweedie, J., (1 June 1987), 'Duvets and Dont's', *Guardian*.
West Africa, (11 August 1986), 'Back to the front line', *West Africa*: 1659.
West Africa, (11 August 1986), Interview with Obasanjo: the Commonwealth and Sanctions.

Appendix A – Official summary of debate

South Africa: Parliament call for sanctions

Thursday, 19 July – Parliament adopted by 228 votes to 114 with 29 abstentions, a resolution condemning apartheid and calling for the immediate introduction of sanctions against South Africa. The key amendment reads as follows:

> Deplores the failure of the European Council to agree on the immediate implementation of any further measures; calls for the immediate implementation by the member states of at least the measures proposed by the European Council for consideration – a ban on new investments, the import of coal, iron, steel and gold coins from South Africa; and calls in addition for the immediate consideration of further measures, notably a ban on the import of agricultural products, gold, uranium and diamonds from South Africa.

Other points in the resolutions include:

- a call for an increase in economic aid to the Southern Africa Development Coordination Committee (sic) (SADCC)
- a call for studies into alternative sources of supply of sensitive products (chrome, vanadium and rhodium)
- the EC ban on oil exports to South Africa to be extended to all oil based products

- a call for a ban on all cooperation between the member states and South Africa in the nuclear field
- a call for the release of Nelson Mandela and all political prisoners.

Derek Prag (Hertfordshire, Dem) appealed to both the South African government and representatives of the black majority to get together. This is the only way apartheid can be ended and peaceful transition to a democratic society ensured.

Full scale international sanctions would not bring about this but merely drive the Afrikaners into the laager. Furthermore, if the five million white people feel threatened they will fight and a bloodbath ending in a victory for the white minority would be the result. As he put it 'It will help no-one for the Left to ride into battle shouting "God for immediate full-scale sanctions, Alf Lomas and St George" '.

Mr Prag did, however, feel that the Community should have ready a graduated series of measures to persuade the South African government to end apartheid.

Vassilis Ephremidis (GR) (COM) too condemned the South African government but he favoured full scale sanctions and considered the motion before the House contradictory and not strong enough.

José Madeiros Ferreira (P) (ERDA) called for more decisive action from the Community and Else Hammerich (DK) (RBW) pointed out that Denmark was the only EC country to introduce trade sanctions.

Lord Bethell (London North West, Dem), on the other hand, took issue with the European Left for exploiting the situation for political purposes. The sensible way forward is to propose measures designed to bring about power-sharing.

Niall Andrews (Dublin, ERDA) backed sanctions taking the view that they had worked in Rhodesia.

Sir James Scott-Hopkins (Hereford and Worcester, Dem) provoked objection on the other side of the House when he accused the Left of stirring up racial hatred. Much of the violence taking place is between black people. Sanctions are negative. Parliament should be backing positive measures designed to help the victims of apartheid, he said.

Ernest Glinne (B) (SOC) spoke in support of independence for Namibia.

Janet Buchan (Glasgow, SOC) describing her visit to South

Africa said everyone she met, including those most likely to be affected, favoured sanctions. She took issue with what she termed the hypocrisy of the Right in pretending there could be any other course of action. She called on the UK Presidency to follow the lead set by smaller countries such as Denmark, Holland and Ireland.

Jorge Campinos (P) (SOC) could not accept that apartheid is capable of evolving. It must be abolished, he said.

Replying for the Commission, Willy de Clercq said that if the South African government failed to accept dialogue then the Community would be faced with no alternative but to take economic measures. This is, however, a matter for the member states meeting in political cooperation.

'*The Week*', 7–10 July 1986. For the official text of the resolution, see OJ No. C227, 8 September 1986, p. 94.

Appendix B – Abbreviations and acronyms

The following abbreviations and terms have been used for countries and international organizations following the usual conventions:

EEC — European Economic Community, currently comprising 12 member states:

B	Belgium
DE	Denmark
FR	France
G	Greece
Gk	Greece
I	Ireland
IT	Italy
L	Luxembourg
NL	Netherlands
PT	Portugal
S	Spain
UK	United Kingdom

Political groupings in the European Parliament (EP)

S	Socialist
PPE	Group of the European People's Party (Christian-Democrat Group)

ED	European Democratic Group
COM	Communist and Allied Group
LDR	Liberal and Democratic Reformist Group
RDE	Group of the European Renewal and Democratic Alliance
ARC	Rainbow Group: Federation of the Green-Alternative European Link
DR	Group of the European Right
NI	Non-attached

Front-line states: comprising 6 states

Angola
Botswana
Mozambique
Tanzania
Zambia
Zimbabwe

SADCC – Southern African Development Coordination Conference, set up 'to liberate our economies from their dependence on the Republic of South Africa', comprise the Front-Line states plus

Lesotho
Malawi
Swaziland

ACP states (Africa, Caribbean, Pacific) currently number 66, and are signatories to the Lomé convention (ACP/EEC).